ROBERT KENNEDY ■ ■
AT 40 ■ ■

ROBERT KENNEDY ∎∎ AT 40 ∎∎

NICK THIMMESCH and
WILLIAM JOHNSON

W·W·NORTON & COMPANY·INC·
NEW YORK

Copyright © 1965 by W. W. Norton & Company, Inc.
First Edition

Library of Congress Catalog Card No. 65-21618

ALL RIGHTS RESERVED
Published simultaneously in Canada by
George J. McLeod Limited, Toronto

Printed in the United States of America

1 2 3 4 5 6 7 8 9 0

To the Game of Politics

CONTENTS

ILLUSTRATIONS

Between pages 160 and 161

FOREWORD

no means an "authorized biography." We didn't intend it to be. It
has become customary for most writers undertaking any literary
effort about Robert F. Kennedy to ask for his approval and arrange
for his cooperation in producing the final manuscript. We did
neither. Indeed, Kennedy told us he wasn't interested in having
any book written on him. When we approached him about our
project in December, 1964, he had just been elected to the U.S.
Senate from New York and he told us, rather bluntly: "I don't want
to talk about what was in my past. I see no purpose in such a book.
There's no interest in me."

As journalists, we had covered his activities in recent years
and were well aware of his varying moods. At times he is dour and
brusque; on other occasions, he is warm, boyish and full of humor.
By St. Patrick's Day, when he marched up Fifth Avenue in New
York City's annual parade honoring the Irish, Kennedy had softened a bit; he informed us that he realized that he couldn't stop
us from writing a book about him. Toward the end of work on the
manuscript, he even showed flashes of friendliness. During a chance
meeting with one of the authors, he asked cheerfully, "How are my
biographers coming along?" On another occasion, he kidded with
one of us, and asked if we were "calling him ruthless on every
page." We told him there were indeed some who called him "ruthless," a word which seems to stick to him like warts.

11

Ultimately we talked with scores of people who know Bobby well—members of his family, people in politics and government, friends, enemies and those who worked for him. If there is a single truth about Robert Kennedy, it is that he inevitably generates intense feelings in those who have worked *for* him or who have been dealt with *by* him. Many people we interviewed expressed impassioned sentiments, ranging from sycophancy to downright hatred. A few were ambivalent and combined praise with hesitant criticism.

We are obligated and grateful to many who told us what they know about Bobby from first-hand experience. Our very first thanks go to Hugh Sidey, White House Correspondent for *Time*. As a journalist, Sidey covered John and Robert Kennedy from 1957 on, and developed a personal friendship with both which grew through the 1960 Presidential primaries and election and during the years of the Kennedy Administration. In addition to Sidey's assistance, we had a great deal of help from the insights and information accumulated about Robert Kennedy over the years by other friends on the *Time-Life* reporting staff. We also made use of the few books already written about Bobby, and of the plethora of magazine and newspaper articles available. Dorothea Bourne has our gratitude for her indispensable research and editorial advice.

We are deeply indebted to the many people we interviewed. Among the newsmen we want to thank are Charles Bartlett of the Chicago *Sun-Times* syndicate; Clark Mollenhoff of Cowles Publications; and Terry Smith of the New York *Herald-Tribune*. Those closely associated with Bobby who helped us include Stephen Smith, Walter Sheridan, John R. Reilly, Ed Guthman, Dean Markham, Pamela Turnure, R. Peter Straus and Robert Morgenthau. For background on New York politics we are obligated to Harry O'Donnell, Paul Buiar and Debs Myers. Especially helpful were ten United States Senators and 12 of their staffers. Among those expressing no special admiration for Kennedy, we must thank Sidney Zagri of the International Brotherhood of Teamsters.

Finally, we want to thank Robert Francis Kennedy himself. While providing no assistance at all, he did not shut us off from any of his friends, family, or associates. Once when an aide of Kennedy's was being interviewed by one of the authors, Kennedy suddenly appeared in the room and asked: "How do I look in your book?" The interviewer replied, "Like a million dollars." Bobby grinned and said "That's awfully low for a Kennedy."

Nick Thimmesch
William Johnson

New York City, August 31, 1965

ROBERT KENNEDY AT 40 ■■ ■■

I
THE FORTIETH YEAR

□ □
□ □

H<small>IS</small> GINGER BROWN HAIR
is visibly gray and the lines of his face have deepened. Robert Francis Kennedy is middle-aged—40 years old on November 20, 1965.

Proverbially, 40 is the year when a man's life begins. In his four decades, Robert Kennedy had already lived through far more than the ordinary man's measure of triumph and tragedy, yet, in a real sense, he was now launched on a new and even more dynamic life—as a U.S. Senator from New York, as a personal force in the national Democratic Party, as the head of the rich and numerous Kennedy clan, and as a presidential possibility in years to come.

His moment of departure into his own future came with shattering suddenness when his brother, President John Kennedy, was shot dead in Dallas. From then on, Robert Kennedy was on his own, and at no time were his past agonies and his future hopes better focused than on January 20, 1965—the day Lyndon Baines Johnson was inaugurated as President on the Capitol steps in Washington.

Johnson's voice was thin and twangy as it sounded over the public-address system, uttering the words of his inaugural address in cadence so slow as to be soporific. His speech was packed with platitudes, filled with a Texan's imagery—"the uncrossed desert . . . the unclimbed ridge . . . the harvest sleeping in the unplowed ground." The talk was of a Great Society and there was eloquence at times;

but the message sounded more like a businessman's prayer than a great leader's inspiration.

Deep in the crowd of dignitaries behind the President sat Robert Kennedy, his face grim and unspeakably sad. He looked a full decade older than he was and, as the President talked on, Kennedy listened with head bowed. Lyndon Johnson's aging bulk, his plain-spoken syntax, his lay preacher's delivery could only emphasize the absence of the dead President Kennedy. Gone was the flat Boston accent; the brilliant oratory; the trim figure; the boyish enthusiasm. The LBJ Ranch had replaced Camelot in the Capital; the Kennedy Years were over.

Yet amid the misery of what-might-have-been, there was a dimension of triumph for Robert Kennedy. Ten weeks earlier he had won the New York Senate seat after an angry, fatiguing campaign filled with cries of "Carpetbagger!" from Republicans and Democrats alike. Even that victory was tainted, for without the assassination of his brother it would not have happened, and after he was sworn in as a Senator, Robert Kennedy said, "I wish the situation hadn't arisen that made me run for the Senate in New York, but I'm looking forward to serving—to serving the people of New York."

Had John Kennedy lived, Robert Kennedy might still have been Attorney General of the United States, confidant to the President and the most powerful man in Washington outside the White House. And his star would still have been dimmed by the shadow of the more personable, more popular, more princely presence of his brother.

On that cold day in January, 1965, as Lyndon Johnson orated amid the pomp and trappings of inauguration and Robert Kennedy sat lonely in a crowd, one irrevocable fact snapped clear: The brilliance of John Kennedy no longer obscured the potential of Robert Kennedy. The roles of the supporting brother, the Second Kennedy, the man behind the man in charge, had vanished with a rifle shot on November 22, 1963. Now, given Robert Kennedy's energy, his drive, his ambition, the sky was the limit. Indeed, on some January day in the future this same Robert Kennedy might himself be making an inaugural address from a lectern before the Capitol of the United States.

Even as a junior Senator (so junior that he is seated in a

newly-installed four-chair row at the very rear of the overflowing Democratic majority's side of the Senate chamber), Robert Kennedy has an advantage over many presidential contenders-to-come. His name, his new political base in populous New York, his known experience with Jack in handling crises of world-shaking magnitude, his family's seemingly endless millions, his own extensive knowledge and tough-minded insight into the intricate machinery of politics— all make him a presidential prospect of awesome proportion.

More than that, Robert Francis Kennedy wants to be President.

Since John Kennedy was murdered, there has been a growing acclaim for Robert. In some ways, it is simply a posthumous transfer of allegiance from the dead to the living. Nevertheless, the Senator from New York has become the keeper of the Kennedy charisma, the great White House hope for multitudes of Americans. His younger, handsomer, easier-going brother, Edward "Teddy" Moore Kennedy, six years Robert's junior and the Democratic Senator from Massachusetts since 1962, has so far attracted no such outpouring of Kennedy worship.

Indeed, the cascading admiration for Robert Kennedy has begun to take on the dimension of a cult. When he was campaigning for the Senate seat in New York against incumbent Republican Kenneth Keating, Kennedy was besieged everywhere by screeching hordes of young people, reaching frantically to touch him, to shake his hand, to snatch a cuff link or a tie clasp or a coat button. Since the election, Kennedy's Senate office has been deluged with no less than 1,000 letters daily—a total that far exceeds the mail received by most Senators even when they are embroiled in the most controversial issues. Kennedy's mail pours in from all 50 states, as well as from dozens of foreign countries.

Some of it consists of maudlin notes of sympathy, packages of stale homemade cookies or plastic flowers sent with requests that they be placed on John Kennedy's grave. But the great majority of letters are full of praise and an automatic, if slightly star-struck, assumption that Robert Kennedy will someday be President. A man from Australia wrote in typical fashion: "Dear Senator Kennedy: I thought it best to write you now as when you are President you will not have time to read ordinary mail." An Indiana minister wrote:

"You are a man of rare talent, and I sincerely hope that the people of the United States will continue to recognize this and eventually elect you to the presidency." A woman from New Orleans summed up the credo of the Robert Kennedy cult when she wrote: "There is a hard core of us throughout the country to whom a Kennedy in government represents the highest form of idealism and integrity . . . This admiration [is] only in part sentiment for your late brother. You are a force in your own right and many of us desire nothing more than Robert F. Kennedy as President. Because of your family, many of us who could be considered idealistic have become involved in politics. We are your People."

To many Americans the mere thought of Robert Kennedy standing at a presidential inaugural lectern is odious. After all, this is the Kennedy who reigned as the *enfant terrible* of the New Frontier, the brash kid brother, the shock-haired, stringy, collegiate-looking fellow whom everyone—parents, wife, headline writers, foreign diplomats and enemies alike—calls "Bobby." Indeed, to give him any other name would be like calling Babe Ruth "George"—although Kennedy's loyal publicity men have long urged reporters to refer to him as "Bob."

Bobby Kennedy is a man of many dimensions, of perplexing complications and of deceptively simple drives. He is a man with a complex commitment to a few thoroughly American, if currently rather passé, precepts such as Family, Faith and Football—not necessarily in that order. Bobby Kennedy is pious in his dedication to the never-finish-second creed of the Kennedy clan, as preached by his multimillionaire father, Joseph P. Kennedy. Bobby is devout in his practice of the Roman Catholic faith. And he is strong in his belief that almost nothing prepares a man better for life's tests than the game of football.

The odds are great that Bobby Kennedy will change very little in his basic beliefs. Presidency or not, he is indelibly stamped with a code of life that gives no credence to defeat and offers no credit for halfhearted devotion to victory.

There is an air of white-knuckled tension about Bobby Kennedy that is intimidating to many people. It springs from his intrinsic, insistent sense of urgency and relentless dedication to the task of the moment. An ordinary man, less driven, begins to feel a secret, gnawing guilt for being unable or unwilling to make the every-ounce-of-flesh commitment that Kennedy somehow wrings from himself.

It turns up in almost everything he does, although there are different manifestations of his drive. Sometimes it is tedious, endless, slogging labor. He once defined the practice of politics this way: "All it is is plain hard work—addressing letters, calling people on the phone, registering voters, making sure every possible thing that could be done has been done." When he managed Jack's presidential campaign in 1960, Bobby whipped himself to work like an indentured servant. Most days he rose before dawn. He rushed about to make early-morning handshaking tours at factory gates; he delivered noon-hour speeches at civic clubs; he appeared at afternoon tea parties, cocktail socials and kaffeeklatsches; and he wound up his days in late-night hotel-room strategy sessions with his staff. He was never known to nap. He seemed never to ease up. Even when the Kennedy campaign plane droned on for hundreds of miles through the night, Bobby prowled restlessly in the aisle, incessantly questioning his aides, testing reporters' reactions to his ideas, refusing to rest until he made sure every infinitesimal thing that could be done had been done. Before it was over, Jack said, "He's living on nerves."

When he was chief counsel of the Senate Rackets Committee during the late years of the 1950's and chasing hard on the heels of corruption in labor unions, Bobby plowed through endless pages of depositions, interviewed dozens of witnesses, traveled thousands of miles himself to make front-stoop contacts with people who could add to the evidence he needed to sell the idea of tough labor legislation. When he was Attorney General, he worked 11-hour days at the Justice Department as a matter of routine, except when he was in the storm center of crisis. Then, in shirt sleeves and with tie askew, he sometimes stayed at his desk for 48 hours without sleep. His proud father said, "Jack works as hard as any mortal man can. Bobby goes a little farther."

There is another side to Bobby's single-minded intensity, and it emerges in a blunt, unyielding, uncompromising set of attitudes that are infuriating and even offensive to others. Because of them, he has been called ruthless. His father, who made millions of dollars and hundreds of enemies in his life, once spoke scornfully about

Bobby's reputation for ruthlessness: "As a person who has had the term applied to him for fifty years, I know a little about it. Anybody who is controversial is considered ruthless. If he takes a stand against something, then he's called ruthless. It's ridiculous. Any man of action is always called ruthless."

Few men are more active or more controversial than Robert Kennedy. He is alive with impatience and filled with distaste for what he considers physical softness or mental sloth. He holds a seemingly simplistic concept about people, pigeonholing them categorically as good guys or bad guys. His wife Ethel once said, "For him, the world is divided into black and white hats. The white hats are for us and the black hats are against us. Bobby can only distinguish good men and bad, good things and bad. Good things, in his eyes, are virility, courage, movement and anger. He has no patience with the weak and the hesitant."

Yet as often as not, his definition of which man fits which hat changes with the practicalities of the moment. His approach is more often tasteless, tactless and tough-guy rude than consciously cruel, for he does not set out with the idea of insulting or infuriating just to cause scars. Bobby Kennedy simply wants what he wants when he wants it. That this characteristic does not make him the best-loved man in Washington is an inescapable fact of his life; he has seemed perfectly content to accept it—and ignore it.

"I am so well aware of being disliked by many that it no longer surprises or disturbs me," Bobby told a correspondent for the Italian newspaper L'Europeo. "I no longer care. On the contrary, I do understand the reason. I have been too closely involved in too many struggles, in too many battles. But there are people who do like me: They elected me, did they not? The poorer people like me. Negroes and Puerto Ricans, for instance. The deprived, if you like. They are for me, I know. For me also are the people who understood President Kennedy, our administration during those two and a half years, and I did not expect to find so many of them. So let the others say whatever they like."

Indeed, Bobby himself usually says—and does—whatever he likes if he feels it is a viable means to achieving an end. During the 1960 Democratic convention in Los Angeles, Bobby was trying to pick up last-minute votes to insure his brother's nomination. He learned that Hubert Humphrey, now Vice President but then a Senator from Minnesota, was thinking of supporting the nomination of Adlai Stevenson, the Democratic candidate in 1952 and 1956. Kennedy met Humphrey, poked a finger into his chest and said in Little Caesar style, "Hubert, we want your announcement and the pledge of the Minnesota delegation today—or else." Humphrey flushed, stabbed his finger right back and growled, "Bobby, you go to hell."

When a reform-minded faction of Democrats threatened to split the New York party during the 1960 presidential campaign, Bobby charged into Manhattan and barked at them: "Gentlemen, I don't give a damn if the state and county organizations survive after November, and I don't give a damn if you survive. I want to elect John F. Kennedy." They were apoplectic when he left, but they supported John F. Kennedy for the presidency.

Even in the august chambers of the Senate, Bobby Kennedy trembles with impetuous eagerness to get what he wants—now. By unwritten tradition, a freshman Senator's maiden appearance on the floor is usually an occasion for ritualistic caution. When John Kennedy made his first speech in mid-1953 he had been a Senator for five months, and he delivered an enormously long, almost pedantic trilogy about the state of the economy in New England and the Federal Government's role in it. Teddy Kennedy's first major address occurred during the 1964 debate over a civil-rights bill—16 months after he took office. Not Bobby. He stood up on February 1, 1965, after just three weeks as a Senator, and introduced an amendment favoring New York to tack onto the Johnson Administration's Appalachia poverty bill. Later there was muttering in the cloakrooms about Kennedy's abrasive conduct, for in his haste, Bobby had neither framed the language of the amendment precisely nor had he bothered to give his New York colleague, Republican Senator Jacob Javits, adequate notice of the fact that he would present the measure from the floor. And that was only the beginning, for in the early months of his freshman Senate year Bobby showed no reluctance about expressing his views—including floor speeches that were sharply critical of President Johnson himself in conjunction with the war in Viet Nam.

Kennedy's relations with the press have always been iffy—

if Bobby thinks he will like what is to be written he is voluble and cooperative. If not, he can be curt, cold or utterly uncommunicative. When a reporter, who is not notably part of the Kennedy press claque, probes too deeply for personal tidbits, Bobby cuts him dead with, "I'm no good at talking about things like that." A newsman interviewed Kennedy while he was swimming in his pool at home in McLean, Virginia, a few years ago. When the reporter asked a question that Bobby did not want to answer, Kennedy simply surface-dived to the bottom of the pool, swam to the other side, climbed out and strode away.

Mincing words simply takes too long in the hurried world of Robert Kennedy. Lawrence O'Brien, a top White House aide to John Kennedy and later Lyndon Johnson's Postmaster General, said, "It takes me half an hour to turn anybody down, and I always hope he'll be halfway home before he realizes what I've told him. But with Bobby, they're in, they've knocked heads and they're out again before they know they're stunned." During Bobby's years on the New Frontier one gag that became popular had a ring of truth to it. One Democrat said to another, "You know, what Bobby Kennedy needs is some humility," and the other replied, "Bobby thinks humility is something in the atmosphere."

Kennedy is not a humble man, nor does he pretend to be. As Attorney General, he would sometimes receive visitors in a disdainful, arrogant posture, staring at them coldly with his feet perched atop the desk. Many people feel a bristling, chip-on-the-shoulder belligerence about him—as if he hears, in a pitch too high for other ears, a constant din of far-off challenges and distant dares to his principles, his courage, his very reason for being. He once summoned New York hoodlum Joey Gallo to Washington for a talk; the flustered Gallo later recounted the meeting this way: "I walk into Kennedy's office and he gets mad at me. He says, 'So you're Joe Gallo, the Juke Box King. You don't look so tough. I'd like to fight you myself.' I hadda tell him I don't fight." Gallo's very existence was an insult to Bobby's sense of morality.

Joseph Kennedy has said, "Bobby feels more strongly for or against people than Jack—just as I do. . . He's a great kid, he hates the same way I do." Later Joseph Kennedy told a reporter that in reality "Bobby is soft—soft on people. All I ever meant to convey is that he has the capacity to be emotionally involved, to feel things deeply, as compared with Jack and that amazing detachment of his."

Bobby's feelings about people cut deeply, and they span the spectrum of reaction from loyalty to love and from dislike to loathing. As a rule, his feelings are not hard to fathom, for he seldom tries to conceal an attitude. (At least, he seldom did when he was not dependent on an electorate for his own job, but that could change somewhat if he consciously seeks a new, less abrasive political image. Despite his legendary label as "the Irish Puritan," Bobby's reaction to any given person is unpredictable. As with most men, it seems less grounded on changeless moralistic principles than it is on Bobby's own personal needs, his prejudices of the moment and his first instinctive snap judgment of an individual.

Kennedy spent six months in 1953 working as a lawyer for the notorious Senate Investigations Subcommittee, run by Wisconsin Republican Senator Joseph P. McCarthy. Because of McCarthy's sinister and often baseless accusations about Communists in sensitive government jobs, an era of fear and distrust spread across the United States. Chief counsel for the subcommittee was a New York attorney named Roy Cohn, who became nearly as famed and feared as the Senator. Bobby personally disliked Cohn from the start and does to this day. As for McCarthy, an old family friend, Kennedy always expressed sympathy. Bobby acknowledged that the Senator was wrong in what he did, but insisted that he was a victim of his own publicity-hunger and of Cohn's influence rather than the demagogue's drives that many historians now claim were McCarthy's personal motivation. Whatever moral or ethical wrongs were perpetrated in the McCarthy era, Bobby judged Cohn and McCarthy from a standard considerably more pragmatic than puritanical.

In his politics, Kennedy has seldom shown any more of an ideological turn of mind than he has in his relationships with people. He has always carried the label of a Democrat in good standing. But members of the liberal wing of the party have been wary of his commitment to their faith. Indeed, in Bobby's politics, practicality and, at times, pure opportunism have seemed motivating forces more than philosophy.

Now that he is in the Senate, and must stand for re-election from liberal-oriented New York, his record will almost certainly be more consistently liberal. But his past record is mottled. Bobby's own relentless pursuit of Teamster Union President James R. Hoffa, whom Kennedy believed guilty of corrupt practices, was suspect in itself to liberals. It sometimes involved bitingly sarcastic cracks from Kennedy when witnesses took the Fifth Amendment during Senate Rackets Committee hearings, and even as Attorney General, Bobby showed a certain insensitivity toward the due-process doctrine of law in trying to get Hoffa. Yet he felt sincerely that he was helping defenseless rank-and-file unionists.

As Attorney General, Kennedy did not rally with any notable enthusiasm behind the Negro cause for civil rights until after the cries for equality became too loud to ignore. Then he plunged in with admirable and typically unswayable dedication.

One of the bills Bobby initiated early in his term at the Justice Department called for loosening the laws against wiretaps used by both state and federal lawmen. It so shocked liberals that Joseph Rauh, then vice chairman of Americans for Democratic Action, said, "To think that with all our hopes, this Justice Department has proposed a worse bill than any presented before." Later Bobby softened the language, but he still supports wiretap legislation.

Through the years, Kennedy has drifted into liberal pastures; yet he has displayed little evidence of a mind given to intellectual speculation about the subtleties or even the truisms that form the political foundations of a free, democratic nation. Once, during the 1960 campaign, he was asked why he was working so hard to make his brother President. Bobby replied flatly, "I'm not doing this only because of the family and because Jack is my brother. I sincerely do feel that this will make a hell of a lot of difference to the country. I really believe that we've gone soft in America, that we've got to wake up."

Tough-talking and impulsive as he seems at times, Kennedy has—as did his brother Jack—a sharp, quick wit. His humor is scarcely of the style to bring guffaws or belly laughs. Many of his best lines are jokes on himself. When he was first sworn in as Attorney General, he held a series of introductory meetings with Justice Department lawyers and always slipped in a wry little how-to-succeed speech that went something like this: "Don't forget, I came to this department ten years ago as an assistant attorney at a salary of $4,200 a year. But I had ability. I had integrity. I had an interest in my job. I stayed late at night. My brother became President. And now I'm Attorney General." After a pause his face would break into a smile and Bobby would add, "Of course, those qualifications were not necessarily listed in the order of their importance."

Shortly after he won his Senate seat amid sarcastic charges that he was a voting resident of Massachusetts who lived in Virginia and had no right to represent New York, Bobby appeared before a Women's National Press Club luncheon. He drew screams of laughter from the ladies when he said, "I can't tell you how happy I am to be here representing the great state of . . . uh . . . uh . . . uh." Later he told them, "I want to assure you that I have no presidential aspirations." He paused, grinned broadly and added, "Nor does my wife—Ethel Bird."

Despite his occasional charm on a podium, Kennedy has never been a true extrovert, even as a performing politician. While campaigning amid excited throngs for the Senate in New York, he often seemed embarrassed and uncertain about just what he was doing amid such yammering commotion. His oratory never fanned flames of emotion in the crowds, although his intonation and gestures were so like the dead President's that it was positively ghostly at times.

Unlike Lyndon Johnson, he never gorged himself on his own public adulation. When he waved to crowds, he used an almost feminine flutter of fingers; his autographs were tiny squiggles, no more than an inch long. Yet Bobby had come quite a way from the youth who appeared before a few people during John Kennedy's 1952 Massachusetts senatorial campaign against Republican Incumbent Henry Cabot Lodge and said: "My brother Jack couldn't be here; my mother couldn't be here; my sister Eunice couldn't be here; my sister Pat couldn't be here; my sister Jean couldn't be here; but if my brother Jack were here, he'd tell you Lodge has a very bad voting record. Thank you."

Other members of the Kennedy clan have all appeared more gregarious, more relaxed, more polished than Bobby. Most of them, including the women, have a stately, elegant bearing that Bobby does not have. He is the runt among the men in the family. Joseph Sr. himself is six feet tall; Joseph Jr., who died in 1944, was a strapping six-feet-two; Jack was six feet, and Teddy is college-linebacker-sized—six-feet-two and 200 pounds. Bobby stands barely five-feet-ten and weighs just 165 pounds when he isn't gaunt from overwork.

His mother, Rose, once said, "Bobby is the seventh of nine children. He grew up in the shadow of Joe and of Jack, with his sisters and Ted, the baby. He was the smallest and thinnest, and we feared he might grow up puny and girlish. We soon realized there was no fear of that."

Indeed, Bobby still looks frail, a little like an Irish choir boy grown old too soon. But he is about as fragile as a roll of barbed wire. His hands are big and broad, with fingers nearly as thick as the fat end of a pool cue. The palms are plated with calluses, particularly during a campaign when he has gripped hundreds of hands in a day. There is a look about him of the sinewy energy, the tenacious strength of a gymnast.

Despite his size (or maybe partly because of it) Bobby won his major 'H' at Harvard playing football. He has never forgotten the exultation of that combat. As Attorney General, he appeared at a banquet meeting of college coaches in Pittsburgh and said earnestly, "Except for war, there is nothing in American life which trains a boy better for life than football."

Even approaching 40, Bobby was playing touch football with the callow ferocity of a fraternity boy. Most people who have played with him find precious little difference between his brand of touch football and war: all is fair as long as Bobby wins. In any game with him it goes without saying that he will be captain, quarterback, signal-caller and passer for his team. On some occasions, he has refused to play at all unless he could choose exactly the people he wants on his team. Sometimes he has refused to count an opposing team's touchdown on the basis of a sudden rules change that moves the goal line back to "the next tree." He has threatened to pick up his football and go home when it seemed his team might lose. One frequent combatant said of Bobby's brand of touch football, "He's really serious about every play. And he's just *got* to win. If you drop a pass or don't intercept one, he really gets mad at you. And if he can't win by running circles around you, he'll argue you dizzy." Kennedy himself has chuckled about the charge that he switches rules in mid-game and said, "They only complain about the rules because they always lose."

Given his mastery of the roughhouse elements of football and politics, there would seem to be little room for gentleness in a man like Bobby. Indeed, it is one of the paradoxes of the man, but this tough Irishman who dares bigtime hoodlums to fight, is like a lean and beardless Santa Claus when it comes to children. He cannot resist them and they find in him a comfortable, comforting person, tender and sincerely interested in their prattle. Except for Bobby's own family or closest friends, it is a side of him seldom revealed to anyone but children.

During his New York Senate campaign, Kennedy often stopped his motorcades or made special forays away from his sidewalk handshaking paths to chat for a moment with children standing along the rim of the crowd. When he was Attorney General, deep in problems, he invited into his office straggling lines of bewildered school kids who were touring the Justice Department. Occasionally he would leap up on his desk, make a little talk about his job, proudly show drawings done by his own children and then spend many minutes coaxing the dazzled youngsters to ask him questions.

At a hospital ward party for kids a few months after John Kennedy was murdered, a little boy spotted Bobby and yelped with ear-splitting clarity, "Hey, Mister, your brother got shot!" Adults gasped. Bobby paused for a moment, stunned. Then he said quietly to the child, "It's all right. I have another brother."

Bobby's carefully controlled but poignant reply masked a sorrow that was indefinably deep. There would never be anyone again like Jack in his life.

Bobby's intense devotion to the Roman Catholic faith was a bulwark during the trauma that followed the tragedy. Again and again in the months after the murder, usually at night or in the rain to avoid gaping tourists, Bobby traveled to John Kennedy's grave in Arlington National Cemetery. There he knelt in prayer. Of all the Kennedys, only his mother Rose has been more devout than Bobby. For years in his youth he served faithfully as an altar boy, and at one point even considered entering the priesthood. Once when he was Attorney General attending St. Francis Xavier church in Hyannis, an altar boy was absent. Bobby volunteered from his pew to serve the Mass and did it to perfection. At home, Bobby and Ethel Kennedy are strict in their insistence that their children say table grace and recite their Rosary each day. And Ethel herself has sometimes startled people at lavish, formal dinners by saying a prayer aloud before she eats.

His Catholicism is as much a part of Bobby as his intensity of purpose. Indeed, religious faith is an underpinning that all the Kennedys have relied on—and they have needed it far more than most families ever do.

John Kennedy's murder was only one link in a horrifying chain of misfortunes that has haunted the Kennedy clan for years. The first son of Joseph and Rose Kennedy—Joe Jr.—was killed during World War II. He had volunteered as pilot of a highly-secret, experimental "drone" plane that was laden with 22,000 pounds of explosives and aimed at Nazi V-2 sites in Europe. Joe Kennedy and his copilot were to parachute out and let the plane explode on its target. It blew up over the English Channel before they got out; no bodies were recovered. In 1948 Kathleen, second oldest Kennedy daughter and widow of the Marquess of Hartington, died in a plane crash in France. The eldest Kennedy daughter, Rosemary, now 45, has been in a Wisconsin nursing home for the retarded since she was 22. On December 19, 1961, Joseph Kennedy himself suffered a stroke that left him partially paralyzed and speechless. And on June 19, 1964, less than seven months after Jack was murdered, a chartered plane carrying Teddy Kennedy to the Massachusetts Democratic Convention crashed in an orchard near Springfield. Two men were killed; Teddy had a broken back. He was strapped to a bed for months, and barely managed to walk into the Senate chambers with a cane in January, 1965.

The night that Teddy crashed, a stricken Bobby stood in the hospital lobby with a reporter. "I was just thinking, if my mother had not had any more children after her first four, she would have nothing now," he said. "I guess the only reason we've survived is that there are too many of us. There are more of us than there is trouble."

Of all the Kennedy men, Bobby was the only one left alive and physically untouched by devastating accident or crippling disease.

II
THE FAMILY'S MAN

□□
□□

OF NINE CHILDREN
born to Joseph and Rose Kennedy, none seemed more irrevocably
committed to Kennedy blood, pride and ties than Robert. Joseph
Kennedy once said, "I always felt that if I died, Bobby would be
the one to keep the family together. Bobby is a disciple of my
theory—if you have your family with you, you have a headstart on
others who must rely on making friends."

The unofficial motto of the Kennedy family is indelibly
branded on each of the clan, and it is by no means calculated to
make a host of friends. Through the years, it was preached repeatedly by Joseph Kennedy, and like him, it is uncompromising
and charged with pride: "Never Take Second Best."

Predictably, such a credo triggered among the Kennedy
offspring everything from fist fights when they were much younger
to savage, stubborn parlor games lasting far into the night when
they were older. No one wanted to finish second. In time, it ignited
a burning loyalty within the family, a dedication to each other (at
least partly as highly respected opponents) so intense that it approached an obsession: a Kennedy—any Kennedy—should not,
indeed could not, be beaten at anything, and anyone who thought
differently might have to reckon with the whole crowd. In public,
Kennedys together seemed metallic and unsentimental; no gushing
Irish blarney was allowed. But their affection for each other was

31

real enough and ran deep enough so that they never felt the need to wallow in it before other people.

The Kennedy children were raised in an unusual environment that included Irish Catholic piety, compulsive competition, strong parental discipline and millions of dollars. Shrewd, hustling Joseph Kennedy, son of a prosperous saloonkeeper, had set out with a monk's discipline and a gambler's instincts to make the Yankee blue-blood-controlled Boston banking world safe for Irishmen.

After graduation from Harvard in 1912, Joseph Kennedy worked briefly as a $1,500-a-year bank inspector, but that was too small for him. When he learned that Boston's Columbia Trust Company was to be merged with another bank, he borrowed $45,000 from friends and relatives, bought controlling interest in the bank and made himself, at 25, the youngest bank president in the United States. Eventually he moved into Wall Street, made some of his millions by inflating stock prices through rumors and well-publicized transactions, then selling short for enormous gains. He anticipated the end of Prohibition with fine, profit-minded insight. In 1933 he cornered the franchise for importing Scotch whiskey and British gin, then got a United States Government permit to bring in cases of liquor for medicinal purposes. When Prohibition was lifted, Kennedy had an almost limitless supply of booze in the country to slake the nation's thirst. He also made millions in oil, Hollywood movies and real estate in Manhattan, Palm Beach and Chicago.

Eventually, Joseph Kennedy was able to make good on an incredibly ambitious promise he had made to himself back in 1915 when his first son, Joseph Jr., was born—that he would accumulate enough money to set up million-dollar trust funds for his children, allowing them to reap a handsome return over the years. True to Joe Kennedy's word, each of the Kennedy offspring is now worth at least $10,000,000.

Joseph Kennedy insisted that there be no strings attached to the money he gave his children, for he was convinced that the kids he raised would be neither corroded nor corrupted by great wealth. "I put them in a position where each one of them could spit in my eye and tell me where to go," he said. "And there was nothing to prevent them from becoming rich, idle bums if they wanted to." There is no record of any Kennedys ever spitting in the eye of their bureaucratic father, and neither is there an idle bum in the bunch.

That may be more to the credit of Rose, for Joseph Kennedy was gone from home a great deal while he built up his early bankroll. She was quite a person in her own right. Educated in good parochial schools, she was the daughter of John F. "Honey Fitz" Fitzgerald, the jolly mayor of Boston who used to do jigs on table-tops after election victories. Honey Fitz provided his pretty, rosy-cheeked daughter with a comfortable environment, even sent her to Europe for two years of musical education and, upon her return in 1910, had her act as His Honor's official hostess since her mother was too shy. Rose and Joseph Kennedy were married in Boston on October 7, 1914, by William Cardinal O'Connell.

Despite the fortune her husband amassed and her own social polish, Rose remained a practical, down-to-earth Irish mother. She has been strict about the practices of her religion, almost never misses daily Mass and has inculcated in her family a sound grounding in Catholicism. She never got a priest or a nun from her family, large and diverse as it was, although she always had hopes. When Teddy, the youngest, was born, Rose thought he might be the one. Later she said, "The Pope (Pius XII) gave Teddy his first Holy Communion. I thought with all those spiritual advantages Teddy might become a priest or even a bishop, but he met a beautiful blonde one evening, and that was the end of it."

Rose believed as much as her husband in the never-take-second-best precept, but she was more gentle in her approach. She felt that once a child caught the idea of what it meant to be a Kennedy, there would be an epidemic. "If you bring up the older children so they do things in a good way, and give them a lot of attention," she has said, "the younger ones are great imitators and will follow the older ones' example." She did not believe in sparing the rod either, and once said, "I think when children are little, physical punishment is rather a good thing. I used to have a ruler and paddled them occasionally because when they are young that's all they understand. As they get older I think you can reason with them and point out why you request them to do certain things."

Rose and Joe raised a family that came to be admired, even envied, by a whole nation. There were grumblings among some outsiders that the Kennedys were too abrasive, too selfish, too conceited and too clannish to be rated as a Perfect American Family. Indeed, to describe Kennedys as an example of "togetherness" is like calling the Green Bay Packers "lovable." But Rose and Joe got results: already their family claims a President, two Senators and a seemingly infinite number of grandsons who might well become either or both.

Even with the ravages of death and bad fortune over the years, the Kennedys rally an impressive roster of people—in numbers, accomplishments and good looks. As of mid-1965 they included: Senator Bobby, married to Ethel (née Skakel), 37, with nine children; Senator Teddy married to Joan (née Bennett), 28, with two children; Eunice, 43, married to R. Sargent Shriver, 49, director of the Peace Corps and head of President Johnson's pet war-on-poverty organization, with four children; Patricia, 41, married to British-born actor Peter Lawford, 40, with four children; Jean, 37, married to Stephen Smith, 38, manager of Bobby's and Teddy's first senate campaigns and also Joe Kennedy's No. One son-in-law for managing the family fortune, with two children, and Jackie, 36, with Caroline and John Jr.

Because of family death and disease, Bobby is now Kennedy-in-Chief. But for years he played a muted, if scrappy supporting role to his older brothers and sisters.

When Bobby was born on November 20, 1925, at the Kennedys' modest two-story home in the Boston suburb of Brookline, his father already had several million dollars and six other children (only Jean and Teddy were still to arrive). Before Bobby was out of rompers, ambitious Joe decided to pull out of Boston, and he loaded everyone into a plush, private railroad car. He moved to Riverdale, New York, in The Bronx and a short time later to a more lavish mansion in the prosperous Westchester County suburb of Bronxville. The father wanted to seek his fortune in more profitable climes than tight-fisted, Yankee-held New England.

Bobby's life became nomadic and he attended no less than 12 different schools. But Joe's millions, plus the love and loyalty within the family, did furnish an unchanging foundation for childhood, and Bobby led a fairly normal little boy's life.

He was a Cub Scout, a knob-kneed terror at sports, an undistinguished scholar, a reasonably profitable breeder of white rabbits in a tool shed (he opened his first bank account with the proceeds from selling rabbits) and the owner of a beloved pet pig named Porky. He once broke a toe when it was crushed beneath an old radiator that he had been forbidden to play with and he hopped about in silent agony for an hour before he dared tell his parents of the accident. He gashed his head against a heavy table when he made a blind, furious charge at his sister Eunice. He had a brief siege of pneumonia that was more irritating than critical because it came at the height of the swimming season.

Bobby embarked on a brief career as a magazine salesman. At first he was full of energy, buoyed by early intimations of the profit motive. He pedaled his bicycle to the homes of Bronxville neighbors, pleading with them in a shrill voice to buy *The Saturday Evening Post* and the *Ladies' Home Journal* each week. He got some customers, but his enthusiasm gradually evaporated. He stopped riding his bicycle and took to covering his route with his magazines stacked in the back seat of the family's chauffeur-driven Rolls-Royce. Eventually, he lost interest entirely and the chauffeur took the route by himself, while unsold magazines rose in stacks that cluttered Bobby's room.

When Bobby was 10 his father, who had been Securities and Exchange Commissioner, was rewarded for personal loyalty and campaign contributions by President Franklin Roosevelt. Joseph Kennedy was named Ambassador to the Court of St. James's and the family moved to London. There Bobby and Teddy went to the Gibbs School. Occasionally they attended parties with Princesses Elizabeth and Margaret Rose. It was a heady, opulent life and at the embassy Bobby was introduced to a number of little boy's idols of the day—including Charles Lindbergh and Douglas "Wrong Way" Corrigan, who had just flown from Brooklyn to Dublin, Ireland, although he said he meant to fly home to Los Angeles.

During the late '30's Hitler was stamping the swastika of

his regime on Europe, but Ambassador Kennedy insisted that the United States should remain isolationist and avoid involvement in Europe's problems. By late 1940, this sentiment was not particularly popular in Washington; Roosevelt happily accepted his resignation and Joe Kennedy brought his family home to Bronxville.

Bobby spent his last two prep-school years in Massachusetts at Milton Academy, one of the best secondary schools in the nation. Still no scholar, he passed with just average grades. He played a grim, hard game of tennis and he quarterbacked the football team. He also lent his voice, unmelodious as it was, to the glee club. (That voice had not improved 20 years later: Bobby was engagingly appalling during his New York State Senate campaign when he sang "We Shall Overcome" with a perfectly straight face and an unchanging monotone.) At Milton Academy, Bobby eventually became fairly popular, but he had some trouble at first. Many of the other students were sophisticated beyond their years and liked nothing better than smoking cigarettes and guzzling beer. Bobby was strait-laced about such things and refused to participate; but he was so good at sports and other extracurricular pursuits that he was finally accepted. He never did take up smoking (except for an occasional cigar now), and when he was 21 he got $1,000 from his father for abstaining from nicotine or liquor.

Through most of Bobby's youth, his brother Joe Jr., 10 years older, had taken more of an interest in the younger Kennedys than Jack did. He taught Bobby to swim, catch a football and sail a boat. Robust, husky Joe was the hero, the fellow to emulate, the one the family figured would be the first President Kennedy. When Joe was killed in 1944, Bobby was grief-stricken.

Only eighteen and barely a year out of Milton, Bobby was attending naval officer candidate classes in New England. His brother's death emphasized Bobby's disenchantment with the mundane way he was spending the war; he was afraid that he was doomed to sit it out on some grassy college campus. Jack had already become a combat hero by saving most of his crew after a Japanese destroyer sank his boat, PT-109, in the South Pacific; and early in 1945, Bobby decided it was high time he, too, got into the fight. As Jack had done before him, Bobby went to Washington and looked up Secretary of the Navy James Forrestal, who had known his father on Wall Street. Through Forrestal's influence, Bobby was promptly released from the officers' training program, made a seaman second class and assigned to a brand-new destroyer, the Joseph P. Kennedy Jr. It was a noble effort to go to war and to honor his dead brother, but for the next six months Bobby did little but chip paint while his ship cruised peacefully about the Caribbean Sea.

Out of the Navy in 1946, there was no question about Bobby's immediate future: Harvard was where male Kennedys went to college and Robert was to be no exception. Both Joe Jr. and Jack had graduated *cum laude*. Bobby made no such marks. "I didn't go to class very much, to tell you the truth," he said. "I used to talk and argue a lot, mostly about sports and politics."

Bobby spent most of his time with the football team. Occasionally, opportunistic, nonathletic Harvard men, dazzled by the Kennedy millions and smitten by a vision of jobs Bobby might be able to offer through his father, tried to cozy up to Kennedy, but he was never a young man to be climbed over—or on.

Attractive and spirited as he was, Bobby dated only occasionally and pretty much avoided rah-rah cocktail parties in the Ivy League. "Nobody who went to them all the time made any real contribution," he said. "What's the use going to those things and drinking? I'd rather do something else."

During his Harvard days, Bobby seemed to be trying to make up for the combat he missed during the war by flinging himself with single-minded drive into football. Slight as he was, he played end on the varsity, competing in a series of David-Goliath matches against eight other beefier, broader men for the position.

Lacking notable speed or nimbleness, Bobby spent hours after practice charging wearily about the field, catching pass after pass from Team Captain Kenneth O'Donnell, who was later to be one of John Kennedy's top White House aides. At one scrimmage in 1947, Coach Richard Harlow chattered angrily at Bobby because he kept missing a block on an opposing tackle. After several failures, Kennedy collapsed. They found he had been playing with a badly injured leg. That year, as usual, the last game of the Harvard season was against Yale; for a man to win his major 'H' in football, he had to get into that game. Forlorn and resigned, Bobby sat on the bench, his leg heavily taped and braced. Then, for the last play of the game, Harlow sent him hobbling in so he could get his letter. Harvard had just scored a touchdown but Yale was leading, 31 to 21. Bobby, injured leg and all, took his kick-off position at right end. The strategy was for Harvard to kick the ball toward the left side of the field so Kennedy would not be involved, but the kicker sent the ball spinning in a short wobbly arc to the right side. A Yale man grabbed it and ran straight at Bobby. Kennedy crashed into the runner, helped tackle him in a windmilling heap of players, then limped off the field none the worse for valor.

When he graduated from Harvard in 1948, Robert Kennedy had a bachelor of arts degree in Government, plenty of warm memories of football—and not much else. "I had led a pretty relaxed life," he said. "I thought I was completely unprepared and ill-equipped, so I decided to go to law school." Obviously, there was no burning urge to become a master lawyer; the decision was made more from default than dedication. Bobby enrolled at the University of Virginia Law School and produced an uneven scholastic record before he graduated 56th in a class of 125 in 1951. He managed to flunk a course in how to use the library, but earned an occasional 'A' in tougher classes.

One of his proud accomplishments at Virginia was helping to revive the Law School Forum, a group which sponsored prominent speakers on campus. Bobby saw to it that old Kennedy family friends, such as Supreme Court Justice William O. Douglas, *New York Times* Columnist Arthur Krock and Wisconsin Senator Joseph McCarthy came to speak. Bobby had to fight a bitter battle to get a Virginia platform for Ralph Bunche, a Negro, Nobel laureate and now United Nations Undersecretary for Political Affairs. Campus segregationists scrapped viciously to block Bunche's appearance, but Kennedy finally won and got a modicum of national publicity for his efforts.

He also invited his father down to talk, and Joe Kennedy proved he had not modified his isolationist politics at all in the 10 years since he quit as Ambassador in London. It was late in 1950 when he appeared at the university; the Korean War was at a high and bloody tide, and Joe Kennedy declared that the United States should pull out of that fight. Worse, Bobby's father flatly advocated leaving Europe to itself—Communist threats notwith-standing. "It is idle to talk of being able to hold the line at the Elbe or the line at the Rhine," he said. "The truth is that our only real hope is to keep Russia, if she chooses to march, on the other side of the Atlantic. It may be that Europe, for a decade or a generation or more, will turn Communistic."

Education for the Kennedys meant considerably more than the fact of being in a classroom. All of them traveled abroad fre-quently when they were young—and it led them to disagree bluntly with Old Joe's views on foreign policy. Bobby had been to the Continent several times while his father was in London and he had been frightened by the goose-stepping troops of Hitler's Germany. After the Navy, he had taken a long tour of Latin America with LeMoyne Billings, a close friend of Jack's during Harvard days but now one of Bobby's pals. In South America, Bobby was shocked at the bleak poverty and the rampant oppression caused by oligarchic society.

Between Harvard and law school, Bobby worked briefly as a foreign correspondent, covering the Arab-Israeli war for the now-defunct Boston *Post*, a paper owned by William Randolph Hearst, another one of his father's friends. Because of Joe Kennedy's pre-1941 views that Nazi Germany should have been left alone, he was suspected of being anti-Semitic. But Bobby was outspoken in his admiration for the Israeli defense against the Arabs, and later said, "They had much more spirit and zest and determination and discipline. I felt the Jews would beat the Arabs."

As Bobby made more trips abroad, he became convinced that the United States should never backtrack from its role of active protector of democratic progress in the world. In 1955, he and Justice Douglas toured Central Asia on a trip they had planned since 1951. They journeyed deep into primitive regions of Soviet Russia which were previously closed to westerners. They were led carefully about by a Soviet-furnished interpreter and steered away from areas where there were forced-labor camps. Yet they wit-nessed Soviet tyranny and bigotry at every hand, and Bobby wrote a piece for *The New York Times Magazine* that proved he had shed any lingering taint of his father's isolationism: "It is, I believe, high time that we in the West understood and spotlighted in the

United Nations and throughout the world this despoliation of freedom, of local autonomy, of rights of minorities."

Robert Kennedy has seldom been attracted to intellectual pursuits—at least not with the genuine and wide-ranging curiosity of his brother Jack. Although Bobby's speeches are frequently larded with quotes from such diverse and impressive sources as Pericles, Mark Twain and Shakespeare, he drones out the quotations with the awkward and monotonous delivery of a high-school valedictorian. He has written three books himself—*The Enemy Within, Just Friends and Brave Enemies*, and *The Pursuit of Justice*. All are pretty much straight-forward recitations of Bobby's own experiences or discussions of moral stands that he feels would better the country.

Esthetics, too, seem to have little place in Bobby's environment, for it is too full of his vigorous commitment to athletics. He is a daring skier, and when he is at one of his favorite resorts in Colorado or Vermont, he often rises before dawn and races down the trails as soon as there is light enough to see. At times he makes three long runs before breakfast.

He is a sailor of untiring tenacity and considerable skill. However strong the wind or choppy the waters, he will sail far off the family beach on Cape Cod from dawn until after dark. If his favorite boat were not all but unsinkable, it would have gone to the bottom of the Atlantic years ago. He swims, hikes and plays tennis with relentless vigor, as if he were determined to squeeze every drop of energy out of his body before he grows an hour older. He seems to thrill to the challenge of any contest—or any conquest.

One of his most challenging—and certainly most publicized—conquests occurred in March, 1965. The Canadian government had renamed a 14,000-foot mountain after the late President; it was part of the St. Elias Range in the rugged Yukon Territory, and it would be called Mount Kennedy instead of East Hubbard (after Gardiner Green Hubbard, the first president of the National Geographic Society). The peak had never been climbed and almost immediately it occurred to Bobby and Teddy Kennedy that the brothers should be in the first party to make the assault.

The National Geographic Society and the Boston Museum of Science had planned an expedition, and the Kennedys asked if they could go along. When Teddy, still disabled after the plane crash outside Springfield in June, had to drop out, Bobby felt compelled to go alone, although he admitted, "I hate heights." A close friend explained Kennedy's insistence on making the climb: "Bob has what might be called an existentialist streak in him—he feels that when a challenge exists, and you have said you will meet it, you destroy yourself if you run away from it."

The idea for the climb was conceived in secrecy, but the news soon dribbled out through innumerable leaks on Capitol Hill, and when Robert finally left Washington much of the world was watching to see if the Kennedy determination would carry him to the summit.

He seemed to be irked, as usual, by the news coverage, but as one member of his family put it, "If Bobby hates publicity as much as he says, then why, for heaven's sakes, does he go out and climb mountains?" Bobby was not so upset about the idea of publicity that he totally ignored it: dozens of color pictures were taken and Kennedy himself wrote an article for *Life* magazine when he came off the mountain.

On March 22, Bobby was flown in a Royal Canadian Air Force helicopter from White Horse, Alaska, to the party's base camp, 9,000 feet up the snow-covered slope of Mount Kennedy. With Bobby were two of the United States' most expert mountaineers—James Whittaker and Barry Prather, veterans of the first American expedition that scaled Mount Everest in the Himalayas —as well as five other experienced climbers. Mount Kennedy was a molehill compared to Everest, but it was a challenge even for veterans in that it had never been climbed.

From the base camp, the route to the top was 10 miles long, with a vertical rise of nearly a mile over ground that was slick with diamond-hard glacial ice and packed with powder snow. Bobby recalled afterward that throughout the climb he had a nagging headache because of the thin air. Once, he dropped through a snow bridge concealing a crevasse. He caught himself chest-deep in the snow, but he was roped to his companions, who pulled him free.

A blizzard raged about their camp the second night out, but the weather cleared by morning of the third day, and the party came within 500 feet of the summit shortly after noon. The day had become radiantly sunny, the temperature about five above zero—unusually warm for the season. Bobby wore sungoggles and a red stocking cap; sharp crampons were clamped to his boots. Ahead loomed a menacing rock wall pitched at a 45-degree incline.

"I began to climb," Kennedy recalled in his *Life* article. "I remembered my mother's last words to me, 'Don't slip, dear,' and the admonition of a friend who had obviously never climbed, 'Don't look down.' . . . And the reporter from a national newspaper covering the climb told me before I began that his paper had just completed my obituary. All of these splendid thoughts raced through my mind."

As he inched higher, his fear of heights gripped him: "I kept thinking, 'How did I get myself into this?' " Two hundred feet from the top, the incline flattened out a bit. His companions, Whittaker and Prather, waved Bobby on and, bulky as an Eskimo squaw in his padded jacket and trousers, Kennedy clambered to the top alone.

While airplanes full of news photographers buzzed overhead like flies, he paused for a moment, then pulled a three-foot pole from his pack. Wrapped tightly about it was a pennant that Bobby had ordered especially for this moment: President Kennedy's family flag—three gold helmets against a black background with a maroon and silver border. Bobby planted it in the snow, then dug a hole to bury other mementos of his late brother: several PT-109 tie clasps, a bound copy of the 1961 inaugural address sealed in a weatherproof container, a gold John Kennedy medallion.

Bobby had intended to leave Jack Kennedy's flag flying from the mountain top, but his companions convinced him that the winds would whip it to tatters in a few hours, so he brought it down again.

Bobby later admitted that he had been frightened, but his companions had nothing but praise for him. "That final sharp ridge looked a lot like Everest," said Whittaker. "While we were on it Bob wanted to look down the face on the left, thousands of feet of sheer drop. It was the kind of spot that sometimes freezes experienced climbers. He leaned on his ice ax and looked over for a while. If he felt any fear, he kept it to himself." Whittaker and Prather had carried extra first-aid equipment along, but Bobby's only injury was a heel blister.

A few fusty critics complained that Kennedy had no business scaling a mountain when he should have been at work in the Senate. Bobby himself would only say that he went for "personal reasons that seemed compelling." When he got back to Washington, he announced he would never go up another mountain, and said, "I'm going to stay on the first floor of my house; I have nine children." His wife, Ethel, asked for her analysis of Bobby's climb, cheerily offered, "I think he wants to take his mind off the fact that he's not an astronaut."

The week after the climb, the Kennedys invited Jim Whittaker and Barry Prather for a three-day visit to their home in Virginia. Between them, Bobby and Ethel quickly proved that, skilled and tireless as Whittaker and Prather might be on a mountainside, they were no match for Kennedys on level ground. The two mountain climbers were beaten to exhaustion by Bobby and Ethel in an afternoon-long game of touch football, and, to add insult to bone-weariness, Ethel trounced Whittaker in a game of tennis. Stiff and weary when it was over, Whittaker said wryly, "I'm heading for the mountains to rebuild my ego."

Ethel and Bobby Kennedy are indeed quite a team. Of their prowess in touch football, Bobby has said with more truth than humor, "Ethel and I can beat anybody." At 37, after 15 years of marriage and nine children (as of mid-1965), Ethel still looks as if she should be putting up balloons for the junior prom instead of running the household of a United States Senator. She is as sassy as a sorority girl who has just captured her umpteenth fraternity pin; it would be hard to imagine a partner better suited to the moods and motivations of Robert Kennedy.

Over the years, Bobby's commitments—whatever they have been—are also Ethel's. And not just in the suburban spirit of I'm-thinking-of-you-over-the-sink-dear. She is there in body, too, as often as not (thanks, in part, to the fact that she has a staff of 17 at Hickory Hill).

When Bobby was the star performer at the Senate Rackets Committee hearings probing corruption in labor unions, Ethel—and sometimes a child or two—turned up in a front-row seat every day, even though she was far along in another pregnancy. When Bobby managed Jack's 1960 presidential campaign, Ethel was out pouring tea and making radiant little sales talks about her brother-in-law. One of her proudest possessions is a map of the United States, peppered with little red dots to mark each town where Ethel made a speech, a post-campaign gift from John Kennedy.

When Bobby was running for the Senate in New York, she once confronted his opponent, Senator Kenneth Keating, before a large crowd at a rally. Keating had just launched an attack on Bobby about the Justice Department settlement of the General Aniline case, which originally involved a Nazi German firm. With disarming friendliness, Ethel poked a finger at Keating's ample stomach and said, "Shame on you for saying my husband is a Nazi lover"—then she rubbed her index fingers together in a shame-on-you sign.

When it comes to gamesmanship, Ethel is every bit as active and, if it is possible, even more appalled at the idea of defeat than Bobby is. "I like competition," she said, "but I like to win better."

Ethel is one of the all-time greats of Kennedy touch football. She can run faster than most men and has developed a swivel-hipped fake that once threw former All-American football star Byron "Whizzer" White off balance and allowed Ethel to slip by for a touchdown pass from Bobby. She is a skier, a sailor, a swimmer and a daring horsewoman (as a girl she once cleared a hurdle six feet nine inches high). On a camping trip in the Colorado mountains a few years ago, she hopped out of her sleeping bag and took a pre-breakfast dip in a nearby stream—even though the ground was covered with fresh snow. She was once asked what her favorite sport was and chirped, "Whatever we happen to be playing at the time."

Properly enough, Bobby first met Ethel Skakel at a ski lodge at Canada's Mont Tremblant. It was 1944; she was 17, and the gauntly good-looking young man from Massachusetts appealed to her immediately. "He was a good human being," she recalled. "Also he was very handsome." Bobby was not swept off his feet; for the next two years he dated Ethel's older sister Pat.

The Kennedys and the Skakels had a lot in common. Like Old Joe Kennedy, Ethel's father, George, was a self-made millionaire; he had controlling interest in the vastly diversified (coal, chemicals, real estate) Great Lakes Carbon Corporation, one of the United States' largest privately owned companies. (Both of Ethel's parents died in a 1955 plane crash.) The family was Roman Catholic and all of Ethel's education was at parochial schools—first at the Convent of the Sacred Heart, then at Manhattanville College of the Sacred Heart in Purchase, N.Y.

At Manhattanville, Ethel was the roommate of Bobby's younger sister, Jean. Before long, she was caught up in the Kennedy milieu—and pleased with the whole idea. During a vacation from school in 1946, Ethel visited Boston, and wound up marching through the 11th Congressional District doing her girlish best to help elect John Kennedy to a seat in Congress. She wrote her college senior thesis on John Kennedy's book, *Why England Slept*, and won an 'A'.

When she graduated in 1949 the school yearbook described her with a precious, but incisive caption that fits the lady now as well as it did then: "One moment a picture of utter guilelessness and the next alive with mischief." And, for Bobby, that finally proved to be just right. On June 17, 1950, they were married amid white peonies, lilies and dogwood blooms at St. Mary's Roman Catholic Church in Greenwich, Conn., Ethel's home town. John Kennedy was the best man.

Charming though she was, Ethel never could find her way to her man's heart through his stomach. During the first years of marriage, Bobby tried hard to convince her that she should give up cooking for good. She resisted—a little. Bobby's point was proved perfectly one night when Ethel had several guests for dinner. Cheerful and seemingly efficient, she had bustled about in the kitchen for a long time before she finally summoned everyone to the table. Ethel had prepared four vegetable dishes and everyone was suitably impressed—until they found out that she had forgotten to cook the meat. At that point she agreed to drop cooking. Nevertheless, in 1960 Ethel was selected "The Outstanding Homemaker of the Year" by the Home Fashion League of Washington, an honor which confused and amused her as much as anyone.

Housekeeping aside, Ethel's view of her life approaches the epitome of domestic womanhood. "Bobby and my children are really the only things that count," she said.

Babies have been an unchanging element in the Kennedy household for 14 consecutive years. Ethel and Bobby were married 13 months when they had their first, and Ethel has been pregnant for almost seven years of her first 15 with Bobby. She never pampers herself and usually continues to play touch football, swim, skate or dance right up to the last minute. In 1952 during Jack Kennedy's Senatorial campaign in Massachusetts, Ethel made a speech one night in Fall River, then drove to Boston and had a baby before dawn.

The size of her family has been a delight to her. "I was one of seven myself," she has said, "and I think a big family is good for children. They have to learn to get along together, to share things. Each one learns he's not the only star in the sky." The Kennedy children are a rambunctious bunch, and most of them bear names that reflect family memories or a fondness for old friends. As of mid-1965, Bobby and Ethel's brood included: Kathleen Hartington (born July 4, 1951); Joseph Patrick III (Sept. 24, 1952); Robert Francis Jr. (Jan. 17, 1954); David Anthony (June 15, 1955); Mary Courtney (Sept. 9, 1956); Michael LeMoyne (Feb. 27, 1958); Mary Kerry (Sept. 8, 1959); Christopher George (July 5, 1963); Matthew Maxwell Taylor (Jan. 12, 1965).

They are made unforgettably aware of the fact that they are Kennedys. Even as tots being pushed gently on a swing, they hear from their father: "Come on, let's swing higher and see if we can't set a new record. A Kennedy shouldn't be scared." They often form a shrill, proud Kennedy cheering section at touch-football games, where they turn up on the sidelines waving pom-poms and screeching the family yell:

> Hear ye, hear ye, read all about it.
> We've got a team and there's no doubt about it.
> Clap your hands! Stamp your feet!
> 'Cause Daddy's team just can't be beat!

Ethel is convinced that the Kennedy method of child-raising is sound. "I try to do what Mr. and Mrs. Kennedy did," she explained. "I try to relate immediate experience to their everyday lives. For instance, at Thanksgiving I get them to talk about why it is a ceremonial day and why we have turkey. I ask them to tell the story of the Pilgrims and name the boats they came on. I get each child to tell what happened to them that day. If we've been on a trip or something, I ask them what states we flew over. If there is anything in the news that I can relate to their level we talk about it.

"Of course, there's also a lot of 'Come on now, eat your spinach.' "

She is careful that her children have a strict upbringing in Roman Catholic piety; she insists that, besides grace at meals, and saying their Rosaries, they read two chapters of the Bible before bedtime. Ethel has always been determined that her kids will not grow up to be namby-pamby prigs, and they all have plenty of scars, bruises and cracked bones to show for their daring. "I think children should be encouraged to learn things young," said Ethel. "Joe rode and jumped when he was four. Sure, there are risks—Kathleen has broken her leg riding. Courtney broke her arm when she fell out of a tree. Joe broke his leg skiing. It's hard, but you have to let them take those risks. Gosh, if they're going to develop independence, they have to do it while they're young. I want my children to grow up with as little fear as possible, because the less fear, the more they can accomplish. This outweighs the risks."

Nothing ranks higher in Bobby's life than Ethel and her rollicking flock of youngsters. During the frenetic moments of the 1960 election campaign, Bobby sneaked away whenever he could to take his older children sailing on the family's Sailfish at Hyannis Port. On the phone with some important person, he may break into the conversation with an abrupt "Hold it, Governor" or "Excuse me, Senator," then leave the phone to extricate a baby squawling beneath a chair or to comfort a little boy with a newly skinned knee.

Ethel was once asked if Bobby really had enough time to relax with his family, and she nodded, "Oh, yes. He's home for breakfast and most weekends, and when he comes in, it's quite lively. All the children jump on his back."

The Kennedys' 140-year-old white brick house near Mc-Lean, Virginia, seems built to spill over with kids. (It was once the staff headquarters of Union Army General George B. McClellan during part of the Civil War, but that austere past history has been overwhelmed and obscured by the exuberant Kennedys.) Ethel and Bobby bought the 10-acre estate in 1957 from Jack and Jackie Kennedy after Jackie had become lonely in the rural countryside; she had lost her first baby and wanted to move into Washington. The place is called Hickory Hill because of the magnificent 300-year-old hickory trees that adorn the area.

It has 15 rooms, seven fireplaces and it is decorated tastefully, although notably without the delicate continental flair that Jacqueline Kennedy has. Hickory Hill is now a reflection of Kennedy family activism. There are dozens of photographs of Kennedys and even the paintings are personal. There is an Utrillo-like painting by John Kennedy—result of an afternoon's "contest" among Bobby, Teddy and Jack. There is an oil by Jackie Kennedy depicting Fun at Hickory Hill. There are portraits of the Kennedy children hung all about the place, and one of Jackie and her sister, Lee Radziwill.

The grounds have plenty of room for Kennedy tennis, swimming and touch football. The place is also speckled with a zoo-like variety of animals' homes, such as corrals, duck pens, dog houses and rabbit hutches.

A census was taken of the animal population some time ago. There were probably substantial changes even before that count was completed, but it included: two horses, four ponies, one burro, two angora goats, three dogs, three geese, two cockatoos, one cat, one guinea pig, 40 rabbits, one turtle, one alligator turtle, 22 goldfish, 15 Hungarian pigeons and five chickens.

The animals join in the family life whether they are invited or not. The rabbits once escaped into the center of a black-tie party, and Ethel had to scamper after them. The burro wandered into the house during a party, but no one even stopped eating. One of the most publicized Kennedy pets was a 59-pound sea lion named "Sandy." He ate 10 pounds of fish daily and lived near the swimming pool. Unfortunately, Sandy did not adjust to Hickory Hill as well as others of the menagerie. "The trouble was," Ethel recalled, "he learned to flip over the pool fence and he started chasing people. He chased my guests all the way to their cars. We finally had to give him to the Washington Zoo. When we visit him, he doesn't pay the slightest attention to us."

Bobby delights the kids with polliwog hunts in the woods and takes them on lizard hunts whenever they visit Joseph Kennedy's home in Palm Beach. Bobby's hands are usually scratched from handling the rabbits at Hickory Hill. As a rule, the only major custodial bow made to the damage the Kennedy animals can do to the grounds occurs in the spring when hoof-marks are smoothed out and lawn is reseeded.

If Ethel ever becomes the wife of a President, there will be a lot of nonplused matrons around the country. As usual, many will be willing and eager to imitate every nuance of the First Lady's approach to clothes, *décor* and hostessing. But there will be a real question about whether they are *able* to be like Ethel Kennedy. She is casualness personified. Her first words are often a hearty "Hi, kid," followed quickly by, "Just call me Ethel." Her methods of entertaining, at least as they have developed in the effervescent years at Hickory Hill, are inimitable.

She is perfectly competent to put on a dignified affair, exquisitely catered and expertly performed in every detail. Yet her unquenchable sense of humor and her bouncy refusal to be cowed or intimidated by constrictive rules of decorum have added a dimension of unpredictability to her parties.

At a St. Patrick's Day dinner one year, Ethel carried out the green theme of the day by putting big, fat, live bullfrogs in her centerpieces. At another lavish formal dinner for 50 guests, she supervised each place setting to glittering perfection, then carefully arranged the place cards so that when everyone sat down there were 24 women at one table, while Ethel sat in queenly, giggly splendor with 25 men at the other.

Entertaining at Hickory Hill is usually lighthearted, to say the least. The swimming pool became a noted addition, although it triggered no great national fad. Falling in the water in expensive formal dress is a rich man's recreation if there ever was one, and the Kennedys did it with newsworthy frequency for a while. Ethel herself fell in during a black-tie affair in the summer of 1962, and Pulitzer Prizewinning Historian Arthur Schlesinger Jr. plunged in to help her out. On another occasion, Bobby shoved Pierre Salinger, White House Press Secretary, over the edge. Pierre remained submerged for nearly a minute, then bobbed placidly to the surface, his dripping cigar still wedged between his teeth. One night, in 50-degree weather, Teddy Kennedy dived in, dinner jacket and all, then refused to change clothes and shivered gamely through the rest of the party. Even Bobby's New York opponent, Kenneth Keating, a social friend at the time, wound up in the water at one affair (long before the 1964 campaign, of course). Arizona's former Republican Senator Barry Goldwater once cracked, "When Bobby Kennedy sends out invitations to a formal party, they read 'black tie and snorkel.' "

Gamesmanship is usually the order of the night at a Kennedy party. They have played everything from charades to kick-the-can to hide-and-go-seek-with-the-lights-out. Touch football prevails at almost any season, or time of day. The night they were to attend John Kennedy's inaugural dances, the Kennedys and their guests played a quick game in the snow—dressed in formal clothes and overshoes.

There is precious little pretension in the Kennedys' cultural life, too. As Ethel once said, "I like films such as 'South Pacific,' shows such as 'My Fair Lady,' books such as 'The King Must Die.' We do not feel easy in the company of highbrows and we do not understand the first thing about music."

The Kennedys' closest friends form a comfortable, relaxed and unbreakable inner circle. Most of them are old pals from school days. Bobby and Ethel have never felt the need to do any social-climbing themselves and they do not allow ambitious climbers into their midst—at least not into the midst of their most favored people.

Yet the list of guests at Hickory Hill and people they have called friends is diverse. At touch football alone, they have taken on at one time or another such varied luminaries as former tennis champion Hamilton Richardson, former Notre Dame quarterback Johnny Lattner, and British Ambassador to the United States Sir

David Ormsby-Gore (who played in a double-breasted, pin-striped business suit). They once entertained poet Robert Frost, then in his 80's, and although they did not urge him into a touch-football game, they did have a parlor poetry-writing contest while he was there. "His were slightly better than the rest," said Ethel.

At one point, Bobby and Ethel started a set of seminar sessions that came to be called "Hickory Hill Tech." They invited ivory-tower New Frontiersmen such as Arthur Schlesinger Jr. and Walt Whitman Rostow to discuss with them their scholarly specialties.

Bobby is close enough to the Boston prelate, Richard Cardinal Cushing, so that he could call him direct in 1962 and ask him to raise money to free the Cuban rebels who were being held hostage by Fidel Castro after the Bay of Pigs invasion (Cushing delivered a cool million). When Frank Sinatra's son was kidnaped in the summer of 1964, Bobby could phone Sinatra at a Las Vegas hotel to relay his personal sympathies and promise the full cooperation of the Federal Bureau of Investigation in the case.

The private life of Robert Kennedy has been rich and variegated. Wordsworth said, "The child is the father of the man." That is certainly true of Bobby, for from the opulence of his childhood he developed an immunity to the meaning of money. Because of Joseph Kennedy's wealth and power, Bobby could accept nonchalantly the fine schools and superb facilities which encouraged his whims and hobbies, and the glittering crowd of influential friends, any one of whom could offer a once-in-a-lifetime handshake to most people.

Success was something Bobby seemed never to worry about. The only question was "What kind?"

III

INITIATION TO CONTROVERSY

□□
□□

THE DECADE OF THE '50's spawned few men of such sensational controversy as Senator Joseph McCarthy of Wisconsin and Teamster Union President James R. Hoffa. McCarthy was a contemptuous politician who used congressional investigation as an instrument of personal intimidation. He attracted a cult of millions who rallied fanatically to his pursuit of so-called subversives in government. Jimmy Hoffa was (and is) the leader of 1,700,000 union members who maintain the nation's transportation lifelines on the highways. Despite charges of corruption, graft and hoodlum-run locals, Hoffa has retained his power—a power that could someday be used to cripple the country if he ever attains his dream of negotiating a single coast-to-coast Teamster contract; it would allow him to stop a million trucks with one strike order.

McCarthy and Hoffa were from different worlds, and their paths never really crossed, yet Bobby Kennedy became entangled in the lives of both. It happened because he at last decided to commit his legal career to the hybrid environment of Capitol Hill as a full-time investigating counsel for congressional committees.

That decision cast Robert Kennedy, attorney-at-law, in a mold far different from the traditional image of U.S. men of the bar. Bobby became less the legal researcher than the painstaking sleuth; less the advocate than the inquisitor; less the defender of justice than the attacker of injustice; less the courtroom orator than the hearing-room interrogator.

For U.S. lawyers at practice in court, the age-old Anglo-saxon "adversary system" is the rule. Opposing attorneys tangle in a contest that is won or lost on their application of legal theory, lawbook knowledge or persuasive argument. They are adversaries because of the intellectual and philosophical demands of jurisprudence; they stand as opponents because, under the system, they must stand for the separate views of opposing clients. It is a stance of the mind more than of the heart.

In Bobby Kennedy's specialized milieu on the Hill, things were neither so constricted nor so formal. His opponents were apt to become not only his adversaries but also his enemies. For Bobby, law could be a matter of emotion as well as intellect.

Bobby's early jobs had come as a result of his being a Kennedy. He had once worked briefly as a rent collector in Boston apartment houses owned by Joe Kennedy's bank. His foreign correspondent's job with the Hearst paper in Boston was based on his father's friendships and influence. When Bobby graduated from the University of Virginia Law School in 1951, there were plenty of doors open for a neophyte lawyer named Kennedy—especially in Washington.

Jack was a Congressman. His father was a member of the blue-ribbon Hoover Commission, which was created by Harry Truman to study reorganization of the Executive Department. Beyond that, there was still a lush hangover of influence from Joseph Kennedy's service as Securities and Exchange Commissioner and Ambassador to Great Britain. (For years, newspapers would refer to Bobby with irksome consistency as "the son of the former Ambassador" or "the brother of the Senator from Massachusetts.")

Bobby might well have picked off a job more glamorous and certainly one more profitable (indeed, he did have interviews with rich law firms in New York), but he started out working for $4200 a year at the Justice Department as an underling attorney in a section that dealt with affairs of internal security. Except for the money, which didn't matter, it was a nice start.

Bobby and two other lawyers were assigned full-time to dig into corruption charges against former members of the Truman

Administration. Kennedy went to Brooklyn and helped present to a federal grand jury a major part of the case against former (1943-47) Internal Revenue Commissioner Joseph D. Nunan. Bobby enjoyed the work and he said later, "It was a real education."

Before he could acquire much more of that kind of education, Bobby was summoned home by an irresistible combination—politics and family. He quit his promising career with the Justice Department and returned to Massachusetts in 1952 to manage Jack's U.S. Senate campaign against incumbent Republican Henry Cabot Lodge. That year Republicans were reaping congressional victories all over the country as Dwight D. Eisenhower swept to the presidency; thus, Jack's victory was particularly satisfying to Democrats and Kennedys alike. Bobby had done a good job, but when the last hurrahs were over he was unemployed. After a short, restless stay at Hyannis Port (and a lecture from his mother about how Kennedys had always worked) he returned to Washington and went job-hunting on Capitol Hill.

He wound up applying for a job with Senator Joseph McCarthy, an old family friend. The Republican Party had surprised even itself by winning its first congressional majority in 22 years, and McCarthy had moved up to the chairmanship of the Senate Government Operations Committee—which included the already notorious Permanent Investigations Subcommittee.

Robert Kennedy had no reason to be ignorant of McCarthy's tactics when he applied for a job. It was January, 1953, and the Senator from Wisconsin was already well launched in his career as self-appointed inquisitor and would-be exterminator of subversives, homosexuals and anyone even slightly suspect of either aberration. Few men in the country had so much power, and none used it so badly.

Three years earlier McCarthy had begun his assault with a speech in Wheeling, West Virginia, waving a bit of white paper that he claimed bore the names of 205 security risks employed by the State Department. From then on, his harangue had crescendoed. McCarthy's message was fraught with irresponsible and unsubstantiated accusations. His assault was loaded with smear and slander. McCarthy called General George C. Marshall a man "steeped in falsehood," whose strategy decisions had supported "the world policy of the Kremlin." McCarthy went on television during the 1952 presidential campaign and managed to imply that there was a link between Democratic nominee Adlai E. Stevenson and Communists.

By 1952, McCarthy had such an enormous following that during the elections of that year many Republican candidates begged for his endorsement. When the 83rd Congress convened in January, 1953, McCarthy's request for money to finance his investigations passed the Senate easily, with almost no objections from either party. Whether Senators were cowed by McCarthy or simply indifferent about a rather ordinary appropriation of funds at that point was a debatable question. But McCarthy's legions, convinced that Communism was a great internal threat, were so vehement that the man could not be ignored.

When Bobby Kennedy began to talk about going to work as a counsel for McCarthy, Jack advised against it even though he was a member of the full Government Operations Committee himself. Father Joe Kennedy felt differently; he was a close friend of the Senator from Wisconsin.

McCarthy, a genial fellow when he wasn't ranting on a podium or intimidating a witness, had often visited the Kennedys at Hyannis Port in the late 1940's. He had swum from the family yacht and endured many hours of Kennedy-style recreation. He had suffered a cracked rib playing touch football and was once summarily removed from the lineup during a family softball game because he committed four errors at shortstop. He had dated Patricia Kennedy in Washington.

Bobby's father had also contributed to McCarthy's 1952 campaign. At the time, there was a rumor that Joseph Kennedy had offered a huge amount of money so that McCarthy—a hero in those days to Boston's Irish Catholic thousands—would not campaign in Massachusetts for Henry Cabot Lodge. Joe Kennedy was angered by the rumor and he spouted off to author Joseph McCarthy (no relation to the Senator) for his book *The Remarkable Kennedys*, "I gave Joe McCarthy a small contribution, sure, but it was only a couple of thousand dollars and I didn't give it to him to keep him out of Massachusetts. I gave it to him because a mutual friend of ours, Westbrook Pegler, asked me to give it to him and because I liked the fight he was putting up against Communists in our government."

Naturally, Joseph Kennedy saw no reason why Bobby should not work for Senator McCarthy.

Neither did Bobby. He had liked McCarthy when he first met him during Law Forum days at the University of Virginia. Moreover, when Bobby was looking for his post-election job, Mc- Carthy himself had given him a spellbinding sales talk about in- vestigations to come and about the need to erase Communism and corruption from government. People who knew him then say Bobby, like his father, was powerfully committed to the idea that Communists were a real menace to America and that they should be rooted out by whatever means necessary. Indeed, Bobby himself later said of the McCarthy crusade, "I felt it was work that needed to be done then."

Altogether, the job with McCarthy was irresistible to a young (just 27) man of Bobby's soaring energy and altruism. He could lend himself to the Right Kind of Goal (fighting Communism) and at the same time indulge in The Vigorous Life (the excitement and sensationalism generated by Joe McCarthy).

Bobby joined the three-man staff of Francis Flanagan, an ex-FBI man who was general counsel for the McCarthy subcommit- tee. Flanagan's investigative crew worked separately from the rest of the legal staff, which was headed by Roy Cohn, a diminutive, droop-lidded lawyer who had just resigned from the Justice Depart- ment to become McCarthy's chief counsel. Coincidentally enough, Cohn and Bobby Kennedy had worked for the Justice Department on matters of internal security at the same time, although they did not know each other then. A brilliant, if abrasive, young man, Cohn had also been an assistant U.S. Attorney in New York and helped prosecute the Government's espionage case against Julius and Ethel Rosenberg, both of whom died in the electric chair after they were found guilty in 1951 of selling United States atomic secrets to Russia.

Roy Cohn's favorite sidekick on the McCarthy subcommittee staff was G. David Schine, a handsome but rather ineffectual son of a multimillionaire who owned a chain of hotels. Schine had once written a treatise called "Definition of Communism" for distribution throughout his father's hotel rooms. He was carried on the subcommittee payroll as a "chief consultant."

From the start, Bobby disliked Cohn and Schine—largely because of their tactics of investigation. The intrepid pair had gone charging off to Europe snooping for books written by Communists (or a reasonable facsimile thereof) in libraries of the International Information Administration; it was an inimitable example of Insolence Abroad. In Washington, the pair had conducted an investigation of the Voice of America that produced all kinds of publicity, but not a great deal of substance—although it did effectively damage the morale of many people working at the Voice. In those days, Cohn & Shine were a television act almost as famous, but not so funny as Amos & Andy. The spectacle was appalling to Bobby. "They were bad, inefficient, inaccurate and untrustworthy," he said later.

While Cohn and Schine attracted headlines across the country and hero-worship among McCarthy's followers, Kennedy was bulldogging his way through other, more mundane investigations. One of his first cases involved Government-purchased palm oil that had hardened and could not be removed from storage tanks. Later, Bobby began probing claims that ships flying flags of the Allied nations had traded with Communist China, although United Nations forces were then fighting in Korea. Late in May, 1953, Kennedy testified before the subcommittee that 162 vessels flying Allied flags had traded with the Red Chinese in the first months of the year and that two ships owned by a British company had actually transported Red Chinese troops along the coast. The British roundly denounced Bobby's report, but Joe McCarthy thought it was a fine piece of investigative work and Arthur Krock, *New York Times* columnist and Kennedy family friend, lauded it as "an example of Congressional investigation at its finest."

All along, the sinister slapstick of Cohn and Schine had the complete backing of Joe McCarthy. In June, 1953, the Senator gave Chief Counsel Cohn control over the entire subcommittee staff, promoting Flanagan to a position with the full Government Operations Committee legal staff. Between them, McCarthy and Cohn ruled with an iron hand, dictating staff hirings and firings as they saw fit.

The three Democratic Senators on the subcommittee, a long-ignored minority, could take it no longer. All of them—Arkansas's John McClellan, Washington's Henry Jackson and Missouri's Stuart Symington—walked out and refused to participate in McCarthy's investigations. By that time, some six months after he started, Bobby Kennedy was sick of the mess, too. With Cohn in charge and Schine an ever-present influence, Bobby told Senator McCarthy that he wanted to quit. At first McCarthy sugar-talked Kennedy and told him that he really did not like Schine very much either and promised that things would proceed differently in the future. For a brief time, Bobby stayed on the payroll but there was no improvement, to his way of thinking. Years later, in his book *The Enemy Within,* he wrote about the Cohn-Schine tactics: "Most of the investigations were instituted on the basis of some preconceived notion by the chief counsel or his staff members and not on the basis of any information that had been developed. Cohn and Schine claimed they knew from the outset what was wrong; and they were not going to let the facts interfere. Therefore no real spadework that might have destroyed some of their pet theories was ever undertaken. I thought Senator McCarthy made a mistake in allowing the committee to operate in such a fashion."

On July 31 Bobby handed in his resignation, saying that he planned to "enter private practice of law at a very early date." Joseph McCarthy wrote him a warm letter, proclaiming that Kennedy had been "a great credit to the committee and did a tremendous job."

Whatever "private law practice" Bobby had in mind when he wrote his resignation letter, he did nothing about it. Instead, he went to work almost immediately as a counsel for the Hoover Commission, where his father was still a member. Bobby helped organize the work of task forces checking into efficiency of the Executive Department. But there was little thunder-and-lightning there, and Bobby quickly became bored, fidgety and short-tempered. After six months, he got an offer from McClellan, Jackson and Symington, who had decided to rejoin McCarthy's subcommittee. They wanted him to be counsel for them—the Democratic minority. Bobby didn't hesitate for a moment. He left the Hoover Commission in February,

1954, and former President Herbert Hoover, who had spent a good deal of time talking with Bobby during those months, wrote to him: "I am sorry to hear you are leaving us. I realize, however, that there is little to do until the task forces have reported and that a restless soul like you wants to work."

When Bobby rejoined the Investigations Subcommittee, the beginnings of the raucous, disreputable spectacle that came to be known as the Army-McCarthy hearings were in progress. McCarthy, Cohn and Schine were pitted against the forces of the United States Army in a shameful spite fight that had started after David Schine was drafted. The Army had claimed that Roy Cohn tried to get cushy posts and extra furloughs for his friend; Cohn and McCarthy denied it, said the Army was riddled with Reds; and the imperious Cohn threatened to "wreck" the Army. The sessions, televised to millions, were full of Cohn's acid, insulting comments and Joe McCarthy's rasping cry, "Point of order!"

Democrats McClellan, Symington and Jackson were in rigid disagreement with McCarthy's entire operation. They had rejoined the subcommittee to register their protests publicly and in person, and they had hired Bobby to frame questions for them, to check legal points and to keep a hawk's eye on the proceedings. It was far from a starring role for Bobby; he seldom spoke up although he often showed up on the television screen, sitting grim and attentive behind the Democratic Senators.

During the hearings, Bobby's dislike for star performer Cohn reached a new intensity. The two clashed once when Cohn was questioning Mrs. Annie Lee Moss, a low-echelon clerk for the Army Signal Corps, whom Cohn suspected of being a Communist. The woman denied it, but admitted that she did know a man named Rob Hall who delivered the *Daily Worker* to her home. She said Hall was a Negro. Without checking, Cohn immediately assumed that she was referring to a Robert Hall who was a Communist organizer in Washington. When Cohn began quizzing Mrs. Moss about Hall, a reporter passed a note to Bobby, telling him that the Communist Mr. Hall was white and that Cohn was talking to Mrs. Moss about the wrong man. Kennedy quickly got up from his chair and whispered to Cohn that he should hold his questions until the matter could be straight-ened out. Cohn refused, so Bobby challenged him in the open hearings and made the angry, embarrassed Cohn admit that he would indeed have to get some "more exact information" before the interrogation went further.

After another session, the two young lawyers got into a did-too-did-not argument that almost led to blows. During the day's hearing, Senator Jackson derided a sophomoric scheme hatched by Private Schine to fight Communism. It was called "Deminform" and would throw everything from itinerant clergymen to girly pin-ups into the battle against Communism. As Jackson's sarcastic questioning continued, Cohn became enraged. When the hearing adjourned, he stalked over to Bobby and snarled. "Tell your friend Scoop Jackson we're going to get him on Monday." Bobby snapped, "Get lost."

Infuriated, Cohn snarled, "You have a personal hatred for one of the principals." Bobby replied, "If I have it's justified." Cohn clenched his fists and asked, "Do you want to fight now?" Bobby strode away through the crowd with Cohn yelling after him, "Do you think you're qualified to sit here? Do you think you're qualified?" When reporters asked him what was going on, Cohn blustered, "Oh, we've got a real cute kid here." Later in a Capitol corridor, Cohn and Kennedy squared off, glaring like little boys who had just insulted each other's favorite ballplayer. No one swung.

Eventually Joe McCarthy stepped down as chairman of the Investigations Subcommittee so that he and Cohn could act as witnesses in defending themselves against the Army's charges. Republican Senator Karl Mundt of South Dakota moved in as chairman. His Republican colleagues were Michigan's Charles Potter and Illinois' Everett Dirksen. Even they began to turn against McCarthy as he sought to disprove the Army's claims.

The hearings dragged on—a sordid spectacle—for weeks with Cohn and McCarthy pitted against the bewildered, inept Secretary of the Army Robert Stevens and his gracious, witty attorney, Joseph N. Welch. Finally the affair ground to an end and after a hiatus lasting most of the summer, the Mundt-led subcommittee came up with reports in August, 1954, in which both the Republicans and the Democrats agreed that Schine's value to the committee as a "consultant" had been all but worthless and that McCarthy had been wrong in letting Cohn try to gain Army favors for his pal. Both reports were based on a 78-page compendium of the evidence objectively compiled by Bobby Kennedy.

By then Cohn had resigned. His star was burned out in Washington, and he returned to New York, where he plunged into law practice and, eventually, a variety of business ventures. However, the bad blood between him and Bobby Kennedy existed for a long time.

Nearly 10 years later, Roy Cohn was indicted on charges of perjury before a federal grand jury that was investigating a stock fraud. Bobby Kennedy was Attorney General then, and Cohn said flatly that the charges against him were just another dimension of Bobby's "personal vendetta." "Everyone who's followed history knows the Attorney General hates my guts," Cohn declared. He also said that his incoming mail had been checked constantly by federal authorities (the Post Office admitted this was true). And he claimed there were Justice Department taps on his phones.

Cohn's attorneys moved to have the case dismissed. Federal Judge Archie O. Dawson denied the motion, but the judge was irritated enough by the Government's actions to say that the whole affair was "shocking" and "smacks more of Russia than the United States." On July 17, 1964, Cohn was found innocent of the perjury charge, and in obvious reference to Kennedy, he told reporters, "I thank God for the United States of America, where no matter who in high places moves against you there is recourse to a jury of twelve Americans."

Despite Bobby Kennedy's loathing for Cohn, he had remained friendly with Joe McCarthy—even during the Senator's most distasteful displays. To Bobby, McCarthy was a subject for sympathy, though he was convinced that the Senator's methods were wrong, Bobby thought there were extenuating circumstances—such as McCarthy's insatiable hunger for headlines and the influence of Cohn and Schine.

Kennedy's attitude was charitable—and, to many liberals, suspect. In an interview with Robert Thompson and Hortense Meyers who wrote a biography of Bobby called *The Brother Within*, he said of McCarthy:

He got so involved with all that publicity—and after that it was the Number One thing in his life. He was on a toboggan. It was so exciting and exhilarating as he went downhill that it didn't matter to him if he hit a tree at the bottom. Cohn and Schine took him up the mountain and showed him all those wonderful things. He destroyed himself for that—for publicity. He had to get his name in the paper. I felt sorry for him, particularly in the last year, when he was such a beaten, destroyed person—particularly since many of his so-called friends, realizing he was finished, ran away from him and left him with virtually no one.

I liked him and yet at times he was terribly heavy-handed. He was a very complicated character. His whole method of operation was complicated because he would get a guilty feeling and get hurt after he had blasted somebody. He wanted so desperately to be liked. He was so thoughtful and yet so unthoughtful in what he did to others. He was sensitive and yet insensitive. He didn't anticipate the results of what he was doing. He was very thoughtful of his friends, and yet he could be so cruel to others.

On December 2, 1954, after heated and lengthy debate both on the Senate floor and across the nation, Joseph McCarthy was finally condemned by the Senate. A special Senate committee headed by Utah Republican Senator Arthur Watkins had been appointed in August, 1954, to look into McCarthy's conduct. The Watkins Committee report was filed late in November. The Senator was condemned—not for his abusive and arrogant investigatory tactics which had really cast a dim light on the Senate as a whole—but for two relatively minor and specific sins: (1) his refusal to appear before the Senate Committee on Privileges and Elections that was probing his finances, and (2) his insulting remarks made during Watkins Committee hearings about other Senators (at the time, Senator Lyndon Johnson described those remarks as being "much more fittingly inscribed on the wall of a men's room").

Bobby has said that he would have voted for McCarthy's condemnation had he been in the Senate, but that the basis for it should have been broader. "I thought he had brought the Senate and the United States into disrepute by his operation of the committee. The whole operation of Cohn and Schine was the core of it."

John Kennedy was not present for the vote condemning Mc-

Carthy in 1954; he was critically ill at the time. He did say that he, too, would have gone along with the Senate vote. But later he explained to his biographer, James MacGregor Burns, why he had never felt he could be outspokenly critical of McCarthy's tactics. "I was rather in ill grace personally to be around hollering about what McCarthy had done in 1952 or 1951 when my brother had been on the staff in 1953. That is really the guts of the matter," said Jack.

Bobby's personal liking for McCarthy never weakened. In 1955, Kennedy was picked by the Junior Chamber of Commerce as one of the nation's Ten Outstanding Young Men. The speaker at the banquet, held in Louisville, was broadcaster Edward R. Murrow, an early foe of McCarthy. Word had been passed that Murrow was going to make an attack on McCarthy. Loyal to his old friend, Bobby left the room while Murrow spoke. (Despite his disenchantment with Murrow on that occasion, Bobby held no long-standing grudge against the broadcaster. In 1961, President Kennedy named Murrow as head of the United States Information Agency. One of Murrow's first acts as a member of the Kennedy Administration was to hire Reed Harris, a one-time State Department information officer who had resigned under a cloud in 1953—a victim of Joe McCarthy's unsubstantiated charges that he was disloyal to the United States.)

The power of McCarthy was dissipated by the Senate act of condemnation. Moreover, in the 1954 elections, Republicans lost control of the Congress again and, of course, McCarthy lost his chairmanship of the Government Operations Committee. When Congress reorganized under a Democratic majority in January, 1955, John McClellan, the austere Arkansan who had taken a great liking to Bobby, took over the chairmanship and he appointed Bobby chief counsel of the Investigations Subcommittee. Joe McCarthy remained a member and, with Roy Cohn exiled to New York, the Wisconsin Senator felt closer to Bobby than he did to his own Republican minority counsel, James Juliana. When McCarthy wanted to get information about specific committee projects, he usually asked Kennedy about them and Bobby helped him wherever he could.

Occasionally Senator McCarthy would talk again about starting a new investigation of his own. But his day was over; he became a hopeless, incoherent drunk in the months before he died. When his funeral was held in quiet, rural Appleton, Wisconsin, on May 7, 1957, Bobby Kennedy flew out from Washington to join the mourners for his friend, Joe McCarthy.

IV
PURSUIT OF HOFFA

THE SQUALID CLAMOR RAISED BY THE UNJUST antics of Senator McCarthy cast the whole practice of congressional investigation in a suspicious light for a while. With his demise, the hysteria over Communists in government mercifully died down and, regardless of how strongly Bobby Kennedy himself may have felt about the threat of Reds in high places, it was no time to resurrect anything even remotely reminiscent of McCarthyism.

The first two years that Bobby served as chief counsel of John McClellan's Investigations Subcommittee, he had put his staff to work digging into conflict-of-interest charges involving men in the Eisenhower Administration. Bobby's investigators hit pay dirt now and then, and eventually caused the resignations of Air Force Secretary Harold Talbott, Interstate Commerce Commission Chairman Hugh Cross and Assistant Defense Secretary Robert Tripp Ross.

By the early summer of 1956, Bobby's work had become routine, and he was getting restless. One warm day Clark Mollenhoff, a top Washington investigative reporter for the Des Moines *Register* and *Tribune*, dropped into Bobby's office, and they got to talking about how dull things were. "Have you got any ideas?" asked Bobby. Indeed Mollenhoff had. He had spent the last few years ferreting out stories of labor corruption and now he told Bobby that he was certain that the hierarchy of the Teamsters Union was riddled with till-tappers.

At first Kennedy was unimpressed. At least two other congressional committees, one headed by Pennsylvania's Republican Congressman Clare Hoffman, had tried to find evidence of dirty work among the Teamsters. Nothing tangible had come from them, although in 1953 Hoffman's staff had turned up signs of suspicious wheeling and dealing involving James Hoffa, then an international vice president. To Bobby, it hardly seemed worth the effort to revive the probe, but Mollenhoff was persistent.

Finally, after the 1956 elections, Bobby decided to take several trips to the West Coast to look into the possibilities of investigating the Teamsters specifically and labor-management corruption generally. He interviewed Teamster officials, policemen, tax accountants, attorneys and newspaper reporters who had covered the Teamsters. With the expert help of his investigative accountant, Carmine Bellino, Bobby dug into the accounts of some locals and eventually decided he was on the trail of something worth formal investigation.

Kennedy himself did some door-to-door gumshoeing. Once, he called at a Teamster official's home and the man's wife answered the door. Bobby was curious about her husband's finances; she refused to discuss the subject. Suddenly Kennedy sniffed the air and caught the aroma of cooking chocolate. Long a connoisseur of anything chocolate, he begged for a sample and, after sipping the sauce, he pronounced it the best he had ever had. Flattered, the woman spilled out some useful information.

Back in Washington, Kennedy and Senator McClellan decided that the Teamsters seemed ripe. They suspected that luxury-loving old Dave Beck, president of the International, had been dipping into the treasury to satisfy his tastes. In addition, they decided that an investigation into corruption in other unions as well as the management of some business corporations would be timely. On January 31, 1957, the Senate created the Select Committee on Improper Activities in the Labor or Management Field (soon abbreviated to the less lofty and more accurate "Rackets Committee"). This special committee was set up for the expressed purpose of keeping the corruption probe within the bailiwick of the McClellan committee, for other Senate committees were interested in that kind of highly publicized work too.

The Kennedys had a good deal at stake in the committee.

One of the four Democratic members was Senator John Kennedy of Massachusetts. And Bobby, as chief counsel, had 55 people on his staff and an investigations budget of $350,000. The ostensible purpose behind the investigations was, as in all congressional committee work, to provide a basis of information from which to draft new legislation—in this case curtailing corruption in labor unions and business management. That was the way it started.

But beyond that, the Kennedys never lost sight of the fact that the hearings—televised and fraught with sensational charges of corruption and brutality as they would be—would give John Kennedy a fine public platform from which to pursue his presidential ambitions. Although John Kennedy was fairly well known to the nation already (owing largely to his near-miss attempt to get the Democratic vice-presidential nomination in 1956), any additional exposure was considered valuable—and particularly in a well-publicized attempt to clean up graft and shady maneuverings among union leaders who held enormous influence over the lives of American working men.

Ironically, Joe Sr. and Jack were at first terribly concerned that any Kennedy involvement in such a probe could be construed as being an anti-labor position and, thus, might be harmful to Jack's presidential hopes. At one point, they even tried to persuade Bobby not to take the counsel's job. But Bobby wanted it badly—and ultimately it proved to be an enormous help to the Kennedys generally and to Jack specifically. Indeed, many astute observers of political subtleties feel that Jack Kennedy's association with the Rackets Committee investigation in the late '50's was one of the major factors in his capturing the presidential nomination in 1960.

Nevertheless, for most people the probe marked the start of a white-hot and long-running feud that pitted the Government against the Teamsters Union, generally, and Robert Kennedy against James Hoffa, specifically.

Jimmy Hoffa's International Brotherhood of Teamsters, Chauffeurs, Warehousemen and Helpers of America reaches every segment of life in the United States. It is essentially an autonomous empire within a democracy, and Bobby Kennedy likes to say that no institution in the country has more potential power—with the single exception of the Federal Government.

In many ways, the 1,700,000 truckers and haulers of the

Teamsters Union hold in their hands the very lifeline of the nation. There is little related to cradle, grave or the years between that Teamsters do not pick up, haul and deliver. If their trucks stopped, the United States could be crippled. Medical supplies, babies' milk, machines, missile parts, even morticians' hearses could be stalled en route.

There is no tougher or more ambitious union leader in the country than Hoffa of the Teamsters. Through the years, he clambered to his $75,000-a-year position as international president with a ruthless, hard-knuckled passion for power that would not be stopped. In recent years, he has gratified that passion more than ever before. Steadily he has moved to construct one monolithic organization from the hundreds of small Teamster locals that have operated in the past as independent baronies. Through a series of district and regional amalgamations, he has put more and more control into his own hands. As of mid-1965, he had not yet achieved his dream of handling a single, nation-wide contract for all Teamsters—but his closest associates admit there was nothing he wanted more.

It is only through the Teamsters' cynical acquiescence to Jimmy Hoffa's leadership that he has retained his power. They could vote him out of office. They don't. Jimmy Hoffa gets them what they want, and even some of Hoffa's bitterest critics admit he has done pretty well for them.

Hoffa has been perfectly candid about his views of commanding a union. "The trouble with most leaders," he said, "is that they want to go to church every Sunday and be recognized as good citizens and be respectable. They don't understand that this is not a respectable business."

Jimmy Hoffa was born the son of a Brazil, Indiana, coal prospector who died of silicosis when Jimmy was four. He had a rugged, hungry childhood. Eventually his mother moved her family to a Detroit slum. Hoffa quit school in the ninth grade, and by the time he was 18, he was unloading boxcars for a wholesale grocer, laboring up to 15 hours a day for 32 cents an hour. Dissatisfied, Hoffa organized the workers and triggered his first strike. When a perishable load of strawberries arrived, Jimmy's men refused to unload it. Within the hour, management capitulated and offered a small raise and insurance benefits.

That was Hoffa's launching pad, and two years later he got an American Federation of Labor charter and moved his group into the Teamsters Union as Local 299. In the hard-scrabbling days of the '30's, Detroit was the nation's seedbed of labor violence, and Hoffa took his lumps from management goons' brass knuckles and policemen's nightsticks. One night he was left for dead in an alley after a gang of anti-union men beat him up with tire chains. Jimmy Hoffa was—and is—a muscle-packed fireplug of a man (five feet five and one-half inches tall, weighing 170 pounds) and he could slug it out with the worst of them.

He was as good at shouldering his way up through the organization as he was at mixing it up on picket lines; and by 1940, Hoffa was the Teamsters' negotiating chairman for the Central States Drivers Council, a group that included truckers in 12 states. Eventually Hoffa reached out from Detroit and made an alliance with Dave Beck, who had built himself an 11-state Teamster barony centered on the West Coast.

Together, they planned the overthrow of International President Dan Tobin, then in his late 70's and a bumbling, ineffectual old fellow after three decades in office. Tobin toppled easily and in 1952, Beck, boosted by Hoffa, was made president; Hoffa became an international vice president. Between them they controlled the biggest, strongest, wealthiest (its assets climbed to more than one billion dollars recently) labor union in history.

When the Rackets Committee hearings began in early 1957, Bobby Kennedy and his investigators had already unearthed some fascinating characters and eye-opening stories about the Teamsters. Because they knew approximately how many witnesses were to be called, network television executives decided the hearings sounded sensational enough to make them a long-run hit. Thus, as the historic, ornate Senate caucus room echoed with its first Rackets Committee revelations, a great tangle of cable, cameras and blinding lights cluttered the space. For weeks, millions of viewers watched in fascination as a pug-ugly parade of witnesses was humbled and hammered by Bobby Kennedy's biting questions.

It turned out to be quite a morality show: Bobby the clean-cut intense Good Guy challenging angry old labor warhorses, slick union attorneys and such dim lights of the underworld as John "Johnny Dio" Dioguardo, Anthony "Tony Ducks" Corallo, Joey Glimco, Jackie Cerone, Tony Accardo and Joey "Caesar" Di Varco.

Bobby played his role perfectly—so perfectly that it soon became apparent that it wasn't a role at all: it was Real Life Bobby. He seemed personally peeved that the Bad Guys facing him had actually cheated and stolen and lied. Soon it seemed that they had become his own cross to bear, that they had challenged his manhood and that he had to retaliate to revitalize the strength of his own moral convictions. Bobby has said of those hearings, "It was like playing Notre Dame everyday." To his fans, as well as his critics, it seemed more like a daily performance of Billy Batson Meets the Purple Gang.

Soon Bobby developed a national following not unlike the cult of kids that worshipped movie actor James Dean. Dazzled bobby-soxers besieged Kennedy for his autograph, fan letters poured in from love-struck women, and strangers reached out to shake his hand in the street. Newspapers also stopped using the old son-of-the-Ambassador and brother-of-the-Senator references after Bobby's name. He and Jack worked closely on the committee, so much so that some Republicans accused Bobby of feeding Jack the best questions. The television coverage, of course, did Jack a lot of good in his still undeclared move toward the presidency; but Bobby's own image was so bright that people would sometimes mistake Jack for Bobby and rush up to offer Jack congratulations on his oneupsmanship against the corruptors.

Heroic as Bobby's performance seemed to his fans, there were plenty of civil-libertarians who felt that Bobby abused witnesses, and they were queasy about his tactics of interrogation. He caused many witnesses (some of them merciless bullyboys in their own bailiwicks) to cringe at the microphone. He often flared up when witnesses took refuge in the Fifth Amendment—sometimes asking purposely insinuating questions, knowing there would be no answer. One day during questioning of Joey Glimco, the president of a Chicago Teamster local, Bobby and Senator McClellan made a particularly vindictive team. The exchange went like this:

KENNEDY (to Glimco): And you defraud the union?

GLIMCO: I respectfully decline to answer because I honestly believe my answer might tend to incriminate me.

KENNEDY: I would agree with you.

McCLELLAN: I believe it would.

KENNEDY: You haven't got the guts to [answer], have you, Mr. Glimco?

GLIMCO: I respectfully decline . . .

McCLELLAN: Morally you are kind of yellow inside, are you not? That is the truth about it?

GLIMCO: I respectfully decline . . .

Criticism of his tactics irked Bobby. "There were from 30 to 120 reporters there and if there had been any such abuses, you'd think they would have come up with one or two examples at the time," he said.

And there was no question that Bobby felt he was on a mighty crusade for the little man in labor unions. As the investigations turned up more and more stories of corruption, extortion, embezzlement, back-alley beatings and murder, Bobby said, "I'm getting a great deal of deep personal satisfaction from these hearings. But at the same time it's one of my most frustrating experiences. The satisfaction comes from exposing these characters. The frustrations come from two things—questioning witnesses you know are lying and trying to keep your temper, and reading letters from union people all over the country who have been wronged in hundreds of ways by petty racketeering on the part of their leaders and knowing there will never be enough time to investigate all the wrongs. We have to stick to the big shots and the big swindles. God knows how long it will take to do just that."

The biggest game the Rackets Committee ever bagged was Dave Beck. Bald and baleful, he looked like an evil Easter egg when he appeared in the spring of 1957. He constantly took the Fifth Amendment and once even refused to answer when Bobby asked him if he knew his own son. (Later Beck's attorney explained that Beck had done that because a court suit was pending against Dave Beck Jr., and discussion of his son before the committee at that point might have been prejudicial.) Constitutional rights notwithstanding, Bobby was angered when Beck refused to testify fully.

"There's a big difference between a petty crook who takes the Fifth Amendment to protect himself and a man like Dave Beck," Bobby declared. "Both certainly have a right to, but because of his responsibility to a million and a half Teamsters and to sixteen million people in organized labor, Beck, I believe, has an obligation higher than just to himself and should answer whatever questions are asked him about his operation of the union."

Eventually Beck was found guilty of grand larceny and he wound up serving time in prison (although he continued to collect his $50,000 a year Teamster pension in jail). Beck quit his union presidency in late 1957 and Hoffa took over.

Rackets Committee hearings continued for three years, produced more than 11,000,000 words of testimony and cost around $1,500,000. Bobby's investigators, led by Walter Sheridan, a former FBI agent, were thorough. For every witness who testified, they interviewed 35 and for every document introduced in evidence, they studied 5,000. Once in a while they slipped. An investigator told Bobby that they thought they had uncovered the facts to prove that a New York building filled with labor-union offices was owned by mobsters. Interested, Bobby ordered further checks; it turned out the building actually belonged to the Kennedy family.

Corruption of one kind or another was uncovered in some 15 unions and 50 companies. The Bakery and Confectionery Workers Union was booted from the AFL-CIO. Top officials disgraced by committee findings quit their posts in the Carpenters Union, the Operating Engineers Union, the United Textile Workers of America and the Meat Cutters Union.

Congress did pass labor reform legislation in September, 1959—a direct result of the Rackets Committee spotlight on corrupt union leaders and lackeys. Bobby played a special, starring television role in getting the bill through. He went on Jack Paar's *Tonight Show* in July, talked engagingly for more than an hour about the need for legislation and pleaded with people to write their congressmen. Bobby's appeal, much of it couched in a withering, hair-raising diatribe against Teamster Jimmy Hoffa (who later filed a $2,500,000 libel suit against the National Broadcasting

Company because of Bobby's remarks), brought a flood of letters to Capitol Hill.

Bobby's fans insisted that it was his appearance that caused passage of the House-initiated Landrum-Griffin Act rather than a later television appeal by President Eisenhower. That wasn't true. Actually, Bobby had been touting the Kennedy-Irvin bill, a measure originated in the Senate with John Kennedy as co-author. A joint House-Senate conference committee finally worked out a compromise bill that included more substance from Landrum-Griffin than from Kennedy-Irvin.

Despite the new labor law Bobby was not satisfied. As the committee wound up its final weeks of work after more than two years, Bobby said, "Candor compels me to say that in the months since the committee began to work, conditions in the labor and management fields have actually grown worse instead of better."

Whether Bobby meant it or not, that statement was translated by many people to mean that James Riddle Hoffa was riding high, and until he was brought down, Kennedy himself would not consider his efforts to clean out labor corruption a real success.

Oddly enough, when Bobby began his official pursuit of Hoffa, the man seemed to be an easy target. Near midnight on March 13, 1957, only weeks after the Rackets Committee began its work, Bobby waited triumphantly in a Washington courtroom as Jimmy Hoffa was escorted in by FBI agents. The two immediately began a spirited, if *non sequitur*, argument over who could do the most push-ups (Hoffa claimed 27, Bobby said 50). Then everyone got down to business and Jimmy Hoffa was arraigned on a charge of violating the federal bribery statute.

According to the Justice Department charge, he had offered a New York lawyer named John Cye Cheasty $18,000 to take a job with Bobby's staff and leak confidential data to Hoffa. Cheasty had notified the FBI and, typical of many Government efforts to get Hoffa over the years, a trap was laid. Cheasty and Hoffa had met on a Washington street and carried out their business while agents photographed their meeting and an FBI man, masquerading as a taxi driver, listened to the conversation. The charge said that when Hoffa was arrested, he "had in his possession documents from the committee files he had just received."

Bobby was so sure the case was airtight that he said he would jump off the Capitol dome if Hoffa was not convicted. Four months later the case went to trial. Hoffa testified that he had only wanted to hire Cheasty as a lawyer, not as an espionage agent, and that he did not even know Cheasty planned to work for the committee. A federal court jury found Hoffa innocent. His attorney, Edward Bennet Williams, cracked to reporters that he thought he might mail Bobby a parachute, and Hoffa did some moralizing about the verdict, "It proves once again if you are honest and tell the truth you have nothing to fear." Bobby blamed Justice Department lawyers for preparing a flabby case.

He tried again to knock Hoffa off his perch with a federal charge that the Teamster had illegally tapped phones and recorded conversations of his own friends and employees at union headquarters in Detroit. At a trial in December, 1957, the jury deadlocked, but when a retrial was held six months later, Hoffa was acquitted.

For a man who cannot abide defeat, Bobby Kennedy was getting a big dose all at once. After nearly a year of hard work and intense investigation, all Bobby and the McClellan committee had accomplished was to tip over Dave Beck and let Hoffa step in as president to run things alone.

Even when the AFL-CIO expelled the Teamsters in December, 1957, because it had not purged itself of "dishonest, corrupt, unethical leaders," Hoffa was unperturbed. It simply meant the $840,000 annual dues the Teamsters had paid to the parent organization were now available for other uses.

The charge that Hoffa harbored and abetted some seamy people in high-level union offices had disturbed the Rackets Committee from the start. At one point, the committee issued a report charging that a criminal record was "prerequisite" for any kind of "advancement within the Teamster firmament."

There was plenty of evidence as the hearings progressed into their second year to prove that Hoffa had no aversion to hoodlums. When extortionist Johnny Dio, who had helped Jimmy with union affairs in New York, went to prison in 1958, Hoffa promised to take care of his family. Joey Glimco, an old Al Capone gang member, held office in a Chicago local. Paul "The Waiter" Ricca, another Capone henchman, was a trustee of a Chicago local. Larry Welsh, convicted of sodomy, was a Detroit Teamster business agent. Zigmont Snyder, convicted of armed robbery, was another Detroit business agent. So was Jimmy Hoffa's brother, Bill, who had been convicted of assault and carrying concealed weapons.

One of Hoffa's chief organizers for a time was a gigantic man named Barney Baker. He admitted to having pals in every crooked cranny of the underworld. At one point Baker and Bobby Kennedy had this exchange:

KENNEDY: Did you know Cockeye Dunne?

BAKER: I didn't know him as Cockeye Dunne. I knew him as John Dunne.

KENNEDY: Where is he now?

BAKER: He has met his maker.

KENNEDY: How did he do that?

BAKER: I believe through electrocution in the city of New York of the state of New York.

KENNEDY: What about Squinty Sheridan? Did you know him?

BAKER: Andrew Sheridan, sir?

KENNEDY: Yes.

BAKER: He has also met his maker.

KENNEDY: How did he die?

BAKER: With Mr. John Dunne.

When Jimmy Hoffa followed Barney Baker to the stand, Bobby asked him if he believed Baker really knew so many hoodlums. "I heard him testify," said Hoffa. Bobby asked, "Does that not disturb you at all about his operation?" Hoffa replied blandly, "It doesn't disturb me one iota."

Unlike dozens of other witnesses, Jimmy Hoffa did not take the Fifth Amendment. When Kennedy asked him a question that seemed tough, Hoffa said he had simply forgotten. At one session he told Kennedy 111 times that certain incidents had slipped his mind.

Frustrated to the point of fury, the committee slammed Hoffa again in a special interim report. Although there was still not enough hard proof of wrong-doing to take him into court, the committee said, "He has betrayed these [Teamster] members so frequently that it has become abundantly clear that Hoffa's chief interest is his own advancement and that of his friends and cronies—a great number of whom are racketeers. The committee is convinced that if Hoffa remains unchecked he will successfully destroy the decent labor movement in the United States."

Asked about that, Hoffa said, "To hell with them. I'll place my record of achievement for the workers beside the record of Jack Kennedy or Bob Kennedy any time."

Bobby quit the Rackets Subcommittee in September, 1959; but Hoffa was strong as ever. Now burning with desire to dump Hoffa, Kennedy wrote *The Enemy Within*, which became a bestseller. (It made about $125,000, including movie rights which were negotiated by shrewd Joseph Kennedy, who used his experience and influence as a one-time Hollywood magnate to clinch the deal.) Bobby used half the book to punch Hoffa, saying he was operating "a conspiracy of evil" and that "a man with Hoffa's power and position and so corrupt cannot survive in a democratic society if democracy itself is going to survive." Hoffa, less literate but no less committed to his hatred, called Kennedy "that spoiled brat, that crum-bum" and promised, "Someday I'm gonna break both his arms."

After Bobby became Attorney General, it seemed that things might take a quick turn for the worse for Jimmy Hoffa. Both Bobby and Jack Kennedy felt the Eisenhower Administration had been derelict in its prosecution of cases the Rackets Committee considered worthy of trial. During the 1960 campaign, Jack had said, "I want to make it very clear that I don't believe the Department of Justice has carried out the laws in the case of Mr. Hoffa with vigor." Now Bobby had at his beck and command the full arsenal of legal, investigative and enforcement powers of the United States Government. And he could use them as vigorously as he wanted against Jimmy Hoffa—with full backing from the President.

No sooner was he in office than Bobby set up a special 15-man unit in the Justice Department to push investigations of labor and management racketeering. The unit was headed by persistent Walter Sheridan, Bobby's Rackets Committee investigative chief, and it soon became known—unofficially, but with some accuracy—as the "Get-Hoffa Squad." That group pursued the Teamster president all during Bobby's Justice Department reign. So did the FBI. So did the Internal Revenue Service. It was an all-out campaign to put Hoffa out of business, and Bobby used every kind of tool—and weapon—at the disposal of his office.

The Justice Department kept up a steady stream of press releases listing new indictments or sinful incidents involving Teamsters. Kennedy himself was shameless in using friendly reporters to propagate an image of Hoffa as a corrupt labor official. (Publicity had long been a favorite tool of Bobby's: once, while he was with the Rackets Committee, he had become so outspoken in his press releases that Senator McClellan had asked him to clear them before he passed them out.)

Teamster officials insisted they were being followed everywhere they went. They claimed their mail was checked before it arrived. They claimed their briefcases were stolen from hotel rooms and that FBI men disguised as bellhops and busboys had infiltrated a hotel meeting of the Teamster board of directors. They claimed their phones were tapped and their offices were filled with electronic eavesdroppers. The Justice Department denied or ignored the charges.

At one point Jimmy Hoffa told reporters just how little privacy he thought he had, "Our phones are tapped and our hotel rooms are bugged. We'd make remarks just to see and the government attorneys would know next morning what we'd said. We're building a new $800,000 office building in Detroit and they come to me and say the whole place is wired and bugged. I say, 'Hell, whaddya expect? Go on and finish the building.' They go to the school and investigate my kid. He's a good kid, if I do say so. They go around to his friends and say, 'How many suits of clothes has Jim Hoffa got? How much money does he carry around in his pocket?' They gave orders to every airline office in the country—when Hoffa makes a reservation, call the nearest FBI office and give the time he takes off and the time he arrives. You wouldn't believe some of the creepy stuff they are pulling."

The Justice Department would not admit to being involved in the creepy stuff. Walter Sheridan says flatly, "People may not believe us, but not once did we use a wiretap or a bug in the Hoffa investigation." Nevertheless, it seemed obvious that Bobby Kennedy had given orders to nail Jimmy Hoffa with a conviction—any conviction—to get him out of the Teamsters presidency. At one point, there were no less than 14 grand juries energetically at work probing Teamster affairs, and Hoffa once insisted that he could count 32 of them digging into his business.

In October, 1961, Hoffa was indicted in Orlando, Florida, on charges of misusing some $500,000 of Teamster funds intended for investment in Sun Valley, a model city for old folks near Cape Canaveral (now Cape Kennedy). Then, in May, 1962, Hoffa was indicted again—this time on federal charges that he had violated the Taft-Hartley Act in 1948 by sharing in a million-dollar payoff from a Michigan trucking firm in return for his guarantee that the company would have no serious labor problems. The charge said that a trucking firm, Test City Fleet in Nashville, Tennessee, benefited from the deal and that it was in reality controlled by Jimmy Hoffa and another Teamster official, the late Owen (Bert) Brennan—although it was nominally owned by their wives. The Sun Valley and the Test Fleet trials were both set for late in 1962.

For months the Justice Department lawyers puzzled over which case they should try first. If Hoffa were convicted in the Sun Valley case, he could be sentenced to 20 years in prison and an $85,000 fine. A Test Fleet conviction would mean a maximum penalty of two years and a $20,000 fine. Finally, Bobby's lawyers decided that the Test Fleet case, to be tried in Nashville, offered the better chance for a fast conviction. The Florida case was put off.

Almost immediately there was an outcry that Hoffa's right to due process had been violated. Fifteen congressmen rose up to complain. Oregon's Democratic Senator Wayne Morse (former dean of the University of Oregon Law School) said it was a clear case of "forum shopping" to find the best climate in which to hold a trial. Republican Congressman Alvin O'Konski of Wisconsin declared that Nashville was a city with "a hostile anti-labor climate." And Democratic Senator J. J. Hickey of Wyoming said, "The administration of justice in this fashion does more to shake the confidence of people in the courts and destroy the efficient administration—to which all interested members of the bar and bench are dedicated—than any other matter." They called for House and

Senate Judiciary Committee investigations into Bobby's pursuit of Hoffa. Some of the congressmen also pointed out that information on the Test Fleet case had been in Government hands for nearly 10 years; it had been dug up originally by the Hoffman Committee. The Justice Department had declined to prosecute—until Bobby took over.

The Test Fleet trial began in Nashville, Tennessee, in October, 1962. It was far from the finest hour of American justice, for before the trial ended, it had turned into a circus of conspiracies and counter-conspiracies. The star performer in the production turned out to be an unsavory character named Edward Grady Partin, a Teamster agent from Baton Rouge, Louisiana, whom Bobby Kennedy's men had planted as a volunteer government spy in the midst of Jimmy Hoffa's confidential circle.

Shortly before the trial started, Partin had contacted the Get-Hoffa Squad to say that he had information they might be able to use. Partin was an ex-convict and jailbreaker who was already acquainted with the squad, having only a short time before been indicted on charges of embezzling $1,600 in Teamster funds. What interested Walter Sheridan most about Partin was the fact that he was trusted and liked by Jimmy Hoffa. Quickly Sheridan arranged for him to take polygraph tests to examine his capacity for telling the truth. Partin passed nicely.

Then Partin made several telephone calls to Hoffa—a couple of which were recorded without Hoffa's knowledge by men from the District Attorney's office in New Orleans. (Sheridan afterward carefully pointed out that the wiretaps were done by Louisiana state officials, not by the Federal Government agents.) Without any particular trouble, Partin got himself invited to Nashville to be with Jimmy.

As the trial progressed, Partin latched on tight to Hoffa and his battery of attorneys and cronies at the Andrew Jackson Hotel. When he could safely slip away, Partin called Sheridan from a telephone booth to tell him what had transpired. Sheridan was well aware that the due process of law doctrine would be violated if Partin told Sheridan anything about conferences between Hoffa and his lawyers. Such information in possession of the prosecution could open the way for a mistrial motion by the Teamsters. Thus Sheridan was careful to insist that Partin not mention anything about the Teamsters' courtroom plans for defense.

This kind of legalistic nicety aside, Partin's position in Hoffa's inner circle soon paid off. One day he told Sheridan that he had overheard a conversation in which Hoffa's men were figuring how to bribe jurors in order to insure a not-guilty verdict for the Teamster president. Sure enough, things began to happen. One prospective juror, already accepted for duty by the prosecution, told Judge William E. Miller that he had been offered $10,000 to vote for acquittal. Miller dismissed him. Then it was learned that the son of another juror was to be offered $5,000 for himself and $5,000 for his father if he influenced his parent to vote in Hoffa's favor. Next, a highway patrolman, husband of a juror, was told that he might find promotion much easier if he talked to his wife about offering up a pro-Hoffa verdict.

Sheridan's men and the FBI were thorough in their undercover operation. Not only was Partin entrenched inside Hoffa's hotel suite, but whenever the Teamster president and his attorneys left the hotel, FBI men and agents of the Get-Hoffa Squad trailed them. No less than fifteen federal men were on duty to follow Hoffa's group. Hoffa became so irritated by the massive surveillance that at one point he hired six off-duty Nashville policemen and paid them each $50 a day to keep an eye on the men who were keeping an eye on him.

Beyond the weird spectacle of watchbirds-watching-watchbirds all over Nashville, there were other odd and mysterious events around the Test Fleet trial of Jimmy Hoffa. After the lists of prospective jurors became known, a spate of strange telephone calls began, in which a voice on the phone would identify itself as a reporter from the Nashville *Banner*, then ask a potential juror, "What do you really think of Jimmy Hoffa?" More than a dozen of those calls were made and, had the federal men not discovered them in time, they too might have created grounds for a mistrial on the premise that the jurors had prejudiced themselves by answering such a flagrant question.

As it turned out, the caller was not a *Banner* reporter—indeed, the FBI never did find out for certain who made the calls. But in the meantime, the publisher of the *Banner*, James G. Stahlman, became so angry about someone using his paper as a cover for such shenanigans that he planned to run a front-page story, denouncing those tactics and offering a $5,000 reward for information identifying the person on the phone. Bobby Kennedy heard of Stahlman's plan and felt that such a story about the calls might also lead to a mistrial. Kennedy telephoned the publisher and tried—unsuccessfully —to persuade him to forget about publishing the story.

To Bobby's intense embarrassment and chagrin, he learned later that the entire phone conversation with Stahlman had been recorded. It was eventually published in the *Banner* in full, and the Teamsters pointed to it gleefully as evidence that Bobby had been trying to influence coverage of the trial.

The Test Fleet trial itself was drab and deadly compared to the convoluted plots and counterplots going on around it. The Government sent 29 witnesses to the stand to back up a painfully detailed case against Hoffa. It was heavy going for the jurors. After three months of complicated testimony, the jury at last got the case. It deliberated for 17 hours, then returned to tell Judge Miller that it was hopelessly deadlocked; the vote had been seven to five for acquittal.

By then, reports of jury tampering had become so numerous that the judge immediately declared a mistrial—and called a federal grand jury to investigate. In May, 1963, Jimmy Hoffa and 10 others were indicted on charges of trying to bribe three jurors. Even then, the Teamsters had no idea that their pal and compatriot, Edward Grady Partin, was responsible for their predicament.

The bribery trial began on January 20, 1964, before Federal Judge Frank W. Wilson in Chattanooga. Again, the hearing was surrounded by a good-sized assortment of FBI men watching Teamsters, as well as Teamsters watching FBI men. Federal men took no less than 732 photographs of Hoffa's coterie as it moved into and out of the courtroom. In return, Hoffa's men took a batch of photographs of people they thought were FBI agents.

Before it was over, Teamster lawyers complained that all the Hoffa-tailing and picture-taking was a gross invasion of privacy. Which it was. But the government agents simply replied that they wanted to keep track of everyone with Hoffa because they weren't sure who was who and they needed positive identification—for future investigations. To keep their surveillance as airtight as possible, the FBI used a network of walkie-talkies and electronic gear to pass the word among agents concerning the whereabouts of "The Big Boy," which was the code word for Hoffa. This time, the FBI was caught red-handed.

Hoffa imported Bernard Spindell, a well-known expert in the craft of wiretaps and bugs. Spindell flew into Nashville, was immediately picked up by an FBI surveillance team and followed to Chattanooga. Teamsters quickly claimed that this proved the Government had eavesdropped on the phone conversations inviting Spindell to Chattanooga, for Hoffa's men believed that was the only way the FBI could have known precisely when Spindell would arrive. Again federal men denied stooping to such lowdown tricks.

But once Spindell got to Chattanooga, he set up his own electronic monitoring equipment and easily recorded a number of conversations between FBI agents as they chattered to each other about Jimmy Hoffa's movements over their communications network. It was most embarrassing to J. Edgar Hoover's usually covert operators when Spindell's transcript was later made public in the press.

All along, the government seemed almost paranoiacally suspicious of everything Hoffa and his colleagues did. Federal men kept an eagle's-eye watch over every little move even inside the courtroom, suspecting a devious plan to influence the jury in the most innocuous actions. For example, soon after the trial began Walter Sheridan noticed that a Catholic priest turned up every day in the front row of the spectators' section. Curious, Sheridan checked on the priest's identity and found that he had been one of the top clergymen in the local Knights of Columbus organization. Sheridan also knew that one of the jurors had been a leading layman in the Knights of Columbus and that he was well acquainted with the priest.

Immediately Sheridan spotted a plot: he decided that the main reason the priest was in the courtroom was to shake hands with Jimmy Hoffa in the presence of that one juror—thus giving the impression that Hoffa couldn't be all bad as long as he was a hand-shaking pal of the clergy.

As Sheridan recalled it, one day before court convened the door to the jury room swung open. The priest stood up. Hoffa stood up. They began to shake hands. But the door closed and the jury didn't come in just then, so both sat down. A moment later the door opened again. Again the priest stood up. Hoffa stood up. They began to shake hands. Again the jury didn't enter at that moment. Then, before anyone had time to shake hands again, Judge Wilson ascended the bench. When the jury did make its entrance, there was no chance to carry out the handshake, for it would not have been in keeping with courtroom decorum as long as the judge was on the bench.

But Sheridan had seen enough. "We called the bishop and told him to get the priest to stay away from the courtroom," recalled Sheridan. "He didn't show up again."

Despite all the Agent 007 interplay, Hoffa was as cocky as ever at the trial. He had had four federal hearings in the last seven years and the score was: Hoffa, 4, Justice Department, 0. Now, he figured that the only solid evidence against him would likely be based on wiretaps, which were inadmissible. Then, two weeks after the trial began, Ed Partin suddenly appeared in court. Until that moment only six people, including Bobby Kennedy, had known of Partin's undercover role.

When Hoffa saw his once-trusted friend, he flushed. As Partin began to unfold his damning story, Hoffa became increasingly nervous. For more than five days Partin remained on the stand —much of the time under withering cross-examination by eight of Hoffa's attorneys. Again and again they tried to disprove Partin's testimony, to make the jury discount it by casting doubt on Partin's character. But Jimmy Hoffa wasn't in doubt; at one point he snarled to an attorney, "That son-of-a-bitch is killing us."

On March 4, the jury announced its verdict: Hoffa guilty on two counts. Judge Wilson sentenced him to eight years in prison and a $10,000 fine.

Bobby was jubilant. So were Walter Sheridan and the rest of the Get-Hoffa Squad. At a victory cocktail party in Washington, the Justice Department investigators presented Bobby with a leather wallet, embossed with the jury foreman's words pronouncing Hoffa a guilty man.

Jimmy Hoffa, of course, was soured. He accused Kennedy of having a $600,000 "slush fund for stool pigeons." (Indeed, the Justice Department had paid at least $1,200 to the wife of Partin the informer for his "expenses.") Teamster attorneys filed a 207-page brief with the Sixth Circuit Court, appealing Hoffa's conviction. That was to be expected.

But along with the Teamsters' appeals, the American Civil Liberties Union filed an *amicus curiae* brief claiming Hoffa had been denied a fair trial because the Government had violated the due-process clause of the Fifth Amendment and the right to counsel provisions of the Sixth. The use of Partin, said the A.C.L.U., was grounds for a reversal of the verdict. He had listened to conversations between Hoffa and his lawyers and "interference with an accused's right to counsel by spying on their conferences vitiates a conviction," said the A.C.L.U. The brief also pleaded that Partin's friendship with Hoffa made the Government's tactics all the more dubious: "It was not the case of a person being allowed to testify to incriminating statements made to a stranger. On the contrary, we have the Government using someone known to be closely associated with a defendant to spy on him and his lawyers."

But for Bobby and the Get-Hoffa Squad, the victory was sweet—and all the more because there was more to come. In June, 1963, a federal grand jury in Chicago had delivered a 53-page indictment charging Hoffa and seven codefendants with fraudulently borrowing more than $20,000,000 in Teamster funds, then using $1,700,000 for their own use in getting out of the Sun Valley development in Florida. (This case, incidentally, was substituted for the one that had been postponed in 1962.)

The trial began in the spring of 1964, dragged on over 90 days and produced some 40,000 pages of testimony. When it ended, the jury brought in another guilty verdict and Hoffa was sentenced to five years in prison and a $10,000 fine. That, too, was appealed, but suddenly the Justice Department had scored two-for-two against Jimmy Hoffa. There was another cocktail party, this time at the 1789, a restaurant in Georgetown. Bobby was so exuberant that he downed several snifters of brandy.

At last Hoffa had been got, although he still held his power post. It seemed unlikely that he would be ousted until—or if—he went to prison. It had taken Bobby seven years of chasing and he really hadn't done very well until he was in a position to command the full force of Government. If nothing else, he had proved himself a dogged, relentless hunter, intent on bringing down his quarry.

Even so, while he was Attorney General, there was a great deal more than a chunky little union leader named Jimmy Hoffa to occupy his mind and test his stamina.

V
THE GREENHORN
ATTORNEY GENERAL

□□
□□

IT WOULD HAVE BEEN
quite a moment for any young lawyer—his first appearance in an
open courtroom. When Attorney General Robert Kennedy began
his maiden presentation on January 17, 1963, his knees were shak-
ing and his voice quavered. In the chamber sat a crowd of Kennedys, as proud and excited as if Bobby were about to pitch both
ends of a double-header at Yankee Stadium. Ethel and four of their
children were there; so were Rose Kennedy, Eunice Kennedy Shriver
and her son Bobby; Jean Kennedy Smith, Senator Teddy Kennedy
and his wife Joan, and Jackie Kennedy.

This was an extraordinary day. For Bobby Kennedy, looking slightly self-conscious in traditional striped pants and morning
coat, was pleading his first case before the Supreme Court of the
United States. It was a complicated, enormously important suit that
dealt with Georgia's county-unit system; it would lead eventually to
the critical Supreme Court decisions changing the apportionment
of state legislatures—a point of legal upheaval that would unaltera-
bly change the structure of American politics.

It was no time to fail, and Bobby did not. After his initial
jitters he relaxed, synopsized his brief as if he had drafted it himself (Solicitor General Archibald Cox and Justice Department Civil
Rights Division Chief Burke Marshall had done it for him), and
adequately answered a few questions from the Court. When he sat

down, his legal career, at last, bore the Good Courtroom Conduct Seal of Approval. It was an auspicious occasion—even historic—in light of the fact that Bobby had been Attorney General of the United States for two years.

The irony that a man of his inexperience should be the nation's No. 1 legal officer had never been lost on Bobby. He had not sought the job. In fact, after the 1960 election, he had no clear idea of what he wanted to do with his future. "It was a kind of crossroads for me and my family," he has recalled. "Should I try to make a fresh start on my own, in a new career away from Washington? If I didn't, where would I be eight years from now? I would be forty-three years old then. Would I be a has-been without any professional niche to fit into?"

As had happened in the past, Bobby's father and his brother, Jack, stepped in to help him make up his mind. In December, 1960, the Kennedy Cabinet was slowly emerging from a platoon of candidates, most of whom were previously untested in high government office. Early that fall Jack Kennedy had suggested that his brother consider being Attorney General, but Bobby had said no. Joseph Kennedy thought there was no reason Bobby should be left out, and as more Cabinet positions became filled, he huffed impatiently, "Now if Bobby will just go ahead, we'll really be in good shape."

One morning in mid-December Bobby went to eat breakfast with Jack, fully prepared to issue another adamant rejection. When he got up from Jack's table, he found that he had agreed to be Attorney General.

The first newspaper stories broke around the Christmas holidays, and the reaction was by no means in the spirit of the season. *The New York Times* editorialized with lofty disdain: "If Robert Kennedy were one of the outstanding lawyers of the country, a pre-eminent legal philosopher, a noted prosecutor or legal officer at Federal or State level, the situation would be different. But his experience as counsel to the McClellan committee, notably successful as he is, is surely insufficient to warrant his present appointment."

New York Herald Tribune pundit Walter Lippmann wrote, "The really debatable point is that the campaign manager has been placed at the head of the Department of Justice. The more usual practice has been to make the chief politician the Postmaster General." President Kennedy himself quipped, "What's wrong with a fellow getting a little legal training before he goes into the practice of law?" The Kennedys were accused of practicing everything from the crudest power politics to the crassest nepotism; letters to the Democratic National Committee ran 100-to-1 against Bobby's appointment.

Neither Bobby nor the President-elect seemed perturbed by the protests. Old Joe Kennedy was, though, and at one point he snapped to a reporter, "Nepotism, my foot! Why would anybody think that Bobby needs a job? He fought this nomination, fought it until he drove Jack and me crazy."

Despite the uproar, when Bobby's appointment came up for confirmation hearings before the Senate Judiciary Committee on January 13, 1961, even Republican members showed little inclination to attack a President's Cabinet appointment without more substantive charges. They did needle the nominee a little about his youth and his shortage of traditional legal background. Late in the hearings, after Kennedy's experience—or lack thereof—had been discussed from several different angles, Nebraska Republican Roman Hruska brought up the subject all over again. "Have you ever chosen a jury or written a trial brief or prepared a set of instructions for a trial in court?" Hruska asked Bobby.

Bobby replied, "I have not. I think I made that clear, Senator." Then he launched into a firm statement, at once apologia and analysis, about his legal background. "I decided at quite a young age that I would dedicate [myself] to work for the Government," Bobby said. "I would not have given up one year of the experience that I have had over the period since I graduated from law school, I would not give up one year to have sacrificed that experience for experience in practicing law in Boston or wherever it might be. I think I have gained invaluable experience, Senator. I am young and I can't make up for the fact that I have only had ten years out from school. But I think that what I have done or what experience I have had in those ten years will be of tremendous help and make a tremendous difference in this new position."

Bobby promised the committee that "politics will play no role whatsoever" in his Attorney Generalship. He said that he hoped

to "attack organized crime" because it was "one of the major domestic problems that we have here in the United States." Asked
what his approach to new civil-rights legislation might be, he answered with candor, if not quite with the zeal of a rights crusader,
"I have not had a chance to study the situation, the laws, in this
whole field. My general philosophy is that we have to move strongly
and vigorously in the field of civil rights. I do not think that this is
a subject or matter that can be solved overnight, however. . . . I
would wait for my instructions and guidance from President-elect
Kennedy on this matter. He is the one that is going to make the
decision, not me."

Kennedy convinced—or more to the point did not *un*convince—the committee that he was a man for the job. Ironically, it
was New York Republican Kenneth Keating who pealed out the
hearing's final paean for Bobby. "I certainly cannot regard either
his youth or his relation to the President as matters of decisive
significance," Keating said of the man who would take away his
Senate seat in less than four years. "There is no doubt in my mind
that Bob Kennedy is an earnest, capable, and dedicated public
servant. Therefore, I will certainly support his confirmation and wish
him every success in the performance of his duties as Attorney General." Bobby got unanimous approval from admiring committee
members, and in the Senate only one man—Republican Gordon
Allott of Colorado—voted against his confirmation.

The duties young Robert Kennedy was about to assume were
defined originally by the Congress in the Judiciary Act of 1789. It
said: "There shall . . . be appointed a meet person learned in the
law to act as Attorney General of the United States who shall be
sworn or affirmed to a faithful execution of his office; whose duty
it shall be to prosecute and conduct all suits in the Supreme Court
in which the U.S. shall be concerned, and to give his advice and
opinion upon questions of the law when required by the President of
the United States, or when requested by the heads of any of the
departments, touching any matters that may concern their departments."

George Washington's first Attorney General was Edmund
Randolph, a crackerjack lawyer and former governor of Virginia.
But the 1st Congress considered the court system to be the prime

structure of federal law, and Randolph did not even have so much as one salaried assistant. The Attorney General was given official Cabinet rank in 1814, but not until 1839 was the post considered busy enough to rate any full-time legal help—one clerk and one messenger. Other executive departments began to form much larger legal sections of their own.

At last, in 1870, with all manner of post-Civil War legal tangles to unsnarl, Congress created the Department of Justice and transferred dozens of lawyers from other departments to the Attorney General's bailiwick. Once created, the department mushroomed to cope with new pressures of current events and congressional legislation. The department has become diverse and now includes: The Office of the Pardon Attorney, which handles nothing but applications for presidential pardons; a Bureau of Prisons, which supervises 30 federal penitentiaries, reformatories or detention camps; the Federal Bureau of Investigation, which was organized in 1908, and is responsible for investigating violations of 200 federal laws, including sabotage, treason, kidnapping, bank robbery, election law and civil-rights infringements; the Anti-Trust Division, which was established in 1903—Teddy Roosevelt's trust-busting heyday—after laws were passed to regulate business greed; the Civil Rights Division, which was set up in 1957 after Congress passed the first civil-rights legislation since Reconstruction.

By January, 1961, when Robert Kennedy moved into the Attorney General's gymnasium-sized office (much larger than the President's in the White House), the Department of Justice had become a vast network of anonymous people laboring over the intricacies of legal detail and law enforcement. There were some 1,700 lawyers and well over 30,000 diverse civil servants, but Bobby was not intimidated in the slightest by the dimensions of his new job.

At 35, he was the second youngest of the 67 men who had held the job before. (Richard Rush, who was to run for the vice-presidency with John Quincy Adams in 1828, was 34 when he became James Madison's third Attorney General in 1814.) Despite the cries about youth, nepotism and inexperience, Bobby plunked himself down in the huge red-leather chair and hoisted his feet up on the enormous desk top as if he had always been there. He brightened up the wood-paneled walls with watercolors and color-crayon sketches by his children, and he hung up a stuffed sailfish he once caught. A football, autographed by members of the Baltimore Colts professional football team, sat conveniently on a shelf, and at moments of high tension, Bobby would sometimes pick it up and play catch with any lawyer or visitor who happened to be handy.

From the start, Robert Kennedy was involved in crises that ranged well beyond even the far-reaching responsibilities of the Justice Department. As John Kennedy's most trusted confidant and most influential adviser, Bobby shouldered the weighty responsibilities behind White House decisions almost as often as the President himself. That role absorbed a good deal of time and nervous energy, but Bobby had wisely picked a group of enormously able men to assist him in the Justice Department.

Among the original members of Bobby's top staff was Byron "Whizzer" White, a former Colorado football star, Rhodes scholar and a brilliant attorney. He was Bobby's No. 1 aide and held the title of Deputy Attorney General until he was appointed as John Kennedy's first nominee to the United States Supreme Court in April, 1962. Nicholas Katzenbach, a onetime law professor at Yale and Chicago universities, was Assistant Attorney General in charge of the Office of Legal Counsel. When White moved on to the Court, Katzenbach became Deputy, and after Bobby quit, President Lyndon Johnson eventually named him Attorney General. Burke Marshall, once a member of a top Washington law firm, was the Assistant Attorney General in charge of the Civil Rights Division. Solicitor General Archibald Cox, a former Harvard law professor, handled the presentation of federal cases before the Supreme Court, as well as other critical legal actions.

Had it not been for the loyalty, to say nothing of the legal talents, of these men, Bobby might well have floundered in his dual role as Attorney General and President's brother. His aides devoted achingly long hours to their work, for each was determined to bolster Bobby wherever he could. Kennedy also made a tireless effort to meet at least some of the faceless thousands employed at the Justice Department; many a bored and weary civil servant was startled in those early months to glance up over the papers in his In box and find a shirt-sleeved Bobby grinning down, his hand extended. "Hi, I'm Bob Kennedy," he would say.

While Bobby served as Attorney General, the sharpest point of anxiety and activity came in the emotion-charged field of civil rights for Negroes. Dissension and dissatisfaction had been building for years, although it had not yet burst into the streets. That would come soon after the Kennedy Administration took power.

During the 1960 primary campaigns, John Kennedy had promised much to the Negro in the way of prospective legislation. At the Democratic nominating convention in Los Angeles that year Bobby, as Jack's campaign manager, had been insistent that a good, rugged civil-rights plank be written into the party's platform. That was done, but by the time it was drafted, Bobby was deeply involved in the backroom delegate-maneuvering it took to insure Jack's nomination. When one of the men working on the rights plank asked him to commit the Kennedy muscle to it, Bobby paused briefly, then said, "It's a tough plank, eh? All right, we'll support it." He had not read it thoroughly, but it made eminently good political sense— just as long as it was tough. By that time there was little chance of snaring many more southern delegates in Los Angeles for Kennedy than were already in the bag; and a strong civil-rights platform plank would have substantial appeal to most of the nation's 20,000,000 Negroes come the campaign.

The strategy worked perfectly. Jack was nominated, and during the campaign against Richard Nixon, the Kennedys continued to promise strong civil-rights legislation. One of the most effective moves of the campaign occurred when Jack telephoned the wife of the Rev. Martin Luther King Jr. King was later to become a Nobel Prizewinner for his Gandhi-like leadership in the Negro rights movement, but at that time he was in an Atlanta jail charged with driving in Georgia without a state driver's license. In his call, Jack relayed his concern to Mrs. King. Bobby went further: he phoned the judge in the case and asked him pointedly if King could be released on bond. King was quickly freed, and John Kennedy enjoyed a splendid press over the incident. Negroes were deeply impressed.

When the election returns were in, it became startlingly clear just how important it had been to gain the support of Negroes. John Kennedy had drawn heavily lopsided majorities from Negroes all over the country. He had carried three essential states—New Jersey, Illinois and Michigan—only on the strength of the overwhelming pro-Kennedy vote cast by Negroes. Without the 63 electoral votes those three states gave John Kennedy, Richard Nixon would have been President.

Naturally, when the Kennedy Administration took over, Negro leaders and followers alike had high expectations. They had already had plenty of lip service and legal folderol. By then the Supreme Court's order to desegregate schools was nearly seven years old, yet in the 11 states of the Confederacy, only 60,000 of 3,000,000 Negro public-school children—barely two percent—were in integrated schools. The 1957 Civil Rights Act, landmark legislation that it was after nearly a century of neglect, had produced little in actual results, and John Kennedy himself had once said of it, "This bill creates no new civil rights, provides no unprecedented judicial procedures and is based on no radical principles of constitutional law." A law passed in the spring of 1960 dealt mostly with voting rights, making it a bit easier for Justice Department lawyers to get at records kept by segregationist registrars. Many Negroes considered that, too, little more than a token to appease them.

By early 1961, a menacing impatience had begun to spread among Negroes throughout the land. Few people—including Bobby and Jack Kennedy—recognized it for what it was: the restlessness that precedes rebellion. Indeed, many Negroes, loyal at least to the idea of civil rights that the Kennedy campaign had promised, were willing to bide their time a while longer.

In April, 1961, Bobby's Justice Department did move with force to reopen the public schools in Prince Edward County, Virginia. Two years before, recalcitrant white officials there had circumvented a federal court order by establishing "private" schools for whites only, which were partially financed by state aid. To open the schools for Negroes, federal attorneys brought suit, with the Government as the complaining party, instead of forcing county residents to do it. It was the first time the Government had sued as plaintiff in a segregation case.

It was an encouraging move (although the schools did not actually open for Negroes until 1963), but it was scarcely the kind of far-reaching action southern Negroes needed to get a solid guarantee of equal schooling, let alone voting rights or access to public accommodations.

After all their promises, the Kennedys' first civil-rights legislative proposal in 1961 was little more than an act to extend the life of the Civil Rights Commission for two more years. The commitment to Negro rights seemed less than wholehearted.

There was a reason for this lack of forcefulness. The Kennedys were grappling with problems of practical politics. First, Jack's thin election victory made them uneasy about trying to move too quickly on controversial points. Secondly, they were trying to maintain a warm and workable relationship with southern Democrats in Congress so that other legislation would have a chance to pass. A bristling civil-rights bill seemed dangerous at that point. The Democrats had sizable margins over Republicans in both Houses—260 to 172 in the House and 65 to 35 in the Senate. Yet without solid southern support, these majorities could crumble. Thus an all-out fight to legislate equality and justice for Negroes— moral and right as it was—seemed just a bit too costly to the Kennedys.

Speeches were cheaper. In May, 1961, Bobby decided it was time to say something strong about the Administration's stand on civil rights. He purposely chose a perilous platform: the law school at the University of Georgia in Athens. The campus had been troubled early in the year after the university's first Negro students, Charlayne Hunter and Hamilton Holmes, enrolled; by spring things were peaceful, but there were still ugly undercurrents.

Bobby labored over his speech, drafting it no less than a dozen times; he knew this would be a tough audience, packed with University of Georgia faculty and students who were well educated, as well as deeply segregationist. As it turned out, Kennedy's message contained no promises for specific legislation or legal actions; but the fact that he spoke from a podium in Dixie rather than in the North made his talk more palatable to Negroes and critical liberals.

"We will not stand by or be aloof. We will move," said Bobby. "I happen to believe that the 1954 decision was right. But my belief does not matter. It is the law. Some of you may believe the decision was wrong. That does not matter. It is the law. And we both respect the law . . . For on this generation of Americans falls the full burden of proving to the world that we really mean it when we say all men are created free and are equal before the law."

Bobby Kennedy had long felt that the best solution to the Negroes' plight would be to guarantee their voting rights. He felt that all other rights would flow from that source and that once they got the vote in the South they could change what they wanted changed through the ballot box.

Logical and legally correct as that was, it represented a misjudgment of the reasons behind the fervor and fever growing among Negroes. As long as many southern registrars purposely flunked them in literacy tests, there could be no assurance of Negro voting rights. In any case, to many southern Negroes the right to register would not ease the devastating emotional punishment they suffered every time they were rebuffed by a "White Only" sign on a drinking fountain, a restaurant, a bus station waiting room. They wanted equality—now. And they wanted a kind of equality that they could taste, touch, see and enjoy.

The first bursts of violence exploded in Alabama within days after Bobby's Georgia speech (although there was no correlation of events). A band of hymn-singing demonstrators from the militant Congress of Racial Equality climbed aboard two buses in Washington on May 4, and headed south. They were determined to make a face-to-face confrontation with the cruel rules of segregation that oppressed Negro travelers there. They called themselves Freedom Riders.

All was quite peaceful through Virginia, North Carolina, South Carolina and Georgia. But when the Riders came to Anniston, Alabama, on Sunday, May 14, they were met by a surly crowd of white hoodlums armed with clubs and bicycle chains. The mob set fire to one bus, roughed up the demonstrators before police arrived and broke up the crowd by firing their pistols into the air. Later the same day, in Birmingham, more Riders were beaten up at a bus terminal. Police arrived 10 minutes too late.

When Bobby learned of the violence, he dispatched his own administrative assistant, John Siegenthaler, a former Tennessee newspaperman. Tension was growing all over Alabama. On May 20, Governor John Patterson promised that he would see to it that the beleaguered bus riders were escorted safely from Birmingham to Montgomery. He did—but when the Riders arrived at the bus terminal in Montgomery, a bloodlusty crowd of jeering whites awaited them. The Riders were attacked and clubbed bloody. Siegenthaler, who had left his car to help a girl who was being beaten, was knocked cold with a club. The mob, now 3,000 strong, savagely assaulted Negroes in the demonstration. Again, police arrived after the worst was over.

By then, Bobby and the President were convinced that Alabamans intended to allow the Freedom Riders to be mauled by mobs and send in police only after blood had been spilled. It would be anarchy in defense of injustice. Early in the week Bobby had alerted squads of federal officers—marshals, Prison Bureau guards, Alcohol Tax men. Now, with the President's approval, he moved 400 of them into Montgomery. Deputy Attorney General White went along to take charge of the operation.

Adding to the tension was the fact that Martin Luther King had decided to go to Montgomery from his Southern Christian Leadership Conference headquarters in Atlanta. Bobby had tried several times to dissuade him, but on the night of Sunday, May 21, King was in Montgomery to conduct a prayer meeting for 1,200 people, including some Freedom Riders, in the First Baptist Church. A nervous band of 150 federal marshals stood on the steps outside and warily watched a menacing mob of whites assemble in the street. Soon the crowd was threatening to burn the church and attack the people within.

In Washington, Bobby calmly quarterbacked the tactics from his office, while Byron White kept him informed of the crisis from a Montgomery telephone. Kennedy was also on the phone much of the night with Governor Patterson, who was in a rage because a federal force, however puny, had been sent to his state. The governor had finally decided to call out his own National Guard to try to stifle the riot at the church, but Bobby had to listen to an interminable string of invective from the state executive. Still, Kennedy remained patient and dispassionate.

At one point, he spoke on the phone with King inside the church; Kennedy was so cool he was almost flip. "Well, Reverend, are you praying for us?" When King expressed fear that the marshals could not hold back the mob, Bobby said, "Now, Reverend, you know that without those federal marshals all of you would be dead as doornails." Indeed, between the marshals and the National Guard, the night passed without serious injury to anyone. Kennedy stayed at his desk until morning. Fearing the violence might break out again, he sent 200 more men to Alabama; then he tried to convince the civil-rights leaders that they should call off their bus rides and let things simmer down. They refused.

Two days later, when the Riders set out from Montgomery, bound for Jackson, Mississippi, they were heavily escorted. Bobby had elicited a promise from Mississippi's Governor Ross Barnett that the Riders would not be hurt. Barnett kept his word: the Riders were protected from physical harm by state police along the highway. But when they tried to enter Jackson's segregated terminal, several were arrested and jailed. That, at least, moved the controversy beyond the fists of hoodlums and put it into the courts—and that was the way Bobby Kennedy thought the situation should be handled.

The Attorney General issued a statement urging that people planning to travel through Alabama and Mississippi delay their trips "until the present state of confusion and danger has passed." Negro leaders felt Bobby had undermined their cause. When he tried to convince Martin King that it was a time for discretion instead of valor, the minister replied, "It's a matter of conscience and morality." Unshaken, Bobby said that such martyrdom would not have the "slightest effect" on Kennedy Administration actions in the field of civil rights. The Freedom Rides continued for more than a year, but they never again triggered such vengeful rioting as during May, 1961, in Alabama.

Less than a week after the tide of violence ebbed, Bobby's Justice Department filed a petition with the Interstate Commerce Commission asking for an order to abolish segregation in airport, bus and train terminals involved in interstate traffic. The order was issued and the "White Only" signs began coming down.

The Freedom Rider outbreak was the first time Bobby had been caught in a fiery confrontation between determined Negro rights advocates and southern white segregationists. Bobby was detached, unemotional and efficient throughout the crisis. His insistence on using a velvet-gloved force of marshals instead of bayonet-wielding troops had required icy nerves. (The President had given his approval to apply whatever force the Attorney General felt necessary.) Together, the Kennedys had made it crystal clear that they intended to preserve order in the South—whether local authorities wanted order or not.

Over the months, the brothers kept chipping away at the civil-rights problem. Some disenchanted Negro leaders felt the chipping tended more to sculpt a political image for the Kennedys than to carve any meaningful openings in the walls of southern segregation.

Justice Department lawyers were filing more and more suits charging voter discrimination, but they were hamstrung by weaknesses in the 1957 and 1960 laws, and they averaged 28 months work on each voting suit before it came to any decision. The Kennedys tried in 1962 to get a bill through Congress that would abolish the literacy test in federal elections. They found they couldn't count on a Senate majority to back it, let alone the two-thirds vote necessary to halt the predictable southern filibuster—so they did not push it very hard. Bobby increased the number of Negro lawyers in the Justice Department from 10 to 50. There was also a good deal of behind-the-scenes involvement by the Government in achieving school integration in such Dixie bastions as New Orleans, Little Rock and Dallas. Bobby made a pointed statement about that: "In school integration there has been a basic change in policy from abstention by the Federal Government—except during crisis or a disaster—to affirmative anticipatory action."

The meaning was clear enough: Bobby and Jack Kennedy did not approve of the Eisenhower Administration's practice of sitting by while explosive racial situations built up, and then overreacting when violence actually occurred by dispatching troops under orders to restore peace at gun-point. The Kennedys were determined to win with persuasion.

The time did come when they, too, had to rely on armed force. But after it was over, they could honestly say that they had waited until they had tried every gentlemanly means of settlement before turning to steel and tear gas. The questions were—had they waited too long and had they been too gentlemanly?

On Saturday, September 29, 1962, a slim, introverted Negro Air Force veteran named James Meredith, 29 years old, arrived to register at the University of Mississippi campus at Oxford. Students and town yokels alike waited for him with savagery in their hearts: here was a Negro bent on invading a heavily defended fortress of segregation. Bobby's Justice Department lawyers had been careful to remove every legal roadblock to Meredith's admission; now they were armed with a federal court order that had gone all the way to United States Supreme Court Justice Hugo Black.

Because Mississippi Governor Barnett relied on redneck support and was a thoroughgoing segregationist himself, Robert Kennedy had tried to arrange a carefully scripted drama whereby the governor could put up a show of protest to Meredith's admission. Then the Negro would be admitted while Barnett's state troopers stood aside and maintained order. This would keep segregationists satisfied with Barnett, prevent the governor from being cited for contempt of court and still put Meredith in Ole Miss.

Unfortunately, a gentlemen's agreement did not fit the occasion. Instead of cooperating, Barnett sent a large force of troopers to the campus to keep Meredith from registering. Lieutenant Governor Paul Johnson (now Governor) confronted Meredith and an escorting squad of two dozen federal marshals and flatly refused to let them pass. After four tries, Bobby decided Barnett would not keep his word. President Kennedy ordered Army troops in the area to stand by and called the Mississippi National Guard into federal service. Bobby ordered 500 marshals to a pre-set staging area in Memphis, Tennessee.

Worried, Barnett phoned the White House and promised the President and the Attorney General that if Meredith turned up Sunday afternoon, Mississippi state police would keep order. That, at least, was the Kennedys' understanding. Marshals, 167 of them, were flown in from Bobby's Memphis force and trucked to the campus on Sunday. They escorted Meredith to Baxter Hall, a dormitory, and left him with a bodyguard of 24 marshals, while the bulk of the force assembled at Ole Miss's Lyceum Building as a decoy to throw would-be rioters off Meredith's track.

As it grew dark on the campus, a yammering crowd of students and local hoodlums began to gather under the trees near the

Lyceum, where Meredith was to register in the morning. Barnett's promised force of state troopers was no longer in evidence. The mob began to move menacingly toward the uneasy line of marshals around the building. Sixty men from Oxford's own newly federalized National Guard marched up to reinforce the marshals. The crowd became enraged. Students set fire to a truck. Eggs, rocks, ragged pieces of cement, hunks of metal piping and gasoline-filled Coca-Cola bottles showered down on the men guarding the Lyceum. Again and again the marshals bathed the mob in choking clouds of tear gas. A group of students drove a fire truck toward the Lyceum and blasted the marshals and guardsmen with water from a high-pressure hose. A squad of marshals charged the truck and fired pistols into the hose.

Inside the Lyceum, Bobby's deputy, Nicholas Katzenbach, spoke tersely over a phone to the Attorney General, who was in the White House Cabinet Room with the President and a few close advisers. As Katzenbach described the desperate scene, Bobby could hear the angry mob in the background. In a low, awed voice, Bobby repeated Katzenbach's words to the President.

Around midnight, Katzenbach said he doubted that the marshals could hold out against the mob. The Kennedys had already decided to crush the rebellion. By 2 a.m., thousands of military police and national guardsmen had descended on the campus in helicopters, jeeps and trucks. Cowed, the mob dispersed.

When Meredith finally registered in the morning, 16,000 troops swarmed over Ole Miss and Oxford. The toll from the night was cruel: two men dead, 166 marshals and more than 40 soldiers injured. The schism between the Kennedys and the South gaped wide, and the world was shocked—again—to see that tear gas and soldiers were necessary to guarantee a United States citizen his legal rights.

The Kennedys caught some criticism for waiting too long to send in troops. There had been clear warnings the day before the riot that mayhem at Ole Miss was likely, but Bobby and Jack had trusted Governor Barnett—after all, he had kept his word about protecting the Freedom Riders in 1961. They had committed themselves to using the lightest federal force possible. As it turned out, they misjudged Barnett's character and miscalculated the fury of

Mississippi segregationists; but the troops at Oxford offered a hard, fair warning to redneck agitators, and many responsible southerners felt the Kennedys had been justified in their action.

The next summer, when another bloody crisis threatened at the University of Alabama in Tuscaloosa because of the enrollment of two Negroes, the situation was well in hand. Governor George C. Wallace performed a face-saving little charade of opposition at the "schoolhouse door," but quickly ran for cover before the grim insistence of Deputy Attorney General Katzenbach and troops of the federalized Alabama National Guard.

Still Negro leaders were neither soothed nor satisfied. A handful of costly victories was not enough. Negroes wanted full freedom—now.

As early as December, 1962, Martin Luther King was at work designing the strategy for a massive, peaceful assault on segregation in Birmingham, Alabama. It was a city so savage in its bigotry that Negroes had come to call it "Bombingham"—there had been no less than 18 racial bombings in the preceding six years. Most Negro residents were cowed and docile. They could not get good jobs. Not a single Negro was enrolled in an integrated school. Yet they seemed willing to go on accepting their oppression as an inevitable fact of life.

With his master plan carefully drawn, King moved from his Atlanta headquarters into Birmingham in the spring of 1963. There blossomed a season of revolt that would soon send the thunder of Negro discontent booming over the nation.

King dispatched hundreds of his followers to march through the streets. Many of them were bright-eyed children dressed in their Sunday best. The Birmingham police, commanded by Public Safety Commissioner Eugene T. "Bull" Connor, blocked their parades, watched sullenly while the Negroes knelt to pray, then hauled hundreds of them off to jail. Demonstrations continued for days. Children were told to bring their toothbrushes when they arrived to march because they would certainly be thrown into jail.

Finally Bull Connor's police loosed police dogs on the marchers. Firemen blasted Negroes with streams of water from high-pressure hoses, sending them sprawling and somersaulting through gutters like overturned beetles. Enraged Negroes hurled bottles and bricks at the police. The scenes in Birmingham were dramatic and unforgettable in May of 1963. Civil-rights marches spread to cities all over the United States. The old hymn, *We Shall Overcome,* became a Negro national anthem; tearful crowds everywhere chanted, "Freedom! Freedom! Freedom!" The Negro cause could no longer be ignored.

In Washington, Bobby Kennedy was moved to new action by the Negroes' militancy. He sent Burke Marshall, head of the Civil Rights Division, to Birmingham, and Marshall eventually helped negotiate a truce. The Attorney General decided to have a meeting with Negro artists and intellectuals in the hope that new lines of communication might be set up. He asked Negro Author James Baldwin to arrange it in Manhattan. Bobby had the impression that most Negroes felt great sympathy toward the Kennedy Administration. He could not have been more wrong. The New York affair disintegrated into a tempermental yammering of accusations and insults. When it was over, Baldwin said acidly, "Bobby Kennedy was a little surprised at the depth of Negro feeling. We were a little shocked at the extent of his naïveté."

Nevertheless, the Kennedys were trying to help. Justice Department lawyers had begun to draft a Kennedy Administration civil-rights package early in 1963. The brothers wanted it long before Birmingham exploded, but there was disagreement with congressional leaders about how far it should go. Fearing that they would get nothing at all if they tried for too much, the Kennedys introduced a bill on April 2, 1963, that was confined almost entirely to voting rights. It included a section that would allow proof of a sixth-grade education to replace a literacy test and another section that would allow court-appointed federal registrars to replace local registrars in areas where less than 15 percent of Negro residents were registered.

In fact, Congress was totally uninterested in acting on that first rights package of 1963. But angry Negro leaders blamed the inertia on the Kennedys. Whitney M. Young Jr., director of the National Urban League, snapped that it was about time the Kennedys "place human rights above regional politics." Martin Luther King said that the only difference he could see between the Eisenhower Administration and the Kennedy Administration was that "an inadequate approach has been substituted for a miserable one." Three thousand Negroes marched on the Justice Department building in Washington one warm day in May, and when Bobby came out on the steps, a spokesman shouted, "We haven't seen many Negroes coming out of there." Bobby picked up a bullhorn and replied, "Individuals will be hired on their ability."

Finally, with multitudes of civil-rights advocates marching everywhere and racial pressures building steadily, the Kennedys sent a new civil-rights bill to Congress on June 19, 1963. It asked for broad new Justice Department powers to bring suits in school-discrimination cases. It requested strong fortification of voting rights. It asked that the Government be permitted to withhold financial aid to any program that practiced racial discrimination.

Most importantly, it contained a section dealing with an injustice that had been one of the sharpest thorns in Negroes' flesh for decades: discrimination in public accommodations. That section of the bill was anathema to white merchants, including many outside the South, for it was to be based on the Interstate Commerce Clause (Article I, Section 8) of the Constitution. It would mean that the Government could bring suit against businessmen who ran segregated establishments on the grounds that they were obstructing interstate business. To many an entrepreneur it represented a blatant new federal encroachment on their freedom to profit as they saw fit.

Over the years, the clause had been utilized no less than 38 times as the foundation for congressional acts to regulate everything from firearms to coal-mine safety to the inspection of chickens. Until now, it had not been used as a tool to insure equal rights.

When Bobby appeared that summer of 1963 to testify before the Senate Commerce Committee, he opened with a ringing statement. "For generations, Americans have prided themselves on being a people with democratic ideals, a people who pay no attention to a man's race, creed or color. That very phrase has become a truism, but it is a truism with a fundamental defect: it has not been true. . . White people of whatever kind—even prostitutes, narcotics pushers, Communists or bank robbers—are welcome at establishments which will not admit certain of our federal judges, ambassadors and countless members of our armed forces."

The Kennedy commitment was terribly late and it had been forced into being by Negroes who took to the streets to dramatize their needs. Civil-rights militants argued that the bill did not go far enough, that Bobby should have insisted on a federal fair-employment-practices section, that he should have demanded that the Justice Department be allowed to intervene in all types of civil-rights suits under the Fourteenth Amendment. Although he was sympathetic, Bobby felt Negroes wanted to get too much too soon.

On August 28, Negro and white civil-rights leaders staged one of the most spectacular mass protests in history. A quarter of a million people, both whites and Negroes, descended on Washington and assembled at the base of the Washington Monument. From there, they marched in stern and peaceful ranks along Constitution and Independence avenues to the Lincoln Memorial. They walked with almost no talking. The one sound from the mass was the shuffle of thousands of feet scraping along the pavement; it seemed as inexorable as ocean surf.

At the Memorial, civil-rights leaders spoke. Negro dissatisfaction with the Kennedy program was etched starkly by Roy Wilkins, the usually even-tempered executive secretary of the National Association for the Advancement of Colored People. "The President's proposal represents so moderate an approach that if any part is weakened or eliminated, the remainder will be little more than sugar water. Indeed, the package needs strengthening," said Wilkins. That same day dozens of marchers went out of their way to picket Bobby Kennedy's Justice Department building.

Even as he was being criticized, Bobby's civil-rights record as Attorney General was growing brighter. The bill that he and John Kennedy prepared did not get through Congress until June, 1964—nearly seven months after the President was killed. Rightfully, much of the credit for its passage was chalked up to the political wiliness of Lyndon Johnson and the compromises written into the legislation by Illinois' Republican Everett M. Dirksen, the Senate minority leader.

Yet Bobby Kennedy was deeply involved all along. In spite of the grief he felt in the spring of 1964 over the loss of his brother, he testified nine times before the Senate Judiciary Committee, nearly all of it in answer to needling questions from southerners. Kennedy and Nicholas Katzenbach together hammered out most of the compromises with Dirksen. Bobby and his Justice Department aides nursed the bill through Congress with tender, loving care. They kept it strong in some areas that conservatives wanted weakened and they were flexible enough to give in to compromise in other sections. All in all, it eventually attracted enough support to get a vote of cloture passed, ending an 87-day Dixie filibuster.

When Bobby resigned to run for the New York Senate seat, he had served 44 months as Attorney General. They were tense, tumultuous times for him and for the nation, and Bobby acquitted himself well as a rule.

True to his promise to the Senate Judiciary Committee before his confirmation, Bobby did steer new anti-racketeering bills through Congress—seven of them. In the year before they passed, government lawyers got only 14 racketeering convictions in federal courts; in the year that ended in June, 1964, there were 325. In one sensational effort to attract attention to the dangers of syndicate crime, Bobby went on television to introduce an aging punk named Joe Valachi before the Senate Rackets Committee. For five days Valachi sang a stool pigeon's medley about life in the Cosa Nostra, an occult crime organization. Valachi, who was under life sentence for murder himself, unfolded tales of an underworld network, complete with recollections of blood oaths and revenge killings. If nothing else, Valachi's testimony provided superb cocktail-party conversation, and to some extent it did focus attention on the ever-widening influence of organized criminals in the nation.

The Justice Department, under Bobby's direction, produced an impressive list of more prosaic, but still important accomplishments. A Kennedy-sponsored act relieved backlog-case congestion in federal courts by authorizing 73 new judges. Another authorized funds that allowed impoverished defendants to have not only an attorney but investigative and psychiatric services as well to bolster their defense; Attorneys General before Bobby had tried for 25 years to get the same legislation. Bobby directed federal prosecutors to speed up the pretrial release of indigent defendants by foregoing bail wherever feasible. He created a new Office of Criminal Justice for the expressed purpose of keeping an eye on unfair practices by prosecutors.

His record of anti-trust enforcement turned out to be less impressive than many people had predicted when he was appointed. In 1961 Bobby had said, "I view the business that engages in such [price-fixing] conspiracies in the same light as I regard the racketeer who siphons off money from the public in crooked gambling or the union official who betrays his union members." The Justice Department did bring several suits against steel companies and electrical-equipment companies on charges of price-fixing. And it applied the anti-trust laws for the first time against banks by successfully challenging a major merger involving Philadelphia firms. The record was not particularly distinguished, however—partly because Bobby's appointment of Lee Loevinger (now a Federal Communications Commission member) as head of the Anti-Trust Division did not work out well and the division was relatively stagnant.

Under Bobby's reign, J. Edgar Hoover, a lawman's legend after 40 years as director of the Federal Bureau of Investigation, was startled to find that someone was actually telling him how to run his agency. It had never happened before, although the Attorney General is by law the man in over-all charge of the FBI. The autocratic old G-man had seen more than two dozen Attorneys General come and go, and he had every reason to believe that he had carved himself an untouchable empire.

Not with Bobby in charge. Obviously operating with the full force of the presidency behind him, he ordered Hoover to stop putting all his best agents on cases involving Communism. Bobby wanted the FBI to get down to work on crime-syndicate operations and civil-rights cases as well. Hoover had no choice but to obey. Later, when Lyndon Johnson became President and Bobby had no special entry to the White House, J. Edgar quickly regained his old-time rule over the FBI—although new emphasis remained where Bobby put it: on crime and civil rights.

Bobby's interest in juvenile delinquency, unsurprising in the light of his warm relationship with children, was a key factor in getting a new Juvenile Delinquency Control Act through Congress; it provided $30,000,000 for a three-year study of the causes and prevention of crime among youngsters. The Attorney General did some curbstone research himself on the subject by traveling into the depths of Manhattan slums to visit with ducktail-and-switch-blade members of a kids' gang called the Viceroys. When John Kennedy created the President's Committee on Juvenile Delinquency and Youth Crime, Bobby was put in charge.

Under Bobby, the Justice Department finally settled in 1963 the long-delayed General Aniline & Film Co. suit. The German firm had been taken over as enemy property by the United States Government from its parent corporation, I. G. Farben, in 1942. Interhandel, a Swiss corporation, filed suit to buy part of the General Analine stock. It was an immensely complex—and contro-versial—case, for some people claimed Interhandel was really a front company for I. G. Farben interests, which had been pro-Nazi during the war. After 21 years the legal brush was finally cleared so the stock could be put up for public sale—including some to Interhandel.

During the steel-price crisis of April, 1962, there was an angry flurry around Bobby when three newspaper reporters were jolted out of bed long after midnight by FBI agents. The lawmen had been sent to uncover the facts about a press statement sup-posedly made by one company president to the effect that a price rise would hurt American business's competitive system. Bobby had ordered the investigation and was blamed for playing Gestapo with the FBI. It was a mean and miserable performance, to be sure, but it was an FBI supervisor, not Bobby, who picked the hour for the call. Still, the use of the FBI for such a picayune mission was a dubious idea in the first place.

Robert Kennedy has also been criticized, rightly, for his part in recommending a few southern judicial appointments that turned sour. No less than three district judges, named on Bobby's say-so and after undiscerning examination of their backgrounds, turned out to be of a segregationist turn of mind. The trio—J. Robert Elliott of Georgia, William H. Cox of Mississippi and E. Gordon West of Louisiana—thus became prickly-pear problems in achieving swift settlement of some civil-rights cases.

Another off-key note in his administration, of course, was Bobby's relentless pursuit of Jimmy Hoffa. When Kennedy left office, the House Judiciary Committee voted to investigate the Jus-tice Department to find out whether Hoffa's rights were trampled on during Bobby's zealous chase. (As of mid-1965, little had been accomplished in that probe.)

Measuring the achievements of one Attorney General against another is an uncertain business, at best. There are many imponderables and countless standards to apply. Yet Robert Kennedy would have to be rated as one of the most effective men to hold the job in the 176 years since its creation. He never did become a lawyer's lawyer; administration and activism were his fortes. He held the post at a critical time in American history, for the civil-rights revolution marked a crucial crossroads for the nation. Kennedy's actions at the turning point, although slow and uncertain at times, were the right ones.

Even *The New York Times,* which had been so critical of his appointment and had already begun a powerful editorial campaign opposing Bobby's Senate candidacy in New York, had kind words for his performance at Justice after he resigned. "He named excellent men to most key posts, put new vigor into protecting civil rights through administrative action, played a pivotal role in shaping the most comprehensive civil-rights law in this country, generally improved the department's efficiency," said the *Times.* "Mr. Kennedy has done much to elevate the standard."

Certainly a good share of the credit for Bobby's high grades as Attorney General must go to the brilliant lawyers he himself brought into the Justice Department. Yet, just as certainly, Bobby Kennedy's own tactics and techniques made his Attorney Generalship a credit to him and, of course, to the Kennedys. It was all the more impressive because of Bobby's never-ending obligation to his brother in the White House.

VI
THE YEARS WITH JACK

□□
□□

SHORTLY AFTER HE BECAME ATTORNEY GENERAL
and well before the critical din about nepotism and inexperience had
died away, Bobby Kennedy tried to explain why he had joined his
brother's Cabinet. "The turning point was my realization that I
just couldn't turn my back on this now," he said. "I wanted to be
a part of trying to make good on the things we promised."

He paused, then added, "And besides, Jack needs someone
he can talk to."

On the basis of that unassuming insight, John Fitzgerald
Kennedy and Robert Francis Kennedy constructed the greatest
brother act in the history of American politics. Certainly the tri-
umphs and troubles of the Presidency—its chilling responsibilities
and its historic decisions, its power and its rich rewards—were
ultimately John Kennedy's alone. Yet the presence of Bobby, his
devotion, his dedication, along with the attribute that Joseph Kennedy called "moxie," were invaluable to the President. Their sister,
Eunice Shriver, said simply, "The two of them shared the presidency." Indeed, Bobby often slipped into the pronoun "we" when
he talked of events and decisions at the White House.

The two were close enough and thought so much alike that
they could rely on a kind of brotherly shorthand in their communication. Legend had it that they spent hours in each other's company, that they conversed by phone much of the time when they

were apart. The fact was that, except for days of crisis, Jack and Bobby sometimes did not see each other more than once or twice a week—and then it would often be at ceremonial functions. On many days they did not talk more than once or twice over the White House hot line hooked up to Bobby's Justice Department office.

When they did meet to talk, their conversations were usually curt and hurried, shorn of lengthy explanations and cautious definitions. Bobby's exact reaction to a situation or an individual could be transmitted to the President by a shrug of the shoulder, a shake of the head, a pause before answering, a mumbled phrase. "It's by osmosis," Jack once said of their mode of communication. "We're both cryptic."

It was often hard for anyone, including Jack and Bobby themselves, to recall which came up with a given idea. "I rely on Bobby's judgment as much as anyone I know—he's good. I listen to him a lot," President Kennedy said. "I frequently take his suggestions. Sometimes I don't." No man in the Government or in politics was closer to John Kennedy than his brother. Yet their relationship did not go as far beyond those professional ties as a good deal of sentimental Kennedy lore would have people believe.

They did not see each other socially with any great frequency. Bobby and Ethel had a different set of friends. Reporters often asked White House aides how many times in a week the brothers dined together, and when they were told no times at all, they would not believe it. When the families were at Joe Kennedy's Hyannis Port settlement, Jack and Jackie usually stayed close to their home, Bobby and Ethel near theirs. In the evenings, Bobby might drop around to Jack's house for a few moments—but usually the subject was White House shop talk.

The brothers were unalike in many ways. Bobby leaned toward action; Jack more toward cerebration. Bobby married Ethel Skakel, cute and vivacious; Jack married Jacqueline Bouvier, cameo-handsome and regal. The image of John Kennedy climbing a mountain, shoving someone in a swimming pool or challenging a Brooklyn hoodlum to a fight was so out of character as to be ludicrous. The idea of Bobby launching into one of Jack's eloquent speeches would stretch the imagination, too. Once while he was speaking before the Foreign Student Service Council in Washington, Bobby tried one of Jack's famed phrases. He said, "You people are exemplifying what my brother meant when he said in his inaugural address, 'Ask what you can do for — uh — uh — do not ask what you can do — uh — ask not what you can do for your country but——' Well, anyhow, you remember his words." The audience roared with laughter and Bobby popped back gamely, "That's why my brother is President."

In some ways, the fact that they were brothers—even brothers reared to cherish the tenacious loyalty that existed among Joseph Kennedy's children—was coincidental to their close relationship during the years of the New Frontier.

Had Bobby chosen to "follow the dollar," as he once put it, the chances are slim that he would have been a President's confidant. Even a President Kennedy's. Had he been running Joe Kennedy's Merchandise Mart in Chicago or playing the stock market or investing in Manhattan real estate, he would have been loved for being a brother, respected for his skill at making a buck, admired for his touch-football prowess. But a power in John Kennedey's White House? Likely not.

"All this business about Jack and Bobby being blood brothers has been exaggerated," said Eunice Shriver. "First there was a big difference in years. They had different tastes in men, different tastes in women. They didn't become really close until 1952, and it was politics that brought them together. That's a business full of knives. Jack needed someone he could trust, someone who had loyalty to him. Jack knew he had a person like that with Bobby around."

By the time John Kennedy really "needed someone to talk to" at the White House the brothers had fought, talked, connived and strategized through all manner of political combat.

Their first effort together came in 1946. Jack was 28, a newly discharged Navy hero; Bobby was 20, also fresh out of the Navy. Jack, still wan and weak from his war experiences, had decided to run for the House seat from Boston's 11th Congressional District; it had been vacated by that charming old crook, James Michael Curley, who had been re-elected mayor of Boston despite the fact that he was found guilty of fraud a few years earlier.

Ironically, in the light of Bobby's later experience in New York, Jack was tagged by entrenched Irish politicians in the 11th as a "goddam carpetbagger" because his residence in the district was a newly rented room in the Bellevue Hotel. Jack entered the Democratic primary against nine opponents.

The Kennedy Clan, along with a group of Jack's college and service cronies, were bustling about to guarantee his election, but Bobby rated no higher than the Kennedy girls in the campaign hierarchy. He was neither frontroom strategist nor backroom string-puller; his job was almost as lowly as scraping paint in the Navy: "I went around buzzing doorbells," he recalled. "I don't remember what I said to people. I guess I just asked them to vote for my brother." He carefully studied the operation of Jack's campaign, as well as of others in the race. Bobby began to formulate his own basic tenet of politics: work hard and you will win. "All they did," he said of the garden-variety Boston politicians he watched, "was sit around talk about it. They never got off their asses."

Jack won the primary, which was equivalent to winning the election, and went on to serve three terms in Congress. Then, in 1952, with what seemed too-much-too-soon brashness, he decided to run for the seat of G.O.P. Senator Henry Cabot Lodge. Lodge had been first elected in 1936 and had a powerful following both nationally and in Massachusetts. Bobby, now a law-school graduate and committed to government work, had risen higher in Jack's estimation and in the family political organization—he was summoned home from his Justice Department job in Washington and given the title of campaign manager. Bobby was 26 then and he looked like a boy who would do better organizing a campus pep rally than a state-wide political campaign.

John Kennedy called the major strategy shots himself, although his father, who remained a closeted family skeleton during that campaign as well as others in the future because of his controversial political image and isolationist leanings, poured in almost as much advice and influence as he did money (close to $500,000).

The role of young Bobby Kennedy was nonetheless an important one. His youthful appearance was deceiving. Ruddy-faced old Democratic warhorses would swagger into Kennedy headquarters, expecting at least a low bow from Bobby in deference to their reputations and years of experience. Not Bobby. He didn't even recognize some of them, which injured their Irish egos and sent them stamping away in anger. When one group got past his cool reception long enough to offer their services, he told them to sit down and lick envelopes. This did not make friends for Bobby among the Derby Hat and Cigar Brigade.

On one occasion, Bobby was sent to deliver a message to Massachusetts' Democratic Governor Paul Dever, who was running for re-election that year. In no uncertain terms, young Kennedy told the governor he had committed an error that could hurt Jack's campaign and that the governor had better be more careful in the future. Apoplectic, Dever ordered Bobby out; then he telephoned Bobby's father and said, "I know you're an important man around here and all that, but I'm telling you this and I mean it: Keep that fresh kid of yours out of my sight from here on in."

Bobby became a kind of one-man firing squad for Jack that year as well as a relentless watchdog. He once received sycophantic assurances from a group of Boston labor leaders that they were doing everything they could to get Jack Kennedy elected. Suspicious, Bobby spent a few hours one afternoon plodding through parking lots at factories. As he had guessed, there were no Kennedy-for-Senator bumper stickers on the cars; he lost no time in rebuking the union chiefs for letting down the Kennedy cause.

Naturally, Bobby left a trail of exasperated old-line Democrats in Massachusetts, but there was an admirably consistent integrity to his performance. He did not ask wardheelers to lick envelopes just to insult them; that kind of work really did have to be done—and Bobby did plenty of it himself. If the pols took it as an insult, too bad.

John Kennedy later said of Bobby's role: "You can't make an omelet without breaking the egg. I don't pay any attention to the beefs. Every politician in Massachusetts was mad at Bobby after 1952, but we had the best organization in history. And what friend who was really worthwhile has he lost? I don't recall."

Robert Kennedy cared only about winning the election for Jack and if people mistook his abrasive manner for ruthlessness, he was bothered not a whit. "I'm not running a popularity contest," he said. "It doesn't matter if they like me or not. Jack can be nice to them. I don't try to antagonize people. But if they are not getting off their rear ends, how do you say that nicely?"

He never did learn to say it nicely. Yet for people willing to work, Bobby had nothing but praise. During the 1952 campaign, he and Jack built a large, loyal organization. Through a statewide network of 286 local leaders, each backed by hundreds of workers, there was a flourishing Kennedy cadre in every corner of the state. John Kennedy had no opposition in the Democratic senatorial primary and he only needed 2,500 signatures on a petition to get the nomination. Instead of settling for that puny figure, the Kennedys proved the power of their fledgling organization by getting a whopping 262,324 signatures.

In their effort to leave no region or specialized bloc untouched, the Kennedys set dozens of girls to work making up typewritten lists of selected interest groups. Eventually there were committees created to offer a specific, individual pro-Kennedy organization for everyone from ethnic loyalists to religious protagonists to professional men. Bobby himself traveled all over Massachusetts ("We tried to organize every town of over 600 voting population") keeping the lines taut. He worked seven-day weeks and 20-hour days; he lost 10 pounds before it was all over.

Bobby also contributed a tactic to the Senate race that became important in John Kennedy's presidential campaign: voter-registration drives. Bobby had pored for hours over police-department address lists of residences, comparing them to lists of registered voters. Bobby found that many streets had virtually nobody registered in areas which should have been thick with Democrats. He launched a state-wide campaign to get voters registered. It paid off: by Election Day 100,000 new names appeared on the lists. John Kennedy defeated Henry Cabot Lodge for the Massachusetts U.S. Senate seat by a bare 70,000-vote margin in 2,300,000 votes cast.

In 1956 Bobby and Jack fought again in tandem to get the Democratic vice presidential nomination at the convention in Chicago. When presidential nominee Adlai Stevenson threw the choice of his running mate to the delegates instead of making the selection himself, Jack Kennedy seemed to have a good chance. The brothers prowled sleeplessly through hotel corridors the night before the balloting, trying to collar votes. Their effort fell short. Nevertheless, John Kennedy crept to within 38½ votes of the nomination, before losing to the much better known Tennessee Senator, Estes Kefauver.

Later Bobby recalled, "I was terribly disappointed to be in a battle and lose, but when that roll call was over, I walked over to see Jack and I told him it was the luckiest thing that ever happened to him."

There were lessons to be learned from the folksy Tennessee glad-hander, who was a living antithesis of John Kennedy. "It really struck me," said Bobby, "that it wasn't the issues which matter. It was the friendships. So many people said to me they would rather vote for Jack, but that they were going to vote for Estes Kefauver because he had sent them a card or gone to their home. I said right there that we should forget the issues and send Christmas cards and go to their homes next time."

Both Bobby and Jack knew full well that the run for the presidency would come in 1960. (Bobby has insisted that he and his brother had never openly discussed it then, but by that special osmosis which characterized their relationship, Bobby was perfectly certain that the presidential campaign was a certainty.)

Right after the 1956 Chicago convention, Bobby took a leave from his Rackets Committee job and spent seven weeks traveling with Adlai Stevenson. He was carried on the rolls as a special assistant to campaign director James Finnegan, but he had no demanding duties. Not to Stevenson anyway. For Kennedy futures, Bobby did make a thorough study of Adlai's tactics and techniques. He was appalled.

For one thing, Stevenson seemed to recoil at backslapping and handshaking in crowds. He seemed timorous or uninterested during speeches from the rear car of his whistle-stop campaign train. His staff did not offer a great deal of cooperation to the press. Stevenson's subtle flaws and major tactical mistakes alike were caught and collected by Bobby for later analysis.

When the Kennedy-for-President campaign began to warm up in 1959, there was no question in Jack's mind about who would head his general staff. Bobby resigned from his high-tension work on the Rackets Committee to finish his book about the investiga-

tions into labor corruption. Then he sprinted on to the nerve-rack-
ing job of electing to the presidency a Senator who was just 42
years old and a Roman Catholic to boot.

Because Jack's age and religion were such powerful factors
against him, he would have to enter the perilous presidential primaries to prove that he could actually pull votes beyond Massachusetts and outside the parishes of Roman Catholicism. The
Democratic convention would not seriously consider nominating
him otherwise. The first primary of major importance was to be in
Wisconsin on April 5, 1960; Kennedy's opponent would be the
ebullient, popular Hubert Humphrey, Senator from neighboring
Minnesota. Bobby spent a frigid week in Wisconsin before the
campaign. He found that the state Democratic organization was
flabby and practically useless; he leaked word to reporters that he
thought Jack should stay out of Wisconsin because Hubert was too
strong. That was a ploy to create an image of John Kennedy the
Underdog. Everyone in the Kennedy camp knew full well that there
was no choice but to make the run in Wisconsin. As Bobby said,
"The American people like an underdog. The campaign people
work better when you are behind. Jack does better."

Besides running the organizational charts-graphs-and-per-
sonnel end of the campaign, Bobby was a tireless performer on the
hustings in Wisconsin. He made tart little speeches to high-school
kids, addressed church ladies' tea parties and spun tales of suspense
and intrigue about Jimmy Hoffa to audiences of farmers in bib
overalls. By the time the primary was held, Jack Kennedy was no
longer an underdog; he won 20½ of the state's 31 convention delegates. Hubert Humphrey felt that his defeat was not truly decisive
and he announced that he would carry the battle into the West
Virginia primary.

Exhausted, Bobby nevertheless flew there the morning after
the Wisconsin primary with Larry O'Brien, a top Kennedy political
brain-truster. West Virginia was a bitter, angry campaign. Both
candidates utilized below-the-belt personal accusations as much as
high-level policy exhortations. Humphrey jabbed constantly at
Kennedy's wealth, hinted that there might be some vote-buying
going on in West Virginia. "I can't afford to run through this state
with a little black bag and a checkbook," he said. (There was no

evidence to prove such a charge.) The Kennedys brought in Franklin Delano Roosevelt Jr., a magic name in long-depressed West
Virginia, and Roosevelt cast one of the most vicious barbs of the
campaign when he attacked Humphrey's wartime status. "He is a
good Democrat," said Roosevelt, "but I don't know where he was
in World War II." (Humphrey was a 4-F.)

Bobby himself did some public sniping at Humphrey. At
one point, he cracked that the Minnesota Senator had "played fast
and loose with smears and innuendoes . . . and I do not intend to
take this kind of abuse indefinitely." Humphrey retorted, "Politics
is a serious business, not a boy's game where you can pick up your
ball and run home if things don't go according to your idea of who
should win. Bobby's statement indicates they're pushing the panic
button."

The major issue—played down by both Kennedy and
Humphrey—was the matter of Jack Kennedy's Roman Catholicism. And without question, this was the crux of Kennedy's attempt
to get the nomination through the primaries route. A win in heavily
Protestant West Virginia would pretty well squash the widespread
and recurrent suspicion that Kennedy could not win the election in
November because of his faith.

When the polls closed on May 10, the Kennedys were convinced that they had lost. Their own statistics pointed to it and so
did much of the curbstone conversation around the state. As scant
early returns began to drift in, Bobby sat tense and irritable in the
Kennedy headquarters, a one-time barbershop in a Charleston
hotel. But after the first sizable returns were in, he began to relax.
Soon it turned into a Kennedy landslide. Two hours after the polls
closed, Ethel Kennedy began taking pictures with a flash camera
and burbled merrily, "Isn't it exciting?" Bobby quipped to reporters, "I couldn't have done it without my brother."

As the victory count mounted, Bobby left Kennedy headquarters and walked through the rain to Hubert Humphrey's hotel.
There, while the saddened Minnesota Senator told his weeping
workers that he was pulling out of the presidential race for good,
Bobby stood at the rear of the room, his arms folded. When Humphrey finished conceding defeat, Bobby walked forward, threw his
arm over Hubert's shoulder and the two men strode through the

drizzle to hear Jack Kennedy make his victory statement at Kennedy headquarters.

The Democratic convention opened in Los Angeles on July 11. Bobby had already laid out an extensive and unprecedented communications network (seven telephones and eight walkie-talkies) connecting the floor of the Los Angeles Sports Arena with the Kennedys' convention command post in a cottage outside. Bobby—aided by family lieutenants such as Teddy and brothers-in-law Steve Smith and Sargent Shriver—had a staff of 50 men who were to keep tabs on the various state delegations until the night of the presidential balloting. The Kennedy shepherds were expected to do nothing else. Some slacked off a bit, and at one meeting, Bobby snapped at them, "We're not out here to go to Disneyland. We're not out here to go to night clubs. We're out here to work. If you're not out here to work, you can turn in your staff badges right now—we've got a lot of people who would like to have them."

On the night of the balloting, Bobby ran things from the cottage outside the arena. Jack would need 761 votes to win; based on his shepherds' counts, Bobby predicted 803. Just before the balloting began, Bobby phoned Larry O'Brien and said flatly, "This is it. We're going to win." Win they did—with 806 votes on the first ballot.

A jubilant Joseph Kennedy told Bobby over the phone, "It's the best organization job I've ever seen in politics."

Next day the Kennedys had to pick a vice presidential candidate. John Kennedy favored Lyndon Johnson—partly because he felt the Senate Majority leader was well qualified to succeed him as President and partly because a Texan on the ticket would pull votes in the South. Johnson showed immediate interest in taking the job when it was suggested by Jack on the morning of July 14, but Johnson asked for a couple of hours to consider it. Early in the afternoon, Bobby went to the Johnson suite in the Biltmore Hotel to discuss the situation with the late Speaker of the House Sam Rayburn, who was Johnson's chief confidant and adviser. At first, according to the recollection of the late Philip Graham, publisher of the Washington *Post*, who was also in the Johnson suite that day, Bobby asked Rayburn if Lyndon Johnson might want to be Na-

tional Democratic Chairman. Rayburn flatly rejected that idea as insulting. Then Bobby brought up the vice presidency again, and
asked if he could talk to Johnson himself.

Johnson refused to see Bobby then, saying he wanted to
talk with Jack. Bobby left. Graham called Jack and was told that
Johnson was the man they wanted. But as the afternoon progressed,
the Kennedys learned that liberal Democrats at the convention
might stir up a floor fight in objection to Johnson's candidacy.
Worried, Jack sent Bobby to the Johnson suite again to tell the
Texan of the impending troubles and ask if Johnson might not want
to withdraw.

Amid the tension and confusion, Bobby's curt delivery of
the message was interpreted by some men around Johnson as a
sign of antagonism from the Kennedy camp. Phil Graham recalled
that he phoned Jack Kennedy and said, "Jack, Bobby is down here
and is telling the Speaker and Lyndon that there is opposition and
that Lyndon should withdraw." Coolly Kennedy replied, "Oh,
that's all right. Bobby's been out of touch and doesn't know what's
been happening."

A moment later Bobby took the phone from Graham to talk
to Jack. As Graham left the room, he remembered that he heard
Bobby say, "Well, it's too late now," then drop the receiver back
in its cradle. From that episode there grew a report that Bobby had
fought against Lyndon Johnson's candidacy, that he and Jack had
bitterly disagreed. Bobby has never been very candid about his role
in the selection of Johnson, but he finally did give this version of
the affair:

"There was no disagreement between my brother and me
on this. We did, however, have our supporters to consider. Our
primary aim at the convention had been to put over John Kennedy
on the first ballot. We had had little time to think about the vice
presidential slot. We'd finally narrowed the field down to [Washing-
ton Senator] 'Scoop' Jackson, [Minnesota Governor] Orville Freeman and Lyndon. When Johnson's name was selected, I pointed
out to my brother that this was going to be very hard to explain to
many of our supporters. Johnson had tried to block us, to fight us
all the way, and the fight had unfortunately gotten personal in the
final stages. I was afraid the news of Johnson's selection to be vice

president would cause the Walter Reuthers, John Baileys and others to collapse. And some of them did fall on the floor when they got the word. We were afraid there would be a floor fight to prevent Johnson's nomination. We didn't know whether he'd be willing to go through a floor fight and all the acrimony again. I was sent as emissary to ask him this. He said he was willing to risk a floor fight to accept the nomination. I went back to my brother with the news."

No sooner was the convention over than Bobby plunged into the election campaign. This time he commanded an army of workers who fanned out across the country to trigger voter-registration drives, whip up audience enthusiasm for Jack's appearances and tune up the intricate workings of state political machines. No one really knew how many people were working for Bobby, but there was a gag at Democratic headquarters that if all of Bobby's legions did vote for Jack he could win on that basis alone. Robert Kennedy's knowledge of details was profound. At one point he asked a lieutenant how things were going in upstate New York; the man replied, "Pretty good," and Bobby bristled. "You know damned well they are not going 'pretty good,' " he said. "I was there yesterday."

To John Kennedy, his brother was the perfect campaign manager. "He's easily the best man for the job," said Jack. "He's the hardest worker I've ever seen. He's the best organizer. He went to work right after the convention. He took no time off. He's fantastic."

Again, Bobby was the hatchet man. He stormed about the country, ferreting out laziness and inept leadership. He was blunt, cold and undiplomatic at times. Yet he handled delicate tasks with equanimity. It was Bobby who informed two old Kennedy friends —Frank Sinatra and United Auto Workers President Walter Reuther—that they were too controversial to play major parts in the campaign. Sinatra was all but gagged entirely; Reuther did less than he might have liked.

Of Bobby's clashes with people during the campaign, Jack said, "I don't think he's as patient as I am. But he's overtired. First he went through the McClellan hearings. Then he wrote his book. And then he joined me. He's living on nerves."

Election night was no less wearing than the campaign itself. Bobby had set up a command post in his home at the Kennedy family compound in Hyannis Port. The place was overrun with long-distance telephones, clacking news tickers and television sets. Bobby had a private line hooked up to Jack's home nearby, but the restless presidential candidate was at Bobby's home much of the time. Through the seemingly interminable night and early morning, the Kennedys' hopes soared, then sank, then rose—slowly and precariously—again and again as the election seesawed to its final result.

Not until far into the morning after Election Day could the Kennedys count themselves winners. And then it was by the threadbare margin of just over 100,000 votes out of more than 68,000,000 cast.

Frazzled though he was when the campaign was finally won, Bobby was exuberant about the adventure ahead. To him, the Kennedy Years would cap the crusade to energize America. It was an electric image, and he said shortly after the election, "We're going to do what we thought Eisenhower was going to do in 1952 and never did—bring in a new spirit to the Government. Not necessarily young men, but new men, who believe in a cause, who believe their jobs go on forever, not just from nine to five. It really makes a hell of a difference. Our campaign was made up of new faces to a large extent, and this Administration will be made up of new faces to a large extent."

There were new faces aplenty on the New Frontier. During the conferences over prospective Cabinet members and key administration assistants at Joseph Kennedy's Palm Beach mansion and in Jack Kennedy's Georgetown house, Bobby was with Jack in the center of the Cabinet selection process. Robert S. McNamara, who had been president of the Ford Motor Company for barely a month, was offered the job of Secretary of Defense. When he seemed reluctant to accept, Bobby talked to him and suggested that there were plenty of legal, proper ways for McNamara personally to divest himself of his stock and yet keep it in his family without violating the conflict-of-interest principle. McNamara refused to consider that, but agreed to join the Kennedy Administration without his Ford stock.

During the search for an agriculture Secretary, the Kennedys had considered Fred V. Heinkel, president of the Missouri Farmers Association, as a prime candidate. John Kennedy interviewed him and was as surprised as he was disappointed to find that Heinkel—ostensibly a farm professional—did not have well-reasoned answers to many key problems. As a double check, the President-elect asked his brother to run over the same ground with Heinkel. When Bobby was finished, Heinkel was out. Instead of an agricultural expert, the Kennedys picked a political friend— Orville Freeman, who had been a solid Kennedy supporter, a good administrator while he was Governor of Minnesota and a city boy from Minneapolis who had no first-hand knowledge of farm problems.

When Bobby was finally convinced that he himself should take a place in the Cabinet, the trust in him that John Kennedy had developed became a bulwark behind the powers of the Presidency. Given the precise, pragmatic nature of John Kennedy's mind, the fact that Bobby was his brother was beside the point. The President was once asked why he leaned so heavily on Bobby, and there was not a hint of brotherly sentiment in his answer: "With Bobby, I have been witness to the testing of his judgment in a hundred crises. I know that he has a tough-minded, clear-thinking approach to the facts. I know how he arrives at his decisions. My confidence in him has emerged over years of watching him make decisions under great pressure without ever letting the pressure affect the outcome."

During the Kennedy Years, Bobby was the man to see in Washington. His influence was so pervasive that Bobby even took over the dispensing of the enormous political patronage of Post Office Department jobs while he was Attorney General. J. Edward Day, who was Postmaster General during the first two years of the Kennedy Administration, recalled that Bobby was so intensely involved in the pork-barrel appointments available through the Post Office that he once phoned Day three times in a single day to discuss "a single rural letter carrier who was to be appointed in a small town in Mississippi in which Bobby was intensely interested." Beyond that, Bobby was Jack's weathervane for politics and his sounding board for decisions. Frequently the President would ask an aide, "Why don't you check it with Bobby?" When Bobby made a suggestion, or even the implication of a suggestion, people jumped. When Bobby spoke, the echoes were heard in the White House Oval Office—if indeed Bobby's words were not actually echoes themselves of the President. When Kennedy Administration men wanted to guarantee presidential interest in a pet program, they made certain that Bobby was interested first.

To the President, Bobby was neither an Eisenhower's Sherman Adams nor a Roosevelt's Harry Hopkins. His position was neither so official nor so definable. His value lay in his loyalty to Jack and his neutrality of judgment. He had no selfish ax to grind, no personal image to polish, no private ambitions to feed from his proximity to the President. If he gave Jack his opinion, the President could be certain that it was an objective one, without greed or personal aggrandizement to warp its meaning or its motivation. In politics an utterly selfless man is all but nonexistent; but in his brother, Jack had an adviser and confidant dedicated to one thing: The Presidency of a Kennedy.

Of course, such a role pulled Bobby into affairs far beyond his Justice Department job—into foreign policy, for example. When John Kennedy had been in office for less than a year, he was asked just how far he would go in using Bobby as a foreign-affairs adviser. "It would depend," said the President. "Certainly not in the details of generating new ideas and policies—the trip to meet Khrushchev [in May, 1961], for example. These are matters that concern the State Department and the foreign-affairs specialists. When the policy was crystallizing, I might talk it over with Bobby in conjunction with the broad world picture."

The Kennedys may have let the experts have the last word in their special fields during relatively routine weeks. But let a crisis whip up to topple the routine and Bobby would appear at the President's side. In the Oval Office, the Cabinet Room or whatever White House command post was in use, Bobby would be there—slouched in a chair, glancing about from beneath his heavy eyebrows, either warily silent or offering curt and pointed observations.

In the anxious, pressure-filled hours of crisis, Bobby was the man the President felt closest to, although every member of the inner circle pooled opinions, advice and ideas to help John Kennedy shoulder his responsibilities.

The Kennedy Administration's first real brush with major crisis—and ultimately major catastrophe—came as the Bay of Pigs invasion was launched against Fidel Castro's Cuba. On April 17, 1961, a force of 1,400 Cuban exiles wallowed onto the beach in landing craft, trying to grab a toe-hold on the island. It should have worked, for invasion tactics had been in the planning stage since the last days of the Eisenhower Administration. The CIA had helped create strategy and trained volunteers in Guatemala. The Kennedy Administration had remodeled the design slightly, and Bobby, who had been in on the scheme all along, agreed that it had seemed a "worthwhile venture."

Within hours after the pitifully undermanned Cuban exile force hit the beach, it was stunned by a battering ram of Castro tanks and jets. Communist forces were much stronger than anticipated and, as John Kennedy received reports of the battle at the White House, he suddenly realized that advance intelligence and military information about the assault had been totally misleading. At once he knew that the invasion strength was too puny to stand a chance of success. There was no hope.

That morning Bobby Kennedy was in Williamsburg, Virginia, to make a speech to managing editors of United Press International. As soon as the enormity of the Bay of Pigs failure dawned on the President, he phoned his brother, told him the bad news and said, "Why don't you come on back and let's discuss it?" The Attorney General made his speech at noon, then flew back to Washington to join the death watch at the White House.

Vice President Lyndon Johnson was there. So were Dean Rusk and Robert McNamara, both of whom the Kennedys respected highly, as well as Central Intelligence Director Allen Dulles and most of John Kennedy's top White House aides. Bobby sat quiet and crestfallen, and spoke only occasionally. Once he said almost angrily, "We've got to do something. We've got to help those men."

The troops trapped on the beach were beyond real help. Two days after it began, the fragile little coup was crushed. During the last bleak hours of defeat, Jack and Bobby Kennedy often talked in undertones—apart from the others. The President had been badly advised and carelessly briefed about the real strength of Castro forces; most of the misinformation had come from the CIA or top military strategists.

In those grim moments John Kennedy was suddenly shaken and a little suspicious of nearly everyone around him—except Bobby. The President even asked his brother if he would become director of the CIA; Bobby declined because he felt it was a job far too sensitive for a member of the family to hold. As the Kennedys took stock of the tragedy, they came to a surprising realization: the whole intricate structure of U.S. national-security agencies and presidential advisers was in a state of organizational disarray.

It was time to redesign the whole national-security hierarchy—from the top down—and straighten out the convoluted channels of communication that existed within it. Beyond that, the President called for a fresh new policy paper on Cuba specifically from the State Department. Ten days later the National Security Council met at the White House, and Under Secretary of State Chester Bowles made the presentation on Cuba. Bobby Kennedy was there (and he would continue to be a regular participant in those NSC meetings). Bowles read page after page of the department's policy paper, which was routine and not notably original. When he finished, Bobby said coldly, "This is worthless." Before the meeting ended, the President had created a special committee, headed by Assistant Secretary of Defense Paul Nitze (now Secretary of the Navy) to come up with something better about Cuba.

For weeks after the abortive Bay of Pigs invasion, Bobby's time was largely taken up with sifting through specific details of the disaster, as well as working out the first steps to reorganize the national-security setup. The President had appointed Army General Maxwell Taylor, whom he called back from retirement, and Chief of Naval Operations Arleigh Burke to make up the study force with Bobby. Taylor and Admiral Burke were years older than Bobby, with decades of military experience, but that did not intimidate the young Attorney General. He considered that he could work as their equal—and in the President's eyes he could.

The incomplete tactical groundwork that had preceded the attack was appalling, and as the study went on, Bobby at last concluded gravely, "Victory was never close." John Kennedy became even more skeptical of his professional advisers. Bobby said, "The President won't assume anything from now on. Simply because a man is supposed to be an expert in his field will not qualify him to the President."

Over the next few months, top people were juggled and jockeyed about. Chester Bowles was sent off to be Ambassador to India. Maxwell Taylor was made a special White House assistant and later became Chairman of the Joint Chiefs of Staff. As soon as CIA Chief Dulles's term expired, he was replaced by John McCone; White House Assistant McGeorge Bundy, formerly dean of the Faculty of Arts and Sciences at Harvard College, was made the contact point for national-security information required by the President. Several State Department task forces were created to put together new foreign-policy ideas for every major problem area in the world.

While the probe and reorganization went on, Bobby had worked inhuman hours. Each morning he arrived at an office in CIA headquarters and pored over Bay of Pigs reports. Late in the afternoon he headed for the White House and private conversations with the President. By sundown he was usually on his way to his Justice Department office where he labored far into the night over the business of being Attorney General. Byron White and his staff tried to lighten Bobby's load. But on many nights Justice Department officials lined up outside Kennedy's office like kids waiting for a double feature, each eager to snatch a moment or two of Bobby's time to get a decision or guiding comment on some critical policy problem.

Yet Bobby's role as foreign-policy adviser—and activist— had barely begun. A month after the Bay of Pigs, John Kennedy was in Paris and again trouble broke out in the Caribbean. This time it was in the Dominican Republic. Long-time dictator Rafael Leonidas Trujillo was machine-gunned to death by rebels. Brutal as Trujillo's government had been, it had at least offered a foundation for civil peace, but now the tiny country was rocked by the threat of a bloody uprising and eventual anarchy. It would be ripe for Communist takeover.

Bobby, with Vice President Johnson and Secretary of State Rusk, quickly set up a command post in a State Department office. From there they implemented a predesigned move to neutralize a rebellion. They gave approval to deploy a force of United States ships carrying battle-ready marines off the Dominican Republic. Their action had complete presidential backing. The show of force at sea did work to prevent any serious attempts at further insurrection, and there was no need to land marines as Lyndon Johnson did in a similar situation four years later.

It was the kind of power-policy participation that people had already come to expect from Bobby. As the months went by, the Attorney General became even more involved in foreign affairs.

In August, 1961, the President was informed that Communists had begun to build a wall between East and West Berlin. John Kennedy was curt and explicit: "Get Rusk on the phone. And go get my brother." As the Berlin crisis became hotter early that autumn, it was Bobby who had a critical private session with Mikhail Menshikov, Soviet Ambassador to the United States. It was Bobby who appeared on the television program *Meet the Press* and calmly defined the depth of the President's determination to keep West Berlin free. "If it comes to that," said the Attorney General, "he will use nuclear weapons." And it was Bobby who sat late one night at the White House and heard the President define his fears about nuclear war: "It really doesn't matter as far as you and I are concerned. What really matters are the children."

In the crisp days of October, 1962, the world came close to exploding in the havoc of nuclear destruction. It happened in a rocket-rattling showdown between the Soviet Union and the United States over a Russian buildup of missile bases in Cuba. It was to be the most horrifying crisis the Kennedy brothers would ever face together.

For weeks before the clash, there were warnings that the bases were being built. One of the loudest voices was New York's Kenneth Keating, who began to express concern about it as early as September 2. On October 10 Keating said flatly, "Construction has begun on at least a half dozen launching sites for intermediate-range tactical missiles." All along, even after the sites were discovered, the Kennedy Administration insisted that Keating's information, gleaned mostly from friendly Cuban refugees, had been erroneous because it was premature.

The President repeatedly said that the buildup was defensive only, that the Russians were putting in anti-aircraft missiles or short-range rockets and that there was really no danger to the continental United States. He told congressional leaders there would be no need for retaliation under these circumstances.

All along, United States reconnaissance planes were flying missions miles above Cuba, snapping roll after roll of photographs of the terrain. Through September, little showed up to cause concern. Then, for a few days in early October, the skies were too cloudy to get good shots of the ground. On October 14, the weather cleared at last; and, suddenly, the Russian plot was revealed: missile bases were nearing completion, and they were for medium-range ballistic missiles (MRBM's), not for defensive weapons. Once installed, the MRBM's would have a range of 1,200 miles, which would carry them easily to Dallas, Kansas City or Washington; each could carry a one-megaton warhead, 50 times the explosive power of the weapon that destroyed Hiroshima.

The aerial photographs offered chilling proof, and the President learned of them from McGeorge Bundy at breakfast on October 15. Before noon, the President summoned a group of men who would be together almost constantly in the next two weeks.

They would make up a special crisis squad that came to be known as the Executive Committee (ExComm) of the National Security Council. Included were Lyndon Johnson, Dean Rusk, Robert McNamara, Bundy, Treasury Secretary Douglas Dillon, Maxwell Taylor, CIA Director John McCone, Under Secretary of State George W. Ball, Deputy Defense Secretary Roswell L. Gilpatric, Ambassador-at-Large Llewellyn Thompson, White House Special Counsel Theodore Sorensen, Assistant Secretary of State for Latin American Affairs Edwin M. Martin, Chief of Naval Operations George Anderson, and, of course, Robert Kennedy. Other Administration aides would be in and out of this select group during the crisis.

The first Executive Committee decision was to pretend there

was nothing wrong. John Kennedy would keep his regular office appointments, and he would even leave Washington for previously scheduled politicking engagements to help Democratic candidates in the upcoming congressional elections. ExComm continued to meet frequently, its members sneaking in and out of White House back doors to avoid suspicion. Bobby Kennedy was at the Executive Mansion nearly as many hours each day as the President.

Soon, high-altitude photographs revealed new gouges in the Cuban earth. Startled experts spotted the beginnings of launching sites that could send intermediate-range missiles (IRBM's) winging toward the United States. The IRBM's were far more menacing than the MRBM's, for they had twice the range and could destroy any city in the continental United States. Many of the medium-range missiles were already implanted and aimed. The IRBM's were not yet in Cuba—but it could not be long. Even then, a small armada of Russian ships was plowing through the Atlantic, carrying a deadly cargo of IRBM's.

ExComm met after dinner on October 17 and discussed the alternatives of reaction. An invasion of Cuba was quickly dismissed. Some ExComm members advocated a surprise air strike that would smash the missile bases. Bobby Kennedy and others were flatly against that. Bobby labeled it "another Pearl Harbor in reverse," a sneak assault that would be damaging to the nation's morale as well as to its world stature. The idea was dropped. Yet something had to be done; Russia had gambled that the United States would not react.

"We all agreed in the end that if the Russians were ready to go to nuclear war over Cuba, they were ready to go to nuclear war—and that was that, so we might as well have the showdown then as six months later," Bobby recalled.

At last the decision was made: a naval blockade would be laid down in the waters off Cuba; United States warships would challenge the Russian freighters hauling the missiles, and if they refused to turn back, they would be sunk. On Monday, October 22, John Kennedy went on television to tell the American people for the first time of the peril and of the decision to blockade Cuba. Already, he had sent off an ultimatum to Soviet Premier Khrushchev. Days of agony and anxiety followed. Later in the week the destroyer *Joseph P. Kennedy Jr.*, challenged a freighter and sent men aboard to inspect her. Soon Russian freighters carrying missiles began to turn back, one by one, as they were challenged. Still, ExComm did not know whether Khrushchev would agree to President Kennedy's demand that he pull the missiles out of Cuba for good. For a time there was no word from the Kremlin; then on Friday, October 26, a secret letter from Khrushchev to the President rattled over teletype machines in the State Department.

The syntax was a bit muddled, but it seemed to offer a peaceful settlement, including withdrawal of the missiles and dismantling of the sites. Then, the next morning, another Khrushchev letter arrived. This one was belligerent and said the Cuban weapons would be removed only on condition that the United States take its missile bases out of Turkey. No one on ExComm was really certain what Khrushchev was up to.

It was Bobby Kennedy who suggested that the President simply reject the second letter so curtly that, in effect, it would cease to exist. Then the President could answer the missive offering a peaceful settlement, blandly assuming that was what the premier really wanted. It was done. On Sunday, October 28, Khrushchev made his surrender total, and Russian technicians began to dismantle the sites. A potential nuclear showdown had been averted.

Through their crises together, Jack's faith in Bobby was confirmed without reservation, and the Attorney General was handed all manner of strange chores in the field of foreign relations. When Aleksei Adzhubi, son-in-law of Nikita Khrushchev and editor of Izvestia, visited Washington, Bobby and Ethel entertained him at Hickory Hill. When Fidel Castro demanded enormous amounts of money, tractors and drugs as ransom payment for Cuban exiles held hostage after the Bay of Pigs invasion, Bobby was the man behind the collection crew for the President. When the Ivory Coast Republic celebrated its first anniversary in 1961, John Kennedy sent Bobby and Ethel over to represent the United States; the pair struggled through conversations in painful French, but they made a hit with President Felix Houphouet-Boigny. When President Kennedy became discouraged over the continuing balance-of-payments mess besieging the nearly bankrupt economy of

Brazil, he sent his brother to Rio de Janeiro to discuss the whole thing with later deposed President Joao "Jango" Goulart.

Jack was smitten with the idea that Bobby was an effective personal emissary, a kind of special Kennedy diplomat—without portfolio but with plenty of that old moxie for getting along with all sorts of foreign dignitaries. (The idea of Bobby the Diplomat must have come as quite an appalling surprise to the legions of ward heelers and lazy political hacks who had felt the bite of Bobby's tongue-lashings during his campaign managing days.)

The President sent Bobby and Ethel off on a four-week world tour in February, 1962; it was billed as "informal," but wherever Bobby went, so too went the power and influence of the presidency. Indeed, when news of the trip first leaked out, the Kremlin quietly suggested that Bobby should stop off in Moscow and possibly have an informal visit with Nikita Khrushchev or other Soviet leaders. The Kennedys turned down the invitation, pleading that Bobby's schedule was too full.

The first major stop was Japan—and there was plenty of excitement. A minor earthquake rattled Tokyo one day Bobby and Ethel were there. When they visited Waseda University, jeering leftist students heckled Bobby so much that he could not be heard. At once, he challenged one of the noisiest of the lot to a debate, but the electric power failed when Bobby tried to make his rebuttal and the microphone went dead. At a later meeting with a Socialist group, Bobby listened calmly as one spokesman accused the United States of being a land of "monopoly capital." Then Kennedy replied: "You have a complete misconception of what kind of government and people we are. This [the United States] is a different country—not what Marx was talking about one hundred years ago."

Bobby made it clear that he was speaking with the sanction of the White House. "My brother, who is the President, wishes me to convey to you his very best regards," he said repeatedly—in Japanese. But he was not all formality and finesse. There was the predictable Bobby tartness, too. At one point he addressed the Japanese Bar Association and lavishly praised Japan's quick recovery from the shambles of war. One of the lawyers thanked him for such "flattery," but Bobby didn't like that word and retorted,

"This is a helluva long way to come just to flatter somebody. I can do that back home." He wanted everyone to know that he meant what he said.

Bobby sang, *When Irish Eyes Are Smiling*, in a back-alley sake house, and in a speech before foreign correspondents in Tokyo, he said wryly, "I had seaweed for breakfast yesterday. To tell you the honest-to-goodness truth it didn't taste bad. When I went to Central Asia with Justice Douglas in 1955, they brought in a goat, very dead, plucked out its eyes and served them to us. Justice Douglas turned to me and said, 'For the sake of America, Bob, make like it's an oyster!' So things have gone up since then."

At a Buddhist temple, priests offered Bobby incense sticks to burn, a traditional practice for visitors. Worried that it might somehow contradict Roman Catholic practice, Bobby asked United States Ambassador Edwin O. Reischauer, "What are the implications if I do this?" Reischauer said, "It just shows respect." "You're sure it won't look as if I'm worshiping Buddha?" he asked. "No, its okay," said the ambassador. Kennedy went ahead with the ceremony, but he was muttering, "If I get kicked out. . . ."

Ethel charmed the Japanese with her ingenuous ways. During one formal speech, she glanced up from her prepared text and laughed helplessly, "Gosh, this sounds like a terrible graduation address." She told officials' wives and secretaries at the U.S. embassy, "I'm so happy to see that you're all living out the President's inauguration speech and deepening American-Japanese relations. You've really gotten your lights out from under the barrel." Ethel tried gamely to speak what little Japanese she had memorized, but sometimes it came out twisted. Once when she was presented with a fan and a scarf she beamed a gracious smile and said in Japanese, "Don't mention it," instead of "Thank you."

In Indonesia, the Kennedys met with more student hostility; someone threw a cold fried egg at Bobby while he was speaking. He still produced a sterling speech about the practicalities of international friendship. "We are going to disagree with Indonesia and you are going to disagree with us," he said. "We should have a foundation, a friendship, so that every time an incident comes up and we do not do exactly what you want, you don't say, 'To hell with the United States.' . . . I'm not asking you to agree with me, but I do ask that there be some understanding of us as we attempt to understand your position. This is not a one-way street, ladies and gentlemen."

Bobby and Ethel continued on to Europe. In Rome, they had an audience with the late Pope John XXIII. In Paris Bobby spent 40 minutes in private conversation with imperious Charles de Gaulle. In the Netherlands he visited with doughty Queen Juliana. In West Berlin he made a speech in which he called the Wall "a snake across the heart of your city." And in Bonn he met with Chancellor Konrad Adenauer.

When Bobby and Ethel got home, there were grumblings, of course. New York's liberal Republican Congressman John V. Lindsay wondered sarcastically "whether this kind of Madison Avenue approach is the stuff of which foreign policy is made." Indeed it wasn't. Yet Bobby's venture into affairs abroad was generally judged a success—which came as an unexpected dividend for even the most fanatic Kennedy-ophiles. After all, who would expect such a performance from a young man who had spent most of his professional life nagging politicians and interrogating witnesses for a Senate committee?

The presence of Bobby added a dimension to the New Frontier that made it unique in the history of presidential administrations. Never before had the nation had an opportunity to watch brotherhood—that most fragile and subtle of human relationships —bloom so publicly before its eyes. If no signs of affection were shown in public, the loyalty between Bobby and Jack could scarcely be missed.

Sometimes it was as simple as a social obligation. Bobby detested the dull formalities of small talk and official parties, but he attended dozens during the years Jack was President—and in many cases he went only because the President could not go. Bobby was a suitable stand-in, clearly the closest thing to having the Chief Executive himself. And if he was sometimes frosty and aloof and often stayed no longer than he absolutely had to stay, at least Bobby did go.

Then there was the lamentably ludicrous occasion of the 50-mile hikes. In February, 1963, harking back to a 1908 order of Teddy Roosevelt's, President Kennedy wondered just how many

American marines could still march 50 miles in 20 hours. Plenty of people besides marines—grandmothers, little boys, college girls, newspaper feature writers—set out to test themselves against that standard.

So did Bobby. Whether he did it more for Jack, or more to satisfy that ever-turbulent competitive spirit of his is hardly debatable; he probably would have tried even if the President's name had been Nixon. He rolled out of bed long before dawn, roused four Justice Department aides to accompany him and set out through the slush and mud along the Chesapeake and Ohio Canal. Bobby was bound for Harper's Ferry, 50 miles away. One by one his companions fell by the wayside—the last one at the 35-mile mark. Bobby trudged the whole distance and made it in 17 hours and 50 minutes. (The best time registered during the national marathon was 11 hours and 44 minutes by a marine in North Carolina.) Next morning, Bobby arose in time for 9 o'clock Mass, then went ice skating with his children.

During John Kennedy's White House days, the brothers learned enormous amounts about each other, but Bobby probably gained far more than Jack from the closeness. As their father said, "Jack used to persuade people to do what he wanted. Bobby orders them to do it." And their sister, Jean Smith, said, "Jack had traveled a great deal in the realms of doubt, whereas Bobby has never explored those regions yet." From Jack, Bobby began to learn the advantages of smoothing off one's rough edges.

Family tragedies brought them closer together too. When Joseph Kennedy had his stroke, it was Bobby who called Jack about it. The two spent hours talking quietly together while Joe Kennedy seemed to hover between life and death.

On August 7, 1963, Jackie Kennedy prematurely delivered Jack's second son, Patrick Bouvier Kennedy, at the hospital at Otis Air Force Base on Cape Cod. The President was summoned. Doctors almost immediately perceived danger signals for the tiny boy, and had him rushed to Boston Children's Hospital Medical Center, where he was placed in a special hyperbaric oxygen chamber. The baby was suffering from a serious lung ailment. The President followed and spent much of the next day there—sitting on a straight-backed chair in a room outside the chamber where the baby fought for life, and peeping occasionally through a small window. Bobby joined his brother that night and when the infant died at 4:04 a.m. on August 9, the brothers left the hospital together—linked tighter than ever through another Kennedy loss.

Despite the baby's death, 1963 had become one of the most dynamic and productive years for the Kennedy Administration. The civil-rights rebellion had at last been recognized for what it was; the battle was at least met—if far from won. A nationwide railroad strike had threatened that summer, but had been headed off at the last minute by congressional legislation requested by the President. In August, the historic nuclear test ban treaty had been signed by more than 100 nations, abolishing weapons tests in the atmosphere.

Men in the Administration were functioning together better than ever. The Kennedy spirit of vigor and good taste had captivated millions.

By November, the Kennedys were already well on their way toward refurbishing the machinery to drive the presidential campaign of 1964—the election that would put John Kennedy back into the White House for another four years. Bobby had said long ago that he did not plan to be the campaign manager again. But no matter what his title, there was little doubt that he would fill the same shoes again. He had held innumerable discussions already with top Democrats, warning them to keep their machines well oiled, their workers primed for the contest to come.

Few people had any real doubts that John Kennedy would win again, but there were political fences to mend. Already in November, the President had been in New York and Florida to see key Democrats and to be seen by crowds in preparation for the 1964 campaign. On November 21, he was to go to Texas, where Democrats were in the midst of a nasty intra-party squabble.

The night before the President left, politics seemed far away. It was a festive, special occasion—the annual White House reception for Justices of the Supreme Court. Seven hundred guests attended and there were bonuses to make it an even bigger night than they expected. For one thing, it was Jackie Kennedy's first appearance as official hostess since the death of her baby almost four months earlier. More than that, it was Bobby Kennedy's 38th birthday. The President was beaming; Jackie was her radiant self again; Bobby grinned and seemed to enjoy it all. It was Camelot-come-to-Washington as only the Kennedys could create it.

The brothers parted with no more than the usual "good night."

In Texas the receptions for a frankly politicking President were beyond all expectations. Large crowds turned out everywhere. The ovations were lusty and natural, and John Kennedy's magic was as strong as ever. The future seemed filled with good—another term in the White House, a New Frontier with the Kennedys stretching on comfortably through 1968, plenty of time for the brothers to accomplish their promises and bring their hopes to reality.

Then, on the morning of November 22, a man named Lee Harvey Oswald carried a rifle wrapped in brown paper to the sixth floor of the Texas School Book Depository building in Dallas. When John Kennedy rode by in his presidential limousine at 12:30 p.m., Oswald shot him dead.

VII
GRIEF AND INDECISION

□□
□□

ROBERT KENNEDY, LIKE MILLIONS OF OTHER AMERICANS, was at lunch when it happened. He was near his swimming pool at Hickory Hill, eating with Ethel and two friends, Robert Morgenthau, U.S. Attorney for Southern New York, and his assistant in charge of the Criminal Division, Silvio J. Mollo. The Indian-summer weather was so pleasant that Bobby had taken a swim before lunch, and he felt good as he talked about one of his favorite subjects—the problem of organized crime.

The meal was not completed when a man, working on the house, walked by, a transistor radio next to his ear, and muttered something about the President being shot. Ethel and Morgenthau heard the man; Bobby did not. Before either could say anything, a maid rushed out of the house to the table and told Kennedy that J. Edgar Hoover was on the White House phone. Bobby went to the phone near the pool. Suddenly, he threw his hand to his face as if to stifle a cry. Ethel rushed and put her arms about him. His head down, his face full of shock, Bobby walked to the table where his guests sat dumfounded.

"The President was shot in Texas," he said. "It may be fatal."

"Oh, my God!" exclaimed Morgenthau. He and Mollo were too stunned to even rise from their chairs. Bobby walked slowly into the house with Ethel. The guests remained behind, not wanting to

137

intrude on his shock and sudden sorrow. In a little while they went in and sat in front of a television set. The announcer gave the impression the President might live. Morgenthau and Mollo leaned forward hopefully, and from behind them came a voice. "He's dead," said Bobby, who had just entered the doorway.

He had been in a series of phone calls. First Lyndon Johnson phoned him from Air Force One, the jet which would bear the dead President's body home. He wanted to take the oath of office in Texas. Bobby checked into it, phoned Johnson back and instructed him to take it immediately aboard the plane. Bobby's anguish and feelings of antipathy toward Johnson were subdued for a moment.

He said little. He paced back and forth, and then, calling his Newfoundland, huge, black Brumus, to his side, walked out onto the rolling lawn, while others stood helplessly watching. His head was bowed. His hands were in his pockets. He walked for nearly an hour, only the dog at his side.

It was Bobby Kennedy's Gethsemane. During his agony, Ethel came out, talked with him as best she could and gave him a pair of sunglasses which he wore, though the skies were gray. He looked at her and said, "He lived such a wonderful life." Soon, Bobby's close friends began to arrive. John McCone, director of the CIA, who lived only one mile away, came to offer his help; he had served as father confessor to Bobby for several years. His old friend and football teammate, Dean Markham, came. So did Justice Byron White, who put his arm around Bobby. Mrs. White kissed him. Sue Markham drove off with her husband to pick up the Kennedy children from school before they heard the news.

One by one the friends came to Hickory Hill and approached the solitary, stooped figure. Bobby braved a cheerful spirit. "There are no long faces here." he said, pursing his mouth, but incapable of masking his sorrow. Then Bobby's eldest children, Joe, Kathleen and Bobby came and hung onto their father's sides as he continued his restless walk. The estate was now ringed with Fairfax County Police.

Torn and numb as he was, Bobby had to perform as head of the family. He talked on the phone with his mother, who urged him to strength. He talked with those who would make funeral arrangements. He talked with his friend, Defense Secretary Robert S. McNamara, who informed him of the arrival time of Air Force One. As the afternoon wore on, his forced bravery disintegrated. He went to his bedroom and there broke down and sobbed while a friend sat quietly by. He changed from his wrinkled light suit to one which was black and heavy. Then he went to the Pentagon, where he boarded a helicopter for the 15-mile trip to Andrews Air Force Base. "Cheer up, cheer up," he told his friends.

At dusk Bobby stood at Andrews Air Force Base as the casket was lowered from the door of the plane. The blaze of flood-lights blanched the horror-stricken face of Jackie Kennedy as she stepped out. Bobby held her hand firmly and led her to the hearse for the trip to Bethesda Hospital. The Kennedys and close friends stayed up all night, Bobby at Jackie's side. He tried to buck up everybody with heavy humor, but it didn't work. At 4:30 a.m. the President's body was placed in the East Room of the White House, now bathed in flare lights. Inside, the mourners stood in prayer. Jackie still wore the blood-stained pink suit.

The next three days is now a montage of endless lines of mourners; of never-forgotten glimpses of Robert Kennedy's grieving face; of Jackie's brave march behind her husband's coffin, her eyes straight ahead but swollen in sorrow; the strange, brilliant sun and vivid splashes of uniformed color; the glitter and sound of band instruments; the somber faces of world dignitaries; the unmistakable Boston accent and intonations of Cardinal Cushing; the magnificent burial scene, with its sweep of people and landscape.

At all times and everywhere, Bobby was at Jackie's side. There was a communion of sorrow. He was with her when she made an unexpected visit to the bier Sunday night at the Capitol; when the President was buried at Arlington; when she returned to the grave just before midnight Monday.

And so a third child of Joseph and Rose Kennedy was now buried. No man in the world was lonelier than Robert Kennedy. On Wednesday, November 27, as President Johnson told the nation, "Let us continue, ..." Bobby sat dazed and sad. The next day, Thanksgiving, which always meant a lively family reunion and house-closing at Hyannis Port, was spent by Bobby and Ethel and their children at Hickory Hill.

The Irish have a saying which advises "laugh with the devil," and perhaps it was this spirit which brought forty or so people to Hickory Hill for Thanksgiving. Bobby appeared in sweater and slacks. There were drinks and chatter among the guests. But Bobby seemed isolated from his own crowd. His eyes bore a haunted look.

His guests were trying to make the occasion as pleasant as possible. One by one they gingerly said hello to him. Then an old friend, columnist Mary McGrory, burst forth, put her arms around Bobby and held him. It was a tense, sad Thanksgiving. Bobby tried to make talk. He asked Walter Sheridan for details of the flare-up between Jimmy Hoffa and his chief lieutenant, Harold Gibbons, who had angered Hoffa by lowering the flag at Teamsters' headquarters and sending the staff home on the day of assassination. In the conversation, Sheridan looked Bobby in the eye and asked, "When are you coming back?" Kennedy replied: "I don't know. I don't have the heart now."

There was immediate speculation about his future. One story declared he would resign as soon as Johnson would release him. Another said he was pondering the vice-presidency, or how he might get it. A Gallup poll, taken in December, showed him the Fifth Most Admired Man in the World—between Albert Schweitzer and Billy Graham. The Kennedy mantle was now fully draped around his shoulders. The Democratic Party was largely a Kennedy Party. Though his brother was scarcely buried, some columnists were discussing the problem the new President and Bobby would have in getting along with each other. Political writers recalled that Bobby was not eager for Johnson to be Jack's running mate in 1960, and that the relationship between Johnson and Bobby had always been cool. Another quick assessment of Bobby's position came from Jimmy Hoffa, who, only three days after the assassination, paid tribute to the dead President, and quickly added that Bobby was now "just another lawyer."

Bobby was still quite a bit more than that. As Attorney General, he faced the priorities of Hoffa, the civil-rights struggle, youth projects and the 1964 election campaign. These challenges were not enough, however, to pull Bobby out of his shock. While newspapermen and politicians speculated about his future, and his closest friends wondered and worried, Bobby wandered erratically in and out of his office at the Justice Department, his expression glazed, his eyes puffed. Some days he took off three hours to have lunch with his family. He had always been a walker, but now he took many walks—around the courtyard at the Justice Department, across the street from the Smithsonian Institution, down Constitution Avenue. Sometimes Brumus was along, but always Bobby's head was down and his hands were in his pockets. Sometimes a federal marshal trailed him.

He was now leader of the Kennedys and devoted more time to all of them. He phoned his father regularly, giving him reports on the family, though the conversation was one-sided because Joseph Kennedy couldn't speak intelligibly. Bobby sent friends to pick up Jackie whenever she wanted to go somewhere. He played father to John Kennedy and Caroline. He stood at graveside again when the President's two deceased infant children were re-interred at Arlington. He and Teddy were on the phone daily, and often had dinner together. Teddy was able to snap back sooner and tried to buck up Bobby. Ethel, watching him stare out windows lost in thought, kept after him to go off on skiing or swimming vacations, no matter how brief. After Thanksgiving, Bobby did go to the Douglas Dillon winter home at Hobe Sound, Florida, but even the sun did not revive him. He smiled some when he greeted 700 underprivileged youngsters from the District of Columbia for whom he gave a Christmas party at the Justice Department. But Bobby felt removed from everything.

One afternoon in early January he sent word around the Justice Department for his top aides to come to his office after six o'clock. He was solemn and grateful as he spoke to them about the past year. He gave each man a pair of Department of Justice cuff links, and then he told them of his brother's feeling of debt to the department. "It sounded like the end," a department official said. "It was a going-away speech . . . as though he was ready to leave." Another aide recalls, "I thought Bobby was going to quit, then and there."

Once the second most powerful man in the nation, Robert F. Kennedy was adrift and aimless. With Teddy and Steve Smith he skied at Aspen, which relaxed him a bit. Gradually, the grief began to lighten. Then, on January 13, at a meeting of the National Security Council, Bobby suddenly smiled. President Johnson, in the voice of a man issuing an important assignment, said, "General . . ." and Kennedy looked at him as if to say, "Who, me?" He thought Johnson meant General Curtis LeMay. But Attorney General Kennedy soon had an assignment: to meet with Indonesia's President Sukarno in Tokyo to persuade him to reduce hostilities toward the neighboring Federation of Malaysia. Kennedy had dealt with Sukarno before. The trip would also show the nation Johnson's concern for Bobby, thereby enticing Kennedy Democrats to Johnson's enveloping embrace. The trip also might snap Bobby out of his despair.

Another reason for dispatching Bobby to the Far East was the new Administration's compelling desire to find out how active Bobby had been in stirring up the Bobby Baker investigation. Some of President Johnson's advisers believed Bobby had finagled several months before to expose Baker and thus embarrass Johnson.

Sukarno is one of those roguish rulers who have prospered in the international political competition of the postwar period. In 1962, with the Soviets backing him, he threatened war if the Dutch would not relinquish West New Guinea. When the Dutch, our NATO ally, looked to us, we shrugged our shoulders in mock neutrality. Sukarno's continued threats brought the United Nations into the situation, and after more of his bullying tactics and many negotiations, the Dutch transferred West New Guinea to a temporary U.N. authority with the proviso that the territory would be turned over to Indonesia in May, 1963. Thus Sukarno, by bluffing U.N. Secretary General U Thant and the Kennedy Administration, had won on the West New Guinea question. Bobby had played an indefinite role in this drama. He had been dispatched by his brother in February of 1962 to Jakarta, the capital of Indonesia, to confer with Sukarno. The American embassy in Jakarta had just been bombed by rioting Indonesians, and there was considerable anti-American feeling. Bobby reassured Sukarno that Indonesia would continue to get U.S. aid, and interestingly enough, the day after

Bobby left Jakarta, an agreement was signed providing for the shipment of $92.7 million in food to Indonesia by the United States under the Food for Peace Program. Indonesia would have to pay only $14 million for the shipment.

Now, in 1964, Sukarno was again threatening war. He wanted to control the newly formed Federation of Malaysia, which he charged was dominated by the British. With the Dutch scalp at his belt, Sukarno could talk tough. On the eve of Bobby's arrival in Tokyo, Sukarno's foreign minister warned that Indonesia might turn elsewhere for financial aid.

The problem was made even more complicated by the fact that the Republic of the Philippines feared the growing strength of leftist elements in the Federation of Malaysia, and did not want a Communist neighbor. In order to assert its interest in the matter, the Philippines resurrected an old legal claim it had made on North Borneo which had been assimilated in the federation. So there were three nations—Indonesia, the Federation of Malaysia, and the Philippines—involved in the dispute. Since the raiders who had crossed the border of Malaysia were Indonesians, and since Sukarno was making most of the noise, it was clear he was the key figure in the crisis. Bobby and Sukarno had gotten along well two years before, and the Johnson Administration hoped Bobby's way of laying it on the line would persuade Sukarno to call off the "volunteer" raiders and negotiate a settlement. Kennedy's public statement, of course, was that the Malaysian crisis "must be decided, resolved and determined by Asian countries, not outsiders."

Bobby had a problem to work on, and he had heartwarming receptions to enjoy. Japanese newsmen saw some humor in their country's being used as a "house of assignation" for Sukarno and Kennedy, but the crowds were really excited to see Bobby. He was the living memory of the late President, and he could be seen, heard and touched. When his plane landed, a banner was waved reading: "We're With You, Bobby!" Bobby smiled and in awkward Japanese said: "Glad to be with you again." He delivered a letter to Prime Minister Hayato Ikeda from Jackie thanking him for attending the funeral. He thanked the Japanese people for their sympathy "in November."

At Waseda University a frenzied crowd of 10,000 gave him

a thunderous reception. He talked of his brother's hopes and ideals, and tears came to Ethel's eyes as Bobby spoke: "He was not only President of one nation. He was president of young people around the world. If President Kennedy's life and death are to mean anything, we young people must work harder for a better life for all the people of the world."

The roaring response of the crowd brought Kennedy's shy smile to full bloom. A friend, Professor Gunji Hosono, remarked, "Two years ago Kennedy looked boyish and full of go. Today he looks older, far more mature and full of signs of deepening wisdom."

He needed these qualities in his talks with Sukarno. Kennedy's entry at the Imperial Hotel the next day caused a jam of 200 newsmen, a squash equalled only when Joe DiMaggio checked in with his bride, Marilyn Monroe, in 1954. Sukarno sat in a heavily draped suite. He was resplendent with his black moslem cap and chest full of military ribbons. He and Bobby talked for 90 minutes, but nothing was settled.

A second meeting was held next day at breakfast, where Bobby and Ethel graciously ate bean-paste soup, dried seaweed, pickled Chinese cabbage and green tea. Sukarno, like most Asians, ate seaweed. Ethel excused herself to visit an orphanage. The second meeting was cordial, but nothing was accomplished.

In the press conference which followed, Kennedy was asked if he would accept the vice-presidential nomination. He smiled and replied, "The question reminds me of my brother. When he was posed with such a question, he used to say that is like asking a girl if she would marry that man if he proposed."

The third meeting between Sukarno and Kennedy was set for five days later, so Bobby used the intervening time to visit other countries. He went to the Philippines, whose position in regard to Malaysia was clear, and whose friendship for the United States was genuine. In Manila, Bobby met with President Diosdado Macapagal and explained that he was trying to organize a meeting with the leaders of the three nations involved in the Malaysian dispute. But the purpose of Kennedy's visit was soon lost in a swell of adulation. Thousands of cheering, jumping girl students engulfed him and Ambassador William E. Stevenson exclaimed, "Why, this is better than bringing Elvis Presley here." Kennedy planted a tree in memory of his brother, and received an honorary degree at the University of the Philippines from its President, Carlos Romulo.

Malaysia was Kennedy's next stop. He had barely arrived when he learned that Prince Norodom Sihanouk, the chief of state of Cambodia, had showed up and wanted to get in on Bobby's forthcoming meeting with the Malaysian Prime Minister Tunku Abdul Rahman. But Kennedy said he did not want Sihanouk in the meeting because he was not a party to the negotiations. Sihanouk was insulted, claimed Bobby had snubbed him and described Kennedy's statement on the impasse as "a model of insolence and hostility presented under a veneer of politeness."

Kennedy and Sukarno then met in Jakarta, and Sukarno agreed to a cease-fire and to meet with the other leaders—President Macapagal of the Philippines and Prime Minister Tunku Abdul Rahman—in an effort to settle the border dispute. The leaders would meet one week later for a final agreement. The government of Thailand invited the leaders to hold that meeting in their capital, Bangkok, which would be a neutral site for negotiations. There was a probationary atmosphere about the whole business, especially with respect to Sukarno's ultimate intentions, but Bobby felt he had done all that was possible. However, the arrangements didn't hold long. Kennedy's plane was still en route to London when Sukarno exhorted a crowd of 15,000 to "go onward, never retreat . . . crush Malaysia!"

Bobby got the news of Sukarno's treacherous outburst when he arrived in London. The British were skeptical and critical of the "settlement," but Bobby was tentatively optimistic. He thought Sukarno might just be making loud noises again and hoped he would comply with the cease-fire arrangements and confine his hostility to the bargaining table.

Back in Washington, President Johnson gave Kennedy a hearty handshake and a brief commendation for carrying out "his assignment constructively and with real achievement . . ." Bobby perked up, even though the trip had had no dramatic success. A few days after Johnson's handshake and commendation, Indonesian guerrillas were shooting away in the Malaysian jungles. On learning of the revival of the feud, Kennedy sardonically observed, "So nothing has been lost but two weeks of shooting and killing."

The trip had distracted Bobby from his grief. He was beginning to form a new memory of his brother, that of a President beloved around much of the world and looked to as an ideal by the young. He would refer to him in those terms many times in the following months.

Bobby's step was now more sure around the Justice Department. It slowly came to him that he had work to do as Attorney General. His old problem—often referred to as Bobby's obsession—in snaring Jimmy Hoffa was being resolved. Walter Sheridan, who had pursued Hoffa with Bobby for seven years, called him daily with reports of how the quarry was being cornered in court in Chattanooga, Tennessee. Each call gave Bobby a lift. Finally, Sheridan called with news of Hoffa's conviction. "We made it!" he exclaimed. For Bobby, this could have been the occasion to holler "whoopee!" But he just smiled broadly, and said, "Nice work, Walter."

Concurrent with the conviction of Hoffa was the gathering momentum of the civil-rights movement. Kennedy kept close to the drafting of the Civil Rights Bill of 1964. The nation was boiling with talk of a "long hot summer," the "white backlash," and never-ending demonstrations. With extremists at both ends making considerable noise and many threats, Bobby found it necessary alternately to criticize those demonstrations which were pointless, spiteful and violent, and to remind the American public that the rights Negroes had been denied must be ensured immediately.

With Hoffa apparently trapped, and passage of the Civil Rights Bill a certainty, Bobby thought more and more about a job other than that of Attorney General. He didn't know precisely what his future would be. In May, he told James Reston of *The New York Times*, "I'm tired of chasing people. I want to go on now to something else."

The Kennedy family, most of all Jackie, took much of his time. She is far from being a hard-bitten public figure. She seems fleeting and soft, an elegant lady in need of protection. Even before the assassination, Jackie's relationship with the Kennedy family had become close. The murder of her husband made it even more so. It was natural that she turned more and more to the man who had been confidant to her husband and was now the head of the

Kennedy family. Bobby was her protector. Whenever she phoned him at the Justice Department all other calls were sidetracked. He and Ethel looked after her children, made them sister and brother to their own. He tousled John Junior's hair, and roughhoused with him. Caroline became big sister to Bobby's smaller children and dedicated her crayon efforts to "Uncle Bobby."

If Jackie needed advice or something done, she called Bobby. When she moved into her new home in Georgetown, Bobby helped her. When she wanted to vacation at Antigua in the West Indies, Bobby went too, along with Princess Stanislas Radziwill and her husband. Bobby tried to interest her in tennis and skiing, and whenever Jackie said she might like to play tennis, he immediately dispatched a tennis-playing friend to pick her up and take her to the courts at Hickory Hill.

The closeness of the two caused gossip, ignored by Bobby and Jackie. It was hard for gossipers to understand how the tragedy, in a special human way, had fused the two who felt the President's loss the most deeply.

Bobby was called on more and more to help define the image of John Kennedy. A reporter once asked him what he missed most about his brother. Bobby's eyes showed the hurt, but he stared at the reporter and answered, "Just that he's not here." When he was in his deepest anguish, Bobby wrote an introduction to the Memorial Edition of *Profiles In Courage*. Part of it amounted to a credo for Kennedys:

"If there is a lesson from his life and from his death, it is that in this world of ours none of us can afford to be lookers-on, the critics standing on the sidelines."

The image of the late President blazed. The name of John Fitzgerald Kennedy was alive, and Jackie and Bobby were its principal instruments. On May 29, the President's 47th birthday anniversary, the family attended a Requiem Mass at St. Matthew's, Washington's Roman Catholic cathedral, then visited the grave. Later that day, in Hyannis Port, Jackie and Bobby joined in a transatlantic memorial telecast. Bobby, in subdued voice, repeated the words of his brother's inaugural message:

"Now the trumpet summons us again—not as a call to bear arms, though arms we need—not as a call to battle, though embattled we are—but a call to bear the burden of a long twilight struggle, year in and year out, rejoicing in hope, patient in tribulation—a struggle against the common enemies of man: tyranny, poverty, disease and war itself."

Everywhere the name was used to title and retitle. Idlewild International Airport became John F. Kennedy International Airport. Despite local protest, Cape Canaveral now bore the late President's name. A 14,000-foot mountain in the Canadian Yukon was renamed Mount Kennedy. Thousands of playgrounds, schools and streets were now "Kennedy." A Chicago expressway took the name. Books, collections of photographs, record albums—some hastily and tawdrily put together—were hot sellers. The Kennedy half dollar sold for 88 cents in Broadway shops. Tasteless knickknacks and mementos were hawked.

Meanwhile there was no harmonious flow of forces at work to get Bobby the vice-presidential nomination. Lyndon Johnson would pick his vice president and he wouldn't leave the decision for any convention to make. Johnson, in the spring of 1964, was trying to create his own presidency, to put his Texas brand on the office. He knew he couldn't be a "co-President" with the Kennedy image and memory. Less than one month after the assassination, Johnson remarked to Ken O'Donnell, "I'll never have a Kennedy on the ticket."

Yet, as the months moved on, the idealized remembrance of John Kennedy strengthened, and took a stronger emotional hold on Democrats. The living projection of that image and memory was Bobby. Therefore, Lyndon Johnson, at this point, could not be publicly disdainful of Bobby.

He and Kennedy frankly did not like one another. Each man's favorite columnist carried on the dislike in print, William White for the President, Charley Bartlett for Kennedy. Each man had friends and allies who would indulge in Washington's pastime of gossip. It became increasingly clear the only situation wherein Johnson would select Bobby as his running mate would be one of political expediency.

Richard Nixon volunteered an assessment of Bobby's chances. In April, he said Humphrey was the obvious choice, unless the polls suddenly showed Johnson facing a genuine fight for re-election. Nixon's logic held that a strong G.O.P. ticket meant the vice-presidential nomination would go to Humphrey. If the Republicans nominated a moderate—and this was becoming a long shot—then Kennedy might make the ticket to hold the northern vote. "If Goldwater is nominated," a Kennedy Democrat predicted, "Bobby doesn't have the chance of a snowball in hell."

No man "runs" for the vice-presidential nomination, particularly when the President is as stubborn as Lyndon Johnson. Though he wanted it, Bobby Kennedy could make no overt moves. He could only view efforts in his behalf with satisfaction.

The first of any consequence was started in snowy Buffalo, the arctic of New York State, where Democratic Boss Peter J. Crotty announced on January 26 that his organization was for Bobby for vice president. Crotty's Erie County Democrats had been the first in the nation to declare themselves for JFK in 1960; and in subsequent elections, they showed New York Democrats how to make gains on the G.O.P.

Then came the New Hampshire primary and the tale of Paul Corbin. Through much of February, it appeared that a write-in campaign for Bobby in New Hampshire would net him more votes for the vice-presidency than Johnson would get for President. The campaign for Bobby was started by his fans in New Hampshire. Then an intrepid admirer of Bobby's named Paul Corbin, from Wisconsin, injected himself into the primary and talked expansively of what he was doing to get him nominated. The rub was that Paul Corbin was an employee of the Democratic National Committee and should not have been taking part in such primaries. The fact Corbin was involved in the New Hampshire situation annoyed President Johnson considerably.

Corbin had long boasted that he planned to spend many years in Washington—eight with President John Kennedy and eight with his successor, Bobby. Corbin was accepted by Bobby more for his loyalty than for his influence in the Democratic Party. His credentials as a spokesman for Bobby were inadequate, his efforts in the New Hampshire primary were inappropriate, and Johnson phoned Bobby to tell him Corbin would have to be fired from the National Committee. Bobby, who appreciates loyalty of the kind Corbin had given him, had saved Corbin's job on one other occasion; but now he had no choice but to agree that Corbin must be dumped.

Even though Corbin was out of the way, there was still a residual problem in New Hampshire in that the effort for Kennedy was gaining support. Bobby had phoned the White House once to find out if President Johnson wanted him to issue a statement discouraging the New Hampshire write-in project. He was instructed to do nothing. But as the weeks went by, the write-in campaign built, and Bobby felt obligated to phone the White House again. This time it was suggested that he say something. Through his Press Secretary, Ed Guthman, Bobby released a statement five days before the primary balloting:

> The Attorney General has said that the choice of the Democratic nominee for vice president will be made and should be made by the Democratic Convention in August, guided by the wishes of President Johnson and that President Johnson should be free to select his own running mate. The Attorney General, therefore, wishes to discourage any efforts on his behalf in New Hampshire or elsewhere.

There was no direct contact between Johnson and Kennedy on this ticklish matter, but each man acted as if he knew he would be living with the other for a long time, like him or not. The Kennedy statement, tardy as it was, amounted to a damper. The word had already been sent to New Hampshire to get out the vote for Johnson. The response to this plea and Bobby's statement were enough to save the President's face. Johnson got 29,635 votes and Bobby 25,861 in New Hampshire. Everybody was relieved.

A few days later, Johnson said nice and loud on television that no Democrat should be seeking the vice-presidency at this time. *Yes, yes* and *amen* were immediately heard from Hubert Humphrey, who declared he agreed with "what everyone knows to be the truth—that the President will take the major part in making this decision."

Suddenly the departed Corbin turned up in his home state, Wisconsin, where another write-in movement for Bobby blossomed. This one, hatched in the back seat of a Greyhound bus by two Milwaukee businessmen, had an unwieldy name: "Draft Robert F.

Kennedy for Vice President of the United States Grass Roots, Ground Swell Committee."

Kennedy is too smart to have encouraged any such flimsy nonsense as this. Yet with Corbin in Wisconsin and the papers full of "feud" talk, the newest committee caught attention. There was a second sigh of relief heard in Washington a week later when one of the bus-riding sponsors resigned and entered a hospital to have his migraines treated. The "Draft Robert F. Kennedy . . . etc. . . . Committee" withered.

Nevertheless, strong feeling for Bobby continued to grow. Wherever he appeared, people's eyes glistened as they reached forward to touch him; it seemed they were trying to reach the late President. Bobby could not avoid the surge of feeling.

In the Spring Bobby toured the nation in what looked like a tacit bid for the vice-presidency. Actually it was a sustaining move to hold the strength Bobby felt his brother's memory deserved. The tour began on St. Patrick's Day in Scranton, Pennsylvania, and what happened in that hard-coal town foretold the receptions Kennedy would get everywhere.

He used the family plane, "The Caroline," and landed on a snowy afternoon at the Scranton-Wilkes-Barre airport, where a crowd of 2,500 broke the police lines and swarmed about the plane. Teen-aged girls screamed. Old people looked up at him expectantly. And the welcoming-committee men from the "Friendly Sons of St. Patrick" were beaming in their black overcoats and emblematic green carnations. Scranton with its large Irish population had always been sure-fire territory for a Kennedy. John Kennedy had made an enormous hit there in 1960.

Bobby spent seven lively hours in the area; helped in a ground-breaking ceremony for the new John F. Kennedy Elementary School; blinked appreciatively at the Casey Hotel when a woman cried "God Bless You, Mr. Kennedy." He loved the crowds and shrugged off the enthusiastic signs reading: "Let's Keep the Johnson-Kennedy Ticket in 1964" . . . "Mr. President, Please Ask Bobby to be Vice President." He went to two St. Patrick's Day dinners, was impressed and heartened when 10,000 people stood in the driving snow on Scranton's streets for a look at him. He shook all the right hands—the judges and U.S. Attorneys and the local

Democrats and Catholic priests. Many teen-aged girls tried to kiss
him. Women managed to kiss his hand and call out, "God Bless!"
But Kennedy's greatest moment was at the Lackawanna County
Friendly Sons of St. Patrick dinner in Scranton. It was a night when
an active, attentive audience of 1,200 heard speakers tell of the
steely will of Irishmen and the great tradition. It was Bobby Kennedy, though, who brought the expressions of feeling and, finally,
tears.

He reviewed the suffering and prejudice the Irish knew, described the American Irish as "the first of racial minorities" here.
He recalled Fred Allen's definition of "lace curtain Irish" as those
who "have fruit in the house when no one is sick." He told of his
own father's dismay, as a young man, with the signs, "No Irish Need
Apply," and how two of his sons had become U.S. Senators and
one, the President of the United States. There were many references
to "the President" or "my brother." Nearing the end of his speech,
he had his audience close to tears, and then, mentioning President
Kennedy again, he said his policies would survive just as the Irish
cause survived the death of Owen Roe O'Neill, "The Liberator."
O'Neill's death in 1649 saddened the Irish nation, and a ballad was
written in his memory. Kennedy read it and when he got to the
following lines, the Caseys, O'Malleys, Rooneys and O'Tooles of
Scranton, Pa. just went to pieces. There wasn't a dry eye in the
house:

> "Oh, why did you leave us, Owen?
> Why did you die?

> "Your troubles are all over,
> You're at rest with God on high,
> But we're slaves and we're orphans, Owen!
> Why did you die?

> "We're sheep without a shepherd,
> When the snow shuts out the sky—
> Oh! Why did you leave us, Owen?
> Why did you die?

In April, Bobby visited the old depressed areas of West
Virginia. He was familiar with the rugged ground, for he and Jack

had campaigned over it successfully in 1960 during the primary. He visited a number of hamlets, including two with the unlikely names of Wetbranch and Drybranch, where the schools had unusually high drop-out rates. At Wetbranch and Drybranch schools, he urged parents to keep their children in school and he urged the youngsters to stick to their studies. He visited an unemployed coal miner named Greenie Mullins who embraced him, shook his own head sorrowfully and said, "We loved your brother. That sure was a dirty trick they did." Bobby also saw a four-year-old girl with cerebral palsy whose mother had been left with six children by a deserting husband. He gave her afflicted child his PT-109 boat tie clasp.

"Coming back to West Virginia for a Kennedy," said Bobby, "is really like coming back home. There is close association with my family, particularly my brother."

He plugged governmental programs for the state and encouraged the impoverished to have hope, quoting a poem President Kennedy frequently used in West Virginia:

> The woods are lovely, dark and deep,
> For I have promises to keep,
> And miles to go, before I sleep . . .
> And miles to go, before I sleep.

Wherever he went in the spring of 1964, he mentioned John Kennedy, and, in effect, relived much of the 1960 Presidential campaign. His brother's aspirations had found great appeal among young people and accordingly Bobby devoted much of his schedule to appearances on campuses. A pattern developed. There would be enormous crowds on his arrival at the airport. Near-hysterical girls would scream, no matter how light or casual were Kennedy's remarks. Indeed, the emotional response to him was so strong that even the adults in his audiences shouted approvingly, whatever his words were.

He visited the South several times, speaking up for civil-rights legislation, and again he received remarkably enthusiastic receptions from college crowds. At Hampden-Sydney, a men's college in Virginia, Kennedy asked his audience how many opposed the pending civil-rights bill. The resounding applause made it clear that nearly all of the students were against the bill. Then Bobby suggested that their opposition was a result of their not knowing the actual provisions of the bill. He told them what he had seen at Negro schools in Virginia, and asked, "How can you watch these little children put their hands over their hearts and pledge allegiance to this country and not want to treat them as citizens?"

Kennedy reminded the white students that six Negro Americans had died recently in South Vietnam. He told of the mixed feelings which a Negro soldier's widow must have after she buries her husband at Arlington National Cemetery, then travels southward and is unable to find restaurant or motel accommodations. After bringing up other touching incidents, Bobby said Negroes would no longer accept such indignities and added, "None of you would put up with all of this either if you were in their place."

He got only polite applause at Hampden-Sydney. But students at West Georgia College at Carrollton, Georgia, applauded for a full minute when he described the conditions Negroes live in and then challenged his audience to ask themselves how they would like to live in those very same conditions. He made another point with his West Georgia audience when he contrasted Georgia, as a state which showed a willingness to work for racial justice, with Alabama and Mississippi, which "have made it quite clear they're not going to do it."

Bobby also visited the interracial schools he and President Kennedy had helped organize in August, 1963, when officials in Prince Edward County, Virginia, closed schools rather than desegregate them. Bobby was surrounded by a hysterical crowd of 1,000 Negroes outside one high school. He was so touched by the show of affection that tears came to his eyes. The Negro children presented him with 9,964 pennies donated for the John F. Kennedy Memorial Library.

In Milwaukee, at commencement exercises at Marquette University, he told graduates "that the most meaningful and rewarding way of achieving involvement [in community] life is in politics, in government service." The Greeks, he said, applied the word "idiot" to the person who did not participate in public affairs. His audience of 12,000 gave him thunderous applause, and the crowd which gathered around him after his speech was so great that Kennedy was unable to retrieve his suit coat. He rode to the airport wearing the gown in which he had received an honorary doctor of laws degree that afternoon.

At Roosevelt High School in Los Angeles, teen-agers and adults alike threw themselves at him, and there were cries of "Viva Kennedy"—which had been a familiar shout in Southern California during the 1960 campaign. Students lifted signs reading, "Bob Kennedy for Vice-President," and a group of Girl Scouts sang, "Oh, Bobby, we love you." At Roosevelt High, and at other schools in Los Angeles that afternoon, Bobby pleaded for students not to drop out. He told one school audience of Negroes and Mexican-Americans: "Don't quit for a temporary job because that's just what it is. Sooner or later, you'll find that job is no more and you will find it harder to get another one, if you're not educated or trained."

That night, June 8, Bobby spoke at the California Institute of Technology, at Pasadena, and made frequent reference to his late brother. He cited the Test-Ban Treaty of 1963 as a significant beginning in the "immense undertaking" of avoiding nuclear war. He said the great irony, however, is that the "surest guarantee of peace" is "the power for war," and explained it was United States power that "achieved the truly momentous victory in the 1962 Cuban missile crisis." In the future, Kennedy said, it will be an understanding of what America stands for, rather than sheer strength, that will convince the world the U.S. is a peaceful nation. This understanding, he noted, does not come about through American expediency. "Far too often, for narrow tactical reasons, this country has associated itself with tyrannical and unpopular regimes that had no following and no future. Over the past twenty years, we have paid dearly because of support given to colonial rulers, cruel dictators, or ruling cliques void of social purpose. This was one of President Kennedy's gravest concerns. It would be one of his proudest achievements if history records his Administration as an era of political friendships made for the United States."

In his conclusion, Bobby quoted from the speech President Kennedy was going to deliver in Dallas on the day of the assassination. The President would have said that while dissident voices will always be heard in our country, other kinds of voices are being

heard in the land today, "voices preaching doctrines wholly unre-
lated to reality, wholly unsuited to the 'Sixties, doctrines which
apparently assume that words will suffice without weapons, that
vituperation is as good as victory and that peace is a sign of weakness." President Kennedy's undelivered speech was, in part, critical
of extremist positions which were being voiced in increasing numbers in late 1963. Bobby himself concluded, at Pasadena: "President
Kennedy felt we deserved better—that as a people and as a country,
we had the strength, courage and fortitude to face the future."

Through all his travels in the spring of 1964, Bobby experienced a show of feeling for the Kennedy name. When he arrived in Syracuse, New York, to dedicate a work-center for high-
school dropouts, the *Post-Standard* headlined his appearance:
BOBBY BRINGS CITY $750,000. This was the amount of money the
federal government had granted to the project, but the 10,000 people who jammed the streets to see Bobby reacted as though Bobby
had given them the money. In Kansas City he stopped at the Little
Sisters of the Poor home for the aged. *God Bless America* was
played on the piano, and many of the old people wept. They told
Bobby they were going to offer masses for him and his family. Indeed, wherever he went that spring, there was a marked show of
sentiment for him by Catholic clergy and lay people. Bobby heard
many a "God Bless You." It was as if all Catholics had lost a
brother who had lived in the White House.

Bobby's travels and speeches and the increasing feeling for
the memory of John F. Kennedy were having a strong effect on the
political attitudes of people. In New York, Bobby's brother-in-law,
Steve Smith, was collecting and watching the results of many private polls being taken among rank-and-file Democrats about their
vice-presidential preference. Kennedy had led nearly every poll,
but by May, his margins had increased so much he was the overwhelming favorite. Some people even wanted Teddy for the vice
president—so strong was the Kennedy feeling—even though Teddy
was three years too young to be eligible for the office. In Missouri,
for example, 37 percent of the Democrats wanted Bobby for vice
president. He was followed by Adlai Stevenson, with 17 percent,
then Humphrey with 11 percent. Another half-dozen possibilities
trailed with only fractional percentages. In Pennsylvania and

Massachusetts, Bobby got 53 percent of the Democratic sentiment, with Stevenson and others trailing far behind. In Michigan, the Detroit *News* poll showed Kennedy the "most preferred" choice for vice president of 54 percent of those who said they would vote for Johnson. Defense Secretary McNamara, whose home is in Michigan, ran a poor second at 16 percent, and Humphrey limped in at 13 percent.

If the vice-presidential nomination were something a man could actually campaign for, Robert F. Kennedy could easily have won it. But Bobby was buffeted by events and possibilities. He considered the idea of being Secretary of State, Secretary of Defense, of being a Senator, or becoming Ambassador to Vietnam. He was a troubled man. "He had difficulty coming to grips with any decision," a member of the Kennedy family explained. "If there ever was a lost soul at that time, it was Bobby. He was out of it. He was hard to talk to on anything."

While he couldn't move inside the party, he could travel, keep his name in the news and grant selective interviews. Late in June, Kennedy spent six hours with *Newsweek*'s Washington Bureau Chief, Benjamin Bradlee, who had been a close friend of John Kennedy's. Bradlee's interview included a kind of summary statement by Bobby about his vice-presidential prospects:

> Actually I should think I'd be the last man in the world he [Johnson] would want . . . because my name is Kennedy, because he wants a Johnson Administration with no Kennedys in it, because we travel different paths, because I suppose some businessmen would object and because I'd cost them a few votes in the South . . . Most of the major leaders in the North want me—all of them, really. And that's about all I've got going for me.

The heart of the matter was the haunting memory of his brother. Bobby told his interviewer:

> I'd like to harness all the energy and effort and incentive and imagination that was attracted to government by President Kennedy. I don't want any of that to die. It is important that this striving for excellence should continue, that there be an end to mediocrity. The torch really has passed to a new generation. People are still looking

for all that idealism. It permeated young people all over the globe. And I became sort of a symbol, not just as an individual.

Some of Bobby's closest friends, particularly Kenny O'Donnell, still on duty as special assistant in the White House, wanted him to fight for it. They were sure Bobby could drum up party support and force Johnson to choose him. Johnson's situation with Bobby was difficult. If he openly opposed him, and allowed a nasty fight to become public, Johnson risked losing favor especially among Catholic voters. To a lesser extent Johnson also risked losing the votes of other northern Democrats still held by the Kennedy memory. Johnson had to avoid any direct confrontation with Bobby.

In mid-July Goldwater was nominated, and there was reason to think he might carry the South. The Democratic Convention was one month off, and Kennedy men pressed as discreetly as possible for their man, who "felt it had all been taken away from him" and was "so dedicated to his brother, he felt obligated to stay near the power center."

Johnson was under increasing pressure to tip his hand. If he waited until the convention, with its John F. Kennedy Memorial film and strong surge of emotion, he risked losing control of his own party. Moreover, Teddy Kennedy, a courageous figure in the hospital, and Jackie Kennedy, a popular figure in any case, let it be known publicly they wanted Bobby for Vice President. Jackie even made the vague remark she would come to the convention to help Bobby. Johnson had to move, surely and firmly.

Whatever his personal feelings against Bobby were, he had to offer an explanation about what he thought of Kennedy as a potential running mate. In his private conversations with Democratic leaders who visited him at the White House, Johnson said he was considering three factors in making his choice: 1. Is the man qualified? 2. What would his nomination mean politically? 3. Will I get along with him?

Johnson told his Democratic visitors he did not think Bobby was the best qualified of the possible candidates. He said he felt Bobby was too controversial, was not a leader, was impulsive, erratic and inexperienced in many government matters. Furthermore,

Johnson told his listeners, he questioned how Bobby, as a potential President, would get along with the powerful people in the nation who become involved with the President. He felt Bobby lacked the capacity to "come reason together." And Johnson explained to the Democratic politicians that, with a Goldwater candidacy, Bobby would add no more to the ticket than Humphrey would. Thus Johnson laid out a rationale which ruled against Bobby, whom he didn't like anyway. Johnson knew he and Bobby were not compatible.

The Kennedy "candidacy," however, worried the President. And he could not be put in the position of publicly designating Bobby as unsuitable for the vice-presidency. His public relationship with Bobby had to remain good for Johnson's own sake. It might have been the rancher in him, therefore, which dictated the strategy that eliminated Bobby. A cowpoke going after a certain steer never tries immediately to single him out of the herd. Instead, he cuts out several at once, and then gets the one he wants. Lyndon Johnson, the Texas politician, handled the matter of Bobby Kennedy masterfully.

On Monday, July 27, Johnson phoned Kennedy and asked him to visit him at the White House. Kennedy demurred, explaining he had to prepare for a trip. Johnson said it was nothing urgent and that Kennedy could come by Wednesday, July 29. On that day, Bobby did see Johnson in his Oval Office. Johnson formally read from a paper, as is his practice whenever he has something important to say:

"Ever since San Francisco, I have been thinking about the vice-presidency. You have a bright future, a great name and courage, but you have not been in government very long. I have given you serious consideration, but find it inadvisable to pick you."

There were a few seconds of silence, and then the President led the conversation to the subject of the 1964 campaign. Both men were cordial. Before the conversation was over, however, Johnson suggested Bobby might want to announce that he was no longer interested in being considered for the vice-presidency. Kennedy declined. As he was leaving the office, he turned to Johnson and said, almost plaintively, "I could have helped you a lot." Johnson grandly assured him he *was* going to help.

Later that afternoon, McGeorge Bundy, a special assistant

to the President, phoned Kennedy and urged him to publicly state he was out of the vice-presidential race. In effect, Bobby told Bundy to go to hell. Bobby had had ambivalent feelings about the vice-presidency all year. When he was thinking clearly, he knew he could not share the presidency with Johnson, as he had with his brother, and certainly could not work under him. Yet, Bobby had an emotional, proprietary feeling about what he and his brother had worked for and accomplished, and what his brother, as President, had stood for. In his emotional moments, Bobby felt the vice-presidency symbolized the continuance of the Kennedy aspirations. The vice-presidency would be the last link between the hope and spirit and youth of the New Frontier and the hulking Great Society. Finally, Bobby did not like to relinquish the last of the power which goes with the presidency and which he had shared. There are small ways in which the loss of power can be felt. When Jack Kennedy was President, Bobby got immediate response from other Administration officials when he put calls through to them. By late spring of 1964, some of the same officials weren't so prompt in calling back. The Texas imprint was being felt.

On Thursday, July 30, the Leader of the Great Society, President Lyndon Johnson, played his cowboy role and made two passes at the steers he wanted to cut out. In the morning, he met the press and while listing the qualifications of a Vice President, proclaimed he should be a man "that is well received in all the states of the Union among all of our people." With the South disliking Bobby, this cut him out. But Johnson made it official with a statement later that day. The press was quickly assembled about suppertime, and Lyndon was all but swinging his lariat. He had reached a conclusion about the vice-presidency; he said, earnestly, "It would be inadvisable for me to recommend to the convention any member of my Cabinet or any of those who meet regularly with my Cabinet."

Thus he had roped out Dean Rusk, Robert McNamara, Orville Freeman—all cabinet members who had been mentioned as vice-presidential possibilities—and the "close ones," such as Adlai Stevenson and Sargent Shriver. The critter he wanted was Kennedy and he got him. Hubert Humphrey and Eugene McCarthy grazed contentedly nearby.

Just to make sure Bobby was roped securely, Johnson had

Death came early to three. Left to right — Jean, Bobby, Pat, Eunice, Kathleen, Rosemary, John and Joseph, Jr.

Bobby wore a warm coat, knickers and knee socks aboard the ship which took him to England where his father was the first Irish-American to serve as American ambassador, March, 1938.

Courtesy, Mrs. Robert F. Kennedy

Three years later, Bobby on the tennis court of his father's estate at Palm Beach, Florida. With him, on the left, is Eunice, and on the right are Teddy and Jean.

Wide World Photos

With his bride in 1950. After a long
honeymoon in Hawaii, there were
many years of Kennedy-style living
at Hickory Hill, Virginia.

Bobby was an undersized, but inde-
fatigable end at Harvard in 1947.

With friend, Senator Joseph R. McCarthy, in 1954. The beginnings were controversial.

Confrontation with Jimmy Hoffa. The investigation which helped launch a presidential campaign.

John Kennedy and Bobby at leisure in 1957. The years in politics tightened the brotherly bond.

Art Rickerby, Life

President Kennedy and the Attorney General.

Huddle at Hickory Hill.
For Bobby, fatherhood is a
natural joy.

Courtesy, Mrs. Robert F. Kennedy

Old Joe was father to nine
children and so is Bobby.

George Silk, Life

The survivors.

Wide World Photos

The civil rights struggle, 1963. After months of dawdling, the Kennedys moved firmly and fast.

Bobby in Asia, January, 1964. Around the world, the name was better known than Coca-Cola.

Courtesy, Mrs. Robert F. Kennedy

Walter Daran

Bobby receiving the New York Democratic nomination for the Senate in 1964. The shy wave, the hesitant smile and the cry of Carpetbagger!

Kennedy campaigning. The kids turned out as if he were a Beatle, but Bobby still worried about the voters.

Cornell Capa, Life

Bobby, Jr., stood at attention, and Joe shook hands while their father got David ready for a parade in the 1964 campaign for the U.S. Senate.

With Hubert Humphrey in Manhattan. When the 1964 campaign got rough, the ride on Johnson's coattail was helpful.

The smiles of unity. Both sides hoped for a thaw.

The Brothers Kennedy in the Senate. New spokesmen for the north? The presidency ahead?

John Bailey, Democratic National Chairman, change the scheduling of the film on John F. Kennedy's life, which was to be shown at the Democratic National Convention. It was originally to be shown the second night of the convention—a Tuesday. Now it would be shown Thursday night, after Johnson had picked his Vice President. The possibility of a Bobby Kennedy demonstration on Tuesday, following the emotional film, was cut off.

The job was done. Bobby was safely eliminated. Some of his supporters were bitter. One said, of Johnson's moves: "He shot us down, the son of a bitch." Johnson's alibi that he wanted to keep his cabinet together was thin. But unexpendability was a lofty enough explanation. The men who had supported John F. Kennedy were more inclined toward rancor directed at Lyndon Johnson than was Bobby. Though he strongly felt his brother's name and hopes should be continued, he knew Johnson's decision and method made sense. There would be no true passing of the presidential power until the "half President" was out of the Administration. Or, as one Kennedy man, still loyal to Bobby but balanced by his position in the Johnson administration, explained it:

"Much of Bobby's success was related to the fact he was the President's brother. Let's be honest about it. Why would Johnson want to compromise his position by accepting a Kennedy into his Administration? It wouldn't be a Johnson Administration then. No man can operate that way. Given Johnson's political history and ego, it had to be someone else than Bobby Kennedy."

Kennedy took his rejection gracefully. Less than a week after Johnson's edict, he spoke to an audience of Democratic Congressional candidates. With a sheepish smile on his face, he said, "I must confess I stand in awe of you," he said. "You are not members of the Cabinet and you don't meet regularly with the Cabinet, and therefore you are eligible for Vice President."

The laughter which followed was healthy, and Kennedy's grin widened when he added, "I decided to send a little note to the Cabinet members in general, saying, I'm sorry I took so many nice fellows over the side with me."

VIII
ENTRY INTO NEW YORK

□□
□□

TEDDY MENTIONED THE NEW YORK SENATE SEAT TO BOBBY as early as January, 1964.

All spring, in New York, Stephen Smith, who manages the interests of Joseph P. Kennedy, Sr. and also serves as a political listening post for all the Kennedys, heard no end of the talk. Through the storm of speculation about the vice-presidency and the gusts concerning other futures for Bobby, there was always the possibility of the U.S. Senate. Steve Smith and the Democratic Party regulars, particularly county leaders or bosses, as they are often called, told Bobby "it's there if you want it." New York's Democrats were panting for a winner, and even Bobby's detractors admitted if he were the candidate, he would be tough to beat.

New York had not elected a Democratic senator since 1950. Under Rockefeller and Javits, Republicanism had prospered in the Empire State, even though there were 500,000 fewer registered Republicans than Democrats. In mid-1964, Republicans had control of both Senate seats; a majority of the congressional delegation; the governorship, and all state cabinet offices save one; a comfortable majority in both houses of the state legislature; and nearly all county supervisors' boards in the state. Only Kansas surpassed New York in terms of elected Republican officials. Furthermore, the New York State Democratic Party was really a series of baronies run by quarrelling chiefs, most of whom could unite only in their opposition to New York Mayor Robert F. Wagner.

Wagner, who had niftily shifted from the Democratic Machine to the Reform Movement, held much of the New York City party strength. But in suburbia, where the Democratic Party was growing, and upstate, where Republicans took too much for granted, the anti-Wagner Democratic officials yearned for a leader with Bobby's name and credentials.

Upstate, Rep. Samuel Stratton, of Amsterdam, who had been elected three times to Congress in a largely Republican district, was anxious to have the Senate nomination for himself. Stratton had long been ambitious for higher office in New York. He had wanted to run for Governor in 1962, but was bumped by his party's leadership in favor of U.S. Attorney Robert Morgenthau, when a study by Pollster Louis Harris proclaimed that Morgenthau would give Governor Rockefeller the stiffest test. Morgenthau's nomination in September of 1962 was a disappointment for Stratton, who now had to run for re-election in a Congressional district which had been gerrymandered one year before by the Republican legislature. But Stratton won easily, in 1962, and became a hero among upstate Democrats. He immediately began straining for the U.S. Senate. An obvious way to show his interest in the seat held by Republican incumbent Kenneth B. Keating was to attack Keating's performance. Since Keating's voting record in 1963 was favorable to the Democratic Administration of President Kennedy, Stratton had to find another way to battle the Republican Senator. He found it in the dispute over the Cuban missile crisis. Keating had long criticized the Administration on the question of Soviet missile installations in Cuba. Stratton, from the House of Representatives, made it his business to counter Keating's attacks on the Kennedy Administration's handling of the Cuban situation. In the public's mind at least, Stratton appeared as the New York Democrat who was opposed to Keating.

This was precisely the reputation he wanted. Stratton was already known as a hard campaigner, a man who slept in the back of his station wagon after a full day of meeting voters and giving speeches. Through 1963 and early 1964, Stratton talked of the growing strength of the Democratic Party in Upstate New York. He also claimed the support of 22 Democratic County organizations. Stratton's intentions were clear: he wanted to run against Keating in the fall of 1964. Early in 1964, when Bobby's name was mentioned for the Senate, Stratton remained quiet. He spoke up on Bobby, however, when Kennedy-for-Vice-President talk reached one of its springtime highs. He solemnly declared Bobby was "the best fitted to assume the heavy burdens of the presidency," and as a vice-presidential candidate "offers our party the best possible chance of a 1964 victory."

During the spring months, the thought of becoming a U.S. Senator from New York was not uppermost in Bobby's mind. It was the vice-presidential situation and other possibilities which occupied his thoughts. Kennedy compulsively, if unobtrusively, kept his hat in the vice-presidential ring. At the same time, he sent up trial balloons for other Cabinet jobs—Secretary of State or Defense. He actually applied in writing for the Ambassadorship to Vietnam, a difficult post which Henry Cabot Lodge resigned in June. President Johnson told Bobby he was needed too much on the Civil Rights front for him to go off to Saigon. The truth was Bobby really didn't know what he wanted. One of his closest friends was amazed with Bobby's sudden interest in the ambassadorship. "Whatever he was doing then," explained the friend, "was very impulsive."

One day in early May, Steve Smith was attending the dedication of a John F. Kennedy school gymnasium on Long Island. Also present was John English, Nassau County Democratic boss, an aggressive young man with a serious face and a distinctive crew-cut. English got right to the point and told Smith that Bobby had to run for Keating's seat. Bobby and the Democratic Party would flourish. Though Smith had heard this before, he relayed English's enthusiasm to a few friends, and soon the Bobby-for-Senate rumor bloomed fully. Spring is the right season for such talk.

Reaction was promising. State Chairman William H. McKeon declared Bobby unquestionably would make a great candidate —a winner, in fact. Mayor Wagner, aware that several powerful county bosses had aligned themselves with Steve Smith in their promotion of Bobby, had to equivocate in his remarks on Kennedy. Wagner knew there was broad support in the party for Kennedy, but he also knew the reform element in the Democratic Party would resist Bobby. So when asked for his reaction, Wagner described Bobby as "my good friend, an accomplished public official who deserves serious consideration" for the Senate. The leadership of the Liberal Party, which can provide up to 500,000 votes for Democratic candidate, was weary of losing Senate seats to the Republicans, and allowed that Kennedy would make a fine candidate.

The trial balloon for Kennedy did not descend unpunctured, however. Stratton angrily announced he was certain Kennedy "wouldn't be part of any such preposterous maneuver," and said New York's Democrats should "not resort to far-fetched and ridiculous gimmicks like this." Stratton wanted his party's convention delegates to meet by June 15 to designate the senatorial candidate. "Obviously," said Stratton, "the Attorney General could not possibly make himself available to meet this June 15 deadline."

In New York City there is a hodgepodge of Democratic clubs and factions which is loosely called "the reform movement." The reformers are bound together in one common interest—namely, to oppose boss-dominated, machine politics. But like most zealots, the reformers tend to factionalize, to disagree among themselves, particularly when they discuss personalities and candidates. Mayor Wagner, for example, did not have the support of reform groups in his early years as mayor, but when bosses—like Carmine De Sapio and Charles Buckley—opposed him in 1961, Wagner was suddenly the "reform" candidate. In May of 1964, Bobby Kennedy certainly did not have the support of reformers, most of whom howled about his friendship with Buckley and the prospect of his coming into New York as a "carpetbagger" candidate. Most reformers lamented the fact that their New York Democratic Party had to go outside its state to find a man.

The New York Times, the state's most important political voice, shared much of the reformers' concern over a Kennedy candidacy. During the May boom for Kennedy, the *Times* sharply remarked:

> There is nothing illegal about the possible nomination of Robert F. Kennedy of Massachusetts as Senator from New York, but there is plenty that is cynical about it . . . The Attorney General has no special knowledge of New York's many complex problems; if he

became a candidate, he would merely be choosing New York as a convenient launching pad for the political ambitions of himself and others.

Bobby was scheduled to be a Massachusetts delegate to the Democratic National Convention, but was indeed eligible to become a U.S. Senator from New York as long as he was a resident of the state on Election Day. The fact that the carpetbagger question emerged in the May enthusiasm for Bobby was a sign the Kennedy candidacy was beginning to be taken seriously. It was important enough that Governor Rockefeller, campaigning hard against Goldwater in the California primary, took time for sharp words about Kennedy. "I would think the Democrats would want a New Yorker for their candidate," Rockefeller snapped. "This looks like the Central Government appointing a Senator for one of the provinces."

The Bronx Boss and longtime Democratic Congressman, Charles A. Buckley, is the symbol of boss rule and machine politics to all New York City reformers. Reformers are ideologists, and Buckley doesn't have an ideological bone in his body. For decades he was content to deliver huge Democratic voting majorities from the Bronx through practical machine politics and a successful system of picking winning candidates. Buckley incensed *The New York Times* as much as he did the reformers. Of New York's six daily newspapers—including the Republican-leaning *New York Herald Tribune*—no paper got more upset over Buckley than the *Times*. His name was the red flag which moved the usually staid *Times* to anger.

On May 20, when Bobby-for-the-Senate talk was lively, Bobby came to New York to speak for Buckley, who was in a tough primary fight for his congressional seat. Kennedy considered Buckley an old political friend who had helped line up New York support in 1960. Bobby felt he should return the favor to Buckley. He gave his speech for the old pol, and newsmen stopped Bobby in a hall and pestered him about his plans for the Senate. What Bobby said made the *Times* and Sam Stratton breathe easily again. Kennedy acknowledged he had discussed with prominent New York Democrats the possibility of running, but he concluded, "All things being equal, it would be better for a citizen of New York to run for the position. I have no other plans than staying on as Attorney General."

This observation was interpreted by the press and many Democratic politicians as a firm disclaimer by Bobby. For Kennedy to endorse Buckley and also to say a citizen of New York should run for the Senate seemed evidence enough Bobby wasn't interested. So other names popped up in the speculation which followed. The Committee for Democratic Voters, a reform organization which examines potential candidates closely to make sure they are "liberal," showed an interest in United Nations Ambassador Adlai Stevenson. But Stevenson's close friends said he would not try for the nomination. And, for the moment, neither would the others mentioned: Dr. Ralph Bunche, a United Nations official; New York County District Attorney Frank Hogan; Queens County District Attorney Frank O'Connor; or Ambassador Averell Harriman, who was really for Bobby. Sam Stratton was the only possible candidate who longed for the nomination, and though he claimed support from 22 upstate counties, it was slender support indeed. Mayor Wagner was hesitant to support Stratton or anyone else at this point.

Then, on June 19, another Kennedy tragedy provided the opportunity for any New York Democrat aspiring for the Senate to make a move. Senator Teddy Kennedy had just voted for the Civil Rights Bill and was in a chartered plane on his way to the Massachusetts State Convention which would nominate him. Shortly after 11 o'clock the plane was making an instrument approach for a landing near Springfield. Suddenly the plane went into a strange climb, then plunged into an apple orchard. Teddy was seriously injured.

Bobby got the word at Hyannis Port, chartered a plane and flew to Boston, where state police drove him and his sister, Jean Kennedy Smith, to the hospital. Bobby hurried through the crowded emergency entrance to his brother's side. Teddy smiled weakly and said, "Hiyah, Bobby." He had three broken vertebrae, two fractured ribs, but no neurological damage or paralysis. Bobby was sad but relieved.

The next afternoon Bobby issued a statement of thanks to the hospital and doctors, and then, with Walter Sheridan, he walked through the growing crowd outside the hospital to a field nearby.

Bobby lay on his back in the grass a little while. Still staring at the sky, he said, "Somebody up there doesn't like us." Then, turning to Sheridan, he wryly remarked, "It's been a great year for giggles, hasn't it?"

Bobby decided that Saturday afternoon in Massachusetts that he would not seek the Senatorial nomination in New York. On the following Monday, in Washington, he made his decision public:

> Over the last several weeks, Democratic leaders and friends in New York and elsewhere have contacted me urging that I seek the Democratic nomination for United States Senator from New York.
>
> Representing the state of New York in the United States Senate is a challenging and important opportunity for public service. I deeply appreciate the loyalty and friendship of those who have urged me to run and who believe I could perform a service for the people of New York.
>
> However, in fairness to them, and to end speculation, I wish to state that I will not be a candidate for United States Senator for New York.

For this, *The New York Times* lauded Kennedy. "It is to his credit," said the *Times*, "that he apparently recognized . . . he had no legitimate claim to residence or to familiarity with problems of the state . . . and also that he made his decision known early enough in the political season that careful consideration can be given to several other candidates . . ."

Democratic State Chairman William McKeon said Kennedy's decision would help Democrats to think better about the Senate race. Sam Stratton said he was "available if the party clearly wants me to run." But the party wasn't ready for Sam. The liberals wishfully hoped that Stevenson would run and so did *The New York Times*. Senator Keating said he was too busy to think about what the Democrats were doing.

His mind evidently made up on New York, Bobby flew to West Germany, where he visited with Chancellor Ludwig Erhard, former Chancellor Konrad Adenauer and other officials. The trip was another of those missions Kennedy, as Attorney General, made in a quasi-official position. He had been invited by the Free University of Berlin to unveil a plaque honoring his brother in City Hall

Square, West Berlin. And though he had no official mission to Poland, Kennedy had advised the State Department he was going to spend four days in Poland on his own after his West Berlin appearance. This announcement caused several gentlemen in the department to grit their teeth because they knew Bobby usually circumvented protocol when he visited foreign countries.

In West Berlin, at the place where the late President had thrilled thousands with his cry, "Ich bin eine Berliner!" Bobby thrilled them again on June 26. His speech was laced with extracts from speeches by his brother and kept close to the theme that J.F.K., more than any other man of his time, was dedicated to the young people of the world. Bobby linked this dedication to the development of freedom in Berlin and West Germany. He quoted Goethe's remark that "The destiny of any nation, at any given time, depends on the opinions of its young men, under 25."

As he concluded, Bobby made some personal observations about the death of his brother. "There were many who felt then that a light had been snuffed out," Bobby said, "that the torchbearer for a whole generation was gone . . . To many, it seemed then, that the world might lapse again into the empty poses and vain quarrels that disfigured our yesterdays, and made of our past a litany of anguish." But Bobby found in his travels the understanding "that the hope President Kennedy kindled is not dead but alive. It is not a memory, but a living force . . . For me, that is the challenge that makes life worthwhile; and I hope it will be the same for all of you."

The response was thundering. There were full-throated cries from the 70,000 people of "Kenn-needee! . . . Bob-bee! . . ." The memory of J.F.K. and Bobby's touching delivery had stirred the Berliners to an outpouring of feeling. Bobby's appearance was an enormous success.

Poland was more complicated. To begin with, the Communist Government wasn't keen on Bobby's traipsing about at the same time Premier Josip Broz Tito, Yugoslavia's Communist boss, was an official visitor—which he was. Then there was a special relationship between the United States and Red Poland which was a sort of mutual looking away. The Poles, even under Communism, are pro-Western. Neither country gets especially tough with the other and often lets well enough alone. Finally, the Church-State relationship in Poland was and is delicate. Bobby arrived at a time when new tension had developed, particularly over Stefan Cardinal Wyszynski, an "enemy" of the State.

Bobby's visit then, carried the potential of troublemaking. While the Communist officials of the Polish Government were loath to say so publicly, they resented Bobby's tour. U.S. officials in Poland were uneasy about the four-day trip out of fear the relationship with their Polish counterparts would be jeopardized. Their fears were substantiated. Before Bobby left Poland, he had shocked and angered Polish Government officials; excited and entertained huge crowds of Poles; broken a half-dozen diplomatic rules; and demonstrated that the Kennedy name and style can really move people.

Kennedy's arrival was like that of a small circus. His party numbered 18, including Ethel and the three eldest children; Princess Lee Radziwill, without her husband (whose brother-in-law, Edmund, is a Polish official); several aides, and a half-dozen newsmen. The government provided only small notice that Kennedy was coming, but people turned out by the thousands to see him. They learned of his visit through radio broadcasts from non-Communist European countries. The word spread that Kennedy was coming.

In Warsaw and Cracow, the crowds were extremely excited. Bobby, Ethel and children sat or stood on the hood and roof of a crawling Soviet Volga limousine. Poles lustily sang a song wishing a life of 100 years for him. He and Ethel responded with "When *Polish* Eyes Are Smiling." With Bobby on the limousine's roof, deporting himself like a political candidate, the American ambassador, John M. Cabot of Boston, sat disgruntled inside. Once, Cabot stuck his head out the window and complained to a Kennedy aide, "Would you please tell the Attorney General that the roof is falling in?"

Kennedy had asked the American Embassy to arrange appearances at a children's hospital, an orphanage and a farm market. He visited them all and also went uninvited to a student graduation ball. At Warsaw's Cathedral, the crowd pushed so hard that Bobby's own children were momentarily lost.

Bobby's fantastic reception eclipsed Tito's visit, and his exploitation of the Poles' enthusiasm at seeing a Kennedy greatly angered Polish officials. The vice-minister of Foreign Affairs, Josef Winiewicz, attended the dinner that Ambassador Cabot gave Bobby for the express purpose of telling the honored guest he had gone too far. Because of the enormous crowds he enjoyed all day, Kennedy was one hour late for the dinner, a tardiness which infuriated Polish Communist brass. They remonstrated with him for playing to the crowds and told him that "Premier Gomulko never does." Bobby replied, "Well, maybe that's the problem." When another official asked Kennedy to speak to the dinner crowd of Communist brass, Bobby snapped, "Please let go of my arm."

Next day, despite advice by Polish officials that it would be "ill advised" for him to visit Cardinal Wyszynski at the Monastary of the Black Madonna, Bobby met privately with the Cardinal for one hour. After consulting with the American embassy, Kennedy decided not to discuss the meeting with the press.

Bobby's visit was so lively that the Polish press asked for a meeting before he left, largely to needle and embarrass him. But Bobby fended off the sharp questions good-naturedly, and was firm when he had to be. When asked why he didn't visit Auschwitz concentration camp, Kennedy replied he had visited many such grisly places, and knew what the Nazis were—he had lost his own brother to them in World War II. Kennedy rendered the United States an important service by stating "there is no doubt" Lee Harvey Oswald, "a misfit," was his brother's assassin. (There was and is great suspicion in Europe over the assassination, many believing it was a racist or fascist plot.) At the end of the meeting, Kennedy was applauded by the Polish newsmen.

Bobby had shaken Polish officialdom, so much so that a glum American embassy official, jealous perhaps of Bobby's striking popular success, said it would take six months to pick up the pieces. It was a bad week for Poland's Communist Party, a great one for Kennedy, and, perhaps, the Democratic Party. For who is the Polish-American who doesn't warm to the news of how Bobby irked the Communist bosses of Poland while being enthusiastically received by the masses of good Polish people?

By the time Bobby arrived home, the political focus was on San Francisco, where a pathetic scramble on behalf of Governor William Scranton was coming to an end. Barry Goldwater was nominated. Nixon's prediction that Bobby's chances for the vice-presidential nomination were greater if a moderate Republican were chosen as the G.O.P. nominee took on substance. Bobby's hope that he might get another Cabinet post was evaporating. In New York, despite Bobby's firm declaration of June 22 that he would not run, there was once again growing momentum for his candidacy. Steve Smith continued to assure New York Democratic leaders that Bobby would eventually say "yes." On July 26, Smith checked upstate county leaders who had met in Syracuse, and learned that only three of the 22 objected to Bobby, despite Stratton's claim of total allegiance.

His own indecision notwithstanding, events were pushing Bobby into the New York candidacy. He had vague thoughts of living in Europe for a year or so, or of teaching, but neither of these possibilities really suited his temperament. He would wind up arguing with academic administrators or, worse, fall into restlessness and indecisiveness if he chose either of those courses. He had announced he would resign as Attorney General in 1964. Days of July passed and finally, on July 29, President Johnson told Bobby he would not be his choice for the vice-presidency. Bobby now had to decide what his own future would be.

One rainy evening in the first week of August, Kennedy's limousine moved slowly through the Washington rush-hour traffic. He stared out the window at government workers huddled under umbrellas and newspapers waiting for buses. A friend sat next to him, and Bobby, his voice heavy with resignation and sadness, said, "I don't think there is much future for me in this city now."

The Cadillac rounded Lincoln Memorial, and crossed the bridge to Arlington Cemetery. The driver spoke to the cemetery guards, "The Attorney General." The flame flickered in the pouring rain at President Kennedy's grave. (Bobby chose rainy evenings, when crowds and cameras stayed away, to visit.) A man held an umbrella. Bobby knelt in prayer for a moment. The wind blew the downpour onto him anyway and soaked his trousers.

That week, because he was torn over New York, he had to talk to old friends: Kenny O'Donnell, Larry O'Brien, Arthur Schlesinger, David Hackett, Averell Harriman. The Senate race did not appeal to him. But the Justice Department held little for him now. Hoffa was convicted and the Civil Rights Bill was now law. He was being urged to run. New York would be a snap. Keating would be clobbered by him. Steve Smith had polls to prove it, and his left ear was red from having the phone pressed to it. He had called every important Democrat in New York, including Mayor Wagner, whom he couldn't move. "To hell with them," Smith told Bobby on the phone. "Come up here and run."

The vice-presidential wisp gone, notions of other jobs or a nonpolitical life discarded, and New York looking riper and riper— Bobby finally decided to run. His mind was made up by August 5, but he wasn't ready for an announcement. He met privately at breakfast with Wagner in Manhattan on August 8. Wagner was noncommittal. He offered neither protest nor support. Bobby was to get considerable opposition from most reformers and in vociferous form. He would also get plenty of support. All in all Bobby had little to worry about. Smith assured him that of the 573 New York Democratic delegate votes he needed for the Senate nomination, it turned out he already had 450 from the various bosses. All Bobby had to do in August was endure the New York political noise; he was nominated before he announced. So he went on a cruise off Maine's shore on the yacht owned by Thomas J. Watson Jr., board chairman of International Business Machines Corporation.

Bobby's first bit of strategy was to hang the responsibility on Wagner, who now knew he would have to have a Kennedy in his New York Democratic Party. Said Bobby, as he left for his cruise, "Under no circumstances would I ever have considered, or would I now consider, coming into the state of New York against the wishes of the mayor." To which the mayor responded, with a straight face, "If he is available, he is the type of person who would make an exceptionally fine candidate. I'm sure that he would win."

Wagner now moved to make sure Bobby wouldn't take over *everything.* President Johnson, in New York for an American Bar Association speech, told Wagner that Kennedy would strengthen the New York ticket. Wagner wanted to be reassured that he was stiil the No. 1 Democrat as far as job patronage and party matters were concerned, that he would be the man consulted on political decisions. Johnson gave him that assurance. Wagner was satisfied. He would play possum in order to keep the unhappy reformers placated. Many of them still believed Wagner himself might announce for the Senate.

New York City's editorial voices were not that naïve. The two papers most influential in state politics, the *Times* and the *Herald Tribune*, now realized Bobby was not only coming, but through the work of Smith and with the problem of a vacuum in the Democratic Party, Bobby was all but nominated. It was the *Times* that got indignant to the point of being flustered. The nation's leading newspaper had assumed, editorially, that Bobby would stay out of New York, but now the assumption was proving wrong. ". . . Mr. Kennedy apparently needs New York," a *Times* editorial said, "but does New York really need Bobby Kennedy?" The *Times* aimed editorial after editorial at him. The Kennedy steamroller, lamented the *Times*, is moving toward "the consolation prize on which the Attorney General has apparently set his heart." It was the design of "selfish bosses" who represented "the nadir of party idealism" who wanted to "ram the impatient young man from Massachusetts down the throats of the party's unhappy top leadership in New York. . . ." The paper noted sadly that there must be a New Yorker who would stand for New York, otherwise, "New York may soon have only one Senator, and Massachusetts three—two of them Kennedys."

The *Herald Tribune* was equally indignant. "The galling part," observed the *Tribune*, "is that so many Democrats are willing and ready to take an outsider who knows little or nothing about New York and who is essentially an adventurer determined to remain in public office as a personal necessity." The fact that Kennedy was a nonresident of New York, the *Tribune* continued, "is abhorrent to tradition. . . . But this is the viciousness hidden under the surface glamour, of Bobby Kennedy's thrust to take over New York." On another day, the *Tribune* called a Kennedy candidacy "bossism gone mad in the obeisant welcome of a carpetbagger. . . ."

In general, the press interpreted Wagner's bland blessing of Bobby as reflecting the bankruptcy of the Democratic Party in New York. With Wagner getting the public credit for opening the state to Kennedy, Adam Clayton Powell, as is his custom, had to throw rocks at his old political enemy, Wagner. "Steingut, Buckley, Crotty and I will decide who will be the next U.S. Senator, or at least the Democratic nominee," Powell thundered, naming most of the State's celebrated bosses in one blast. As for Kennedy, Powell modestly declared, "I urged him three months ago to make the race."

Stratton now discovered and publicly announced that he had the support of 40 counties—not 22—around the state. Stratton's promoter, Schenectady County Chairman George Palmer, angrily warned, "Naming an outsider for Senate in New York could set a precedent which would later be exploited by reactionary well-heeled Republican conservatives. . . . What is to stop a reactionary oil or mining tycoon from deciding that he would like to buy himself a Senate election in some small and poor Republican farming state?"

This possibility did not cross many Democratic minds in New York. Most knew the potency of the Kennedy name. True, there was a handful of reform Democrats who were in anguish over the thought of Bobby's becoming Senator. They saw him as a man not to be trusted; as a reactionary in newly acquired liberal clothing; as Joe's son; as the man who used inquisitorial and unfair tactics to get Hoffa. These people relished reading Gore Vidal's 1963 *Esquire* piece on Bobby, including this assessment: "Bobby's view of men and actions is a good deal closer to that of Barry Goldwater than it is to that of President Kennedy."

The majority of those who questioned Bobby's liberalism were Jewish. Hence, some fast work by a number of Bobby's Jewish political friends was necessary. R. Peter Straus, the energetic president of a New York City radio station, WMCA, and William Haddad, a former Peace Corps executive, tried to persuade influential liberal Jews that Bobby was all right. The Liberal Party's Alex Rose and David Dubinsky—both prestigious names—spent considerable time on the phone with the message that Bobby is a good liberal, and besides, he's a winner. What Kennedy also needed at this point was an endorsement from a highly respected Jewish liberal whose credentials were unquestioned. Mrs. Herbert Lehman would have been excellent but she demurred. She remembered how Bobby had told New York Democratic leaders in the 1960 campaign: "I'm not interested in Senator Lehman, Carmine De Sapio, Mike Prendergast or anyone else. All I'm interested in is Senator Kennedy being elected President."

Stratton fumed, the reformers fussed, Bobby cruised off the Maine coast (but kept in touch by phone) and Wagner sat. The script called for Wagner to state his support, however grudgingly. Next Bobby would announce. Then he could wallow in the flood of huzzahs from bandwagon Democrats. Bobby really had no competition. Those reformers who hated him futilely continued to plead with Adlai Stevenson and Wagner to run. But Stevenson wasn't interested. Wagner wanted to continue as mayor. Sam Stratton's boasted strength was imaginary; the Democratic Party upstate is largely Irish and clamored for Kennedy.

The truth was that no Democrat of substance and political strength wanted to be U.S. Senator from New York badly enough to give Bobby competition.

His ingress was made even more simple because of the noisy but feckless opposition of the reformers. About half of this reform movement, the vocal half, whom Bobby later described as "hating everything and everybody, including each other," complained loudly that he was ruthless, unprincipled and tyranically selfish and ambitious. Unruly little meetings were held. Several spokesmen for this wing of the reform movement were quoted regularly in front-page stories of New York City's papers. Emissaries of the movement visited Wagner, demanding that he do something to stop Kennedy. Wagner patiently explained he stood foursquare behind the reform movement and was reserving decision on Bobby. The exasperated reformers who claimed the liberal grail did everything but what they had to do—namely, line up Democratic delegates who would back a candidate other than Bobby. So while the controversy over Bobby raged, Steve Smith and other Kennedy men enlisted delegates, more than 700 by August 16; a total of 563 was needed to nominate. Smith had captured nearly all the "regular" Democrats, and all he needed to make Bobby's nomination a landslide was one final push from liberal quarters on his behalf.

Smith had been through the whole business about Old Joe and the "ruthless" Kennedys in 1960 when he worked for Jack Kennedy in New York. Many reformers and the leadership of the Liberal Party, had come around to certify Jack Kennedy and now were disposed to bless Bobby. Their attitude was, "Why not? He'll win, won't he?" Bobby's intermediaries assured them he wore no boss's collar. He would take the bosses' support but not their orders. To cinch it for Bobby, Smith arranged for 12 apostles of liberalism in the New York Democratic Party to declare publicly for Bobby. These are the kind of reliable Democrats who fork over big campaign money, pay $1,000 to join the President's Club, and are considered prestigious, liberal and sound.

They were: Averell Harriman; Arthur Krim, President of United Artists; Roswell Gilpatric, former Deputy Secretary of Defense and a prominent lawyer; Mrs. Albert D. Lasker, philanthropist and a member of the East Side liberal group; Mrs. Edward R. Murrow; Howard Samuels, upstate industrialist and promoter of the Democratic Party; Robert Benjamin, an associate of Krim's; John Snyder, who, as President of U.S. Industries, Inc., is one of the kings of automation; and Abraham (Abe) Feinberg, a hosiery baron, who helped make Jack Kennedy palatable to Jews in 1960; Isador Lubin, former State Industrial commissioner and Mrs. Lubin; and George Backer, businessman and former aide of Harriman's.

The public blessing of these estimable Democrats mitigated criticism that Bobby was the bosses' hand-picked candidate. Bobby had the bosses' ardent backing anyway. They liked his no-nonsense view of politics. Bobby talked their language, made no pretense of being a reformer. Boss, to Bobby, means a political leader who knows what's going on. Thus he had the support of these bosses (or leaders, depending on semantics): Adam Clayton Powell; Charles A. Buckley; Peter Crotty; Stanley Steingut; John English; Westchester's Bill Luddy; Daniel P. O'Connell, the octogenarian who controls the city of Albany, and State Chairman William McKeon, who failed to disguise his partisanship for Kennedy.

Stratton, who had thought he would luck into the nomination the same way the Republican Party's moderates thought Rockefeller and Goldwater would fight to a standstill, grew desperate and increasingly strident. "It's morally wrong," he preached bitterly, "for someone to move into New York and try to represent it. What makes it even more callous is that it's obvious that the only reason he's interested in New York is because the door was shut to him for vice president."

One of Stratton's political allies is Congressman Otis G. Pike, whose district embraces the far reaches and potato fields of Long Island, an area dominated by Republicans who like Pike's maverick tendencies. It was in Pike's interest to holler and stamp his foot over Bobby. Pike thundered it would be "wrong, wrong, wrong" for Bobby to represent New York. "We are doing a great disservice to the entire concept of representative government," Pike said, "if . . . we nominate as the Senator from New York a man who on August 24 is listed at the Democratic National Convention as the delegate from Massachusetts." While Pike and Stratton complained about a newspaper "blitz" of news stories for Kennedy, both were likewise being given considerable space in the papers—a fact which later did not hurt their congressional campaigns in districts dense with Republicans.

The advent of a Kennedy in New York provided press excitement. Even though Kennedy had delegates to spare, the news stories were laced with intrigue and struggle. The newspaper drama centered on the state's most important Democrat, Mayor Wagner.

Wagner's genius is that he can operate like a mongoose among snakes in the world's most frenetic and perplexed city and get away with it. He is one of the most underrated men in American politics. For five years he labored to "de-boss" his party in New York, and had a measure of success. Now he was faced with the intrusion of a figure who could easily overshadow him. Wagner knew early that Bobby would be nominated, but Wagner had to be the last to endorse him because Wagner had to *appear* to oppose any last hope of the bosses. And he had to wait until all eyes turned for the final nod to make Kennedy the No. 1 Democrat in the state.

He was Robert F. Wagner, the reluctant endorser. When Kennedy came to meet him one morning at Gracie Mansion, the mayor was one hour late. Bobby paced the lawn with Steve Smith. Nearby was a Conestoga wagon and chefs preparing for a Johnson-for-President barbecue that evening. The mayor was expressionless after the meeting. And in the days following, he looked anxious reformers straight in the eye and told them he was undecided. He and Kennedy steered the news stories toward August 21.

On that date, a Friday, selected so it would spill over into the weekend and Sunday papers, reluctantly Robert Wagner stood before newsmen and uttered 800 words, rich with analysis and explanation.

"I have pondered long and conferred broadly," the Mayor began and then he allowed that there had been considerable interest in Bobby Kennedy for Senator. The mayor solemnly explained he had discussed this matter with Bobby and many others, including men with "impressive credentials for public service." Wagner disclosed that he himself had been asked to run, but had modestly demurred. It was Bobby whom people wanted and "there can be no question of his personal eminence—of the appealing nature of his great public achievements, nor of the dazzling magic of his name."

Then, like a college student who got C-plus in debating, Wagner acknowledged there were objections to Kennedy, but after all, a sophisticated state like New York "has taken to its bosom millions from abroad and from other parts of the country, giving our state constant infusions of new blood. . . ."

Finally the mayor was positive Bobby would work with him and others in the "revitalization and democratization of our party organization." Translated, the phrase meant the fight against bossism. The mayor had salvaged what he wanted.

The Democratic National Convention in Atlantic City was the following week, and a fine week it was for a Kennedy to move publicly for elective office. Had Bobby's vagrant dreams been fulfilled, on Tuesday, August 25, following the touching film on his brother, there would have been enormous outpouring of delegate sentiment for him to be vice president. But the National Committee and Lyndon Johnson had intervened, and so Bobby was at Gracie Mansion in New York City. The grass was scuffed by television trailer trucks. Six painters on the roof stopped their work to watch and listen. A hundred people milled about. All eyes were on the porch door.

Bobby came down the steps with Ethel and Mayor Wagner. He wore a gray, pin-striped suit, the black tie of mourning. He looked serious, and his voice trembled as he began:

"The search for enduring peace and for enduring prosperity begun by President Kennedy . . ." Bobby's hands shook, but he jabbed his right forefinger down onto the paper. He got by the part where he said he would run, but he swallowed when he said, "I recognized that some voters have misgivings about . . . a man . . . who has left the state and who has only recently returned." He jabbed hard again when he told about his parents' New York City apartment and his own schooling in Bronxville.

He wanted to make sure that New York, "the greatest state in the Union," played a leading role at the federal level in solving U.S. problems. He lamented the fact that there had been no Democratic Senator since Herbert Lehman and pledged his talents to New York if he were nominated.

Afterward, Kennedy told newsmen he would not attack Keating's record; he would live in New York, nominated, elected or whatever; noted that Albany was closer to many places in Massachusetts than New York City was; and acknowledged the "carpetbagger" issue needed discussion. Then, his hands clasped behind him, Bobby walked around the greensward, shook hands with starry-eyed people who gathered outside the black grille fences, and played with two of his dogs, enormous creatures named "Panda" and "Battle." Out front, seven pickets carried placards reading: "Go Home Bobby . . . New York For New Yorkers."

In the company of newsmen and Justice Department friends he boarded the "Caroline," and when the plane was airborne, stripped off his coat, rolled up his sleeves and paced the aisle. He talked with everybody about politics. He asked newsmen what Keating's plans were for upstate and city campaigning. What were the ethnic percentages again? New York Teamster Boss Johnny O'Rourke will support me? Good! Then he sat in Jack Kennedy's favorite seat, ordered hot soup, drank it, and ordered more. A newsman, an old friend of the late President and Bobby, saw the similarities and grimaced. "I can't take it. I won't be able to cover this campaign," he said.

At the Democratic National Convention in Atlantic City, Bobby immediately went to Averell Harriman's suite. The press was barred as the New York party faithfuls trooped up, bosses, union leaders, and regulars. There were no reformers in the suite. A photographer who managed to get inside was asked to throw away the pictures he took of Bobby and the bosses. Bobby and Ethel led a procession to the Kennedy Library exhibit on the boardwalk where a large movie screen perpetually showed the late President giving his "Ich bin eine Berliner" speech. Tears came to Ethel's eyes. Bobby's jaw muscles tightened and his eyes moistened slightly. People crowded round.

Upstairs, in the Ritz Carlton, the Democratic mayor of Niagara Falls, E. Dent Lackey, was crying "carpetbagger." Mayor Lackey said, "He has come in here riding an aura of an assassinated President we all adore. I don't believe anyone should ride an aura this way. I don't believe in dynasties."

Lackey's outburst was one of the few flawed moments of the week for Bobby. He went to a reception in his honor, where thousands jammed the room for two hours. The New York *Post's* publisher, Dorothy Schiff, called, "Over here, Arthur, over here," to White House Adviser Arthur Schlesinger, Jr. Congressman Emanuel Celler came by, as did Mrs. Anne (Henry II) Ford and her daughters. Serge Obolensky, leader of New York society's "Russian Rat Pack," Steelworkers' President Dave McDonald, Carmine De Sapio, Eddie Fisher, and scores of party hacks—all were there. The chairmen begged Bobby to campaign in their counties. Bobby stood up high, looked over the swarming room, smiled and cried out kiddingly, "I'm glad to see so many bosses here."

But Thursday was Bobby's big day in Atlantic City. It began simply enough with an appearance before the Kentucky delegation. Newsmen who accompanied him observed that he seemed a little unsettled, withdrawn and more shy than usual. Four years before, at the Democratic National Convention in Los Angeles, he had been completely wrapped up in the task of marshaling delegates for his brother's nomination. Now, in 1964, he was a guest of the convention and would speak to the entire convention only after Lyndon Johnson had been nominated for President. He tried to loosen up a little as he stood before the Kentucky delegates, and reached for one of the familiar remarks about the size of the Kennedy family. "We all want to thank you," he said in what was intended to be humor, "Jackie, Ethel, Pat, Eunice and Jean. Now there are only five or six of us left."

Bobby had attempted to make a funny crack about the clan, but emotion robbed his voice of the witty edge. There were low gasps from the Kentucky delegation and only a few laughed. Even the newsmen, accustomed to observing the full range of human emotion, squirmed a little. Wherever Bobby went that day, he mentioned the late President and a hush resulted. In the afternoon there was a reception for Jackie Kennedy given by Ambassador Averell Harriman, and Bobby stood at her side in the reception line. There were tears in the eyes of many who went through the line.

As Lyndon Johnson had anticipated, the day centered more and more on the Kennedys. The screaming of a crowd on seeing Jackie caused a young woman to run through a plate-glass door; she fell to the cement, her head awash with blood. Nuns pushed against police ropes. Hundreds crushed against the ring of men surrounding Bobby as he inched his way from hotel to hotel along the boardwalk. Then came the night and Bobby's official appearance.

The entire Convention Hall began to stir as Senator Henry Jackson introduced Bobby, and then people stood up and cheered and applauded. By the time Bobby rose, the hall was one enormous roar. Five thousand delegates and alternates stood and cheered and cheered and cheered. Wave after wave of emotional sound broke over Bobby's stooped figure as he stood behind the speaker's lectern. Occasionally he uttered, "Mr. Chairman . . ." but each time the waves increased, and then were punctuated with "WE WANT KENNEDY." Kennedy banners were waved. The convention was caught up in one great outburst of deep feeling. For 13 minutes it went on, Bobby doing little to stop it. He bowed his head, bit his tongue, and unsuccessfully fought the tears back. Hundreds of delegates shed tears along with him as the film was shown. He smiled a little at those portions showing the J.F.K. wit. When the touching strains of "Camelot" were played, Bobby's hand went to his mouth, just as it had that November afternoon at Hickory Hill.

He had to attend one more Democratic convention, this one on September 1. New York's Democrats, 5,500 of them, crowded into an impossibly hot and dusty armory at 34th Street and Park Avenue in Manhattan to nominate a United States Senator they had long been yearning for. The gathering was disorderly, noisy and colorful. There was a blare of Dixieland music, hundreds of bright balloons, ear-piercing klaxons, much shouting and cheering, straw hats and outlandish costumes.

Mayor Wagner sat on the platform, his face a study in Germanic sweat. Carmine De Sapio, retiring as New York State National Committeeman, wore his usual dark glasses, and sat nearby. The convention chairman used a claw hammer on the podium in an attempt to maintain order because the gavel was missing. Above, grouped in a bright cluster, were a dozen members of the Kennedy family. They waved at the swarming delegates on the floor as though they had always lived in New York, not Massachusetts. Sign-waving delegates sat in the galleries around them.

Below the Kennedys and the bunting which decorated the gallery rails, was the jam of delegates, many drinking beer from cans and booze from paper cups. The roll calls of delegates were confused and so were the polls of the delegations. A college student stood up and startled those who could hear him by nominating Adlai Stevenson for Senator. The bewildered chairman, unprepared for introduction of Stevenson's name, nodded to the student and continued to gavel with the claw hammer. Newsmen, soaked in sweat and other fluids, joked about the discordant proceedings. One reporter cracked that if any delegate could honestly claim he heard one speech all the way through he should be awarded the governorship or some other suitable prize. The 1964 New York State Democratic Convention needed only Al Smith, some garters on the men's shirts, and H. L. Mencken to put it in another time. Only the presence of the rigging and tangle of television and radio made it contemporary.

The business before the occupants of the 34th Street armory had really been transacted that morning in a hotel where the State Committee had met. The committee dealt with the fact that Robert Kennedy was not a registered Democrat in New York. Congressman Abe Multer merely introduced a resolution authorizing the committee to allow a Kennedy nomination in order "to avoid controversy and to have a minimum of debate."

At the Convention Sam Stratton pleaded for one last time with the delegates. He declared that Kennedy "isn't even a qualified voter in the State of New York . . . is not an enrolled member of our party. . . . We are setting a far-reaching precedent here." Stratton saw a Kennedy candidacy as discouraging to young people "if famous names and favored circumstances mean a man rises in his party." And he said Kennedy wasn't an automatic winner. He saw an insidious parallel with Nixon's gubernatorial try in California. "Everybody knew Nixon wasn't interested in the governorship, that he was interested in something else."

But Stratton's say was to no avail. The pro-Bobby resolution passed by a five-to-one margin. Later, at the armory, the sweat-soaked delegates finally nominated Bobby by six to one. The speeches, lost in the welter of noise, had some interesting passages.

Congressman Pike, in nominating Stratton, rebuked his own party for its capitulation in selecting Kennedy. He scorned the use of a great "name" to win elections, cited the Morgenthau candidacy where "the illustrious son of an illustrious father [got us] one of the most illustrious shellackings of our illustrious history." He quoted the *Times*, repeated the warning that Massachusetts might have three senators and quoted Adam Clayton Powell's boast that he and other bosses would "name the senatorial candidate." He paused for attention, but didn't get it, when he implored delegates to consider principle. "To those of you who have said privately, 'I know the principle is wrong, but I think he's a winner,' my candidate would say, sadly, 'I understand' [but] principles are like muscles—if you don't use them they atrophy, they wither and they die."

Impassioned as Pike was, neither his speech nor any of the others stirred anyone. The delegates did not want to be bothered. They came to drink beer, visit their friends and get the confounded business of nominating Bobby over with. "That's what we came for, isn't it?" said a Brooklyn gent as he scuttled another beer can. In the balconies the signs waved, pro and con: "Boston Bobby Go Home!" . . . "A Great State Needs a Great Man!" . . . "We Back Bobby!"

In his nominating speech Mayor Wagner droned on about "our candidate . . . a man whose name will add luster to the Democratic ticket of New York . . . whose voice will be heard throughout this land when he raises it in the Senate. . . . All Democrats were proud of the wielder of the nation's sword of justice . . . adviser and brother of the martyred President for whom few of us are beyond the reach of tears. . . ." Naturally such a man is more than welcome in New York, the mayor declared.

The "Mustache Stompers," a whoop-it-up Dixieland band,

whanged away at *Hello, Dolly*. The galleries hollered, the beer cans rolled. A huge portrait of Bobby in shirt sleeves bore the slogan: "Let's Put Bob Kennedy to Work for New York!"

When balloting came to a merciful ending, the band struck up *When Irish Eyes Are Smiling*. The giddy delegates rose as one, expecting Bobby, but, false alarm, it was Sam Stratton to say he accepted the verdict of the convention and wished Bobby well. At this point, the last semblance of order dissolved, and several dozen people, who belonged in their seats or on the convention floor, clambered onto the platform. Those authorized to be on the platform were now jostled around and their chairs were knocked over. Averell Harriman was desperately trying to remain near the center of the platform as Kennedy was summoned to make his appearance and acceptance speech. It took a wedge of his aides and supporters to clear the way for him as he climbed onto the platform. He was wearing his senatorial striped dark suit. The music played on, and the demonstration went 12 minutes, fed by shouts of "We want Bobby!"

Feebly Kennedy lifted his arm. Wagner tried to show him how. Bobby looked especially shy and his eyes were far away. He finally got to his speech. He mentioned President Kennedy and the late Herbert Lehman, then paused for applause. He spoke of his state, New York.

"Where we fail," he cried, "the nation fails. Unless the races can learn to live peacefully in Manhattan, how can they do so in our other large cities? Unless we can bring new industry into Amsterdam [Stratton's home town], where workers have the skills, how can we expect to do so in Appalachia, where they lack them? Unless we meet the cost of education on Long Island, how can we do it in any growing part of suburbia?"

Now his right hand sawed the air as his brother's had hundreds of times. "I know where I stand," Kennedy cried stridently. "I am for Lyndon Johnson. I am against Barry Goldwater. No other candidate for the Senate from New York is willing to make either statement. . . ." (Senator Kenneth B. Keating, had stated he would neither support nor oppose Goldwater.)

. . . "I am aware of the difficulties I face in seeking this office . . . My candidacy establishes no precedent. There have been very similar cases around the country and here in New York. The first Senator from New York, Rufus King, was from Massachusetts. He served the state well."

He pursued the theme that New York deserves Democratic representation in the Senate, a senator "who will not only vote but initiate." Bobby ended with a quote from John Peter Zenger. "It is not the cause of New York alone that we are trying," Bobby quoted. "It is the best cause. It is the cause of liberty."

The Democrats, all candidates for tubs and showers after five hours of milling around and beering it up, applauded and cheered in appreciation that it was over.

Bobby waved and focused on a klieglighted section of the right balcony. There were Ethel and seven of Bobby's children; Eunice Shriver and her 10-year old son; Patricia Lawford and son Christopher; and Steve Smith's wife, Jean. The Kennedy women were splendid and sparkling. The "Mustache Stompers" hit *Happy Days Are Here Again* with what they had left. Eunice smiled broadly, acknowledged Bobby's wave with a responding wave of her own white-gloved hand. The Kennedys were back at it again.

IX
CAMPAIGN FOR THE SENATE

□□
□□

IT WAS AUDACIOUS OF KENNEDY to run for the Senate in New York. He was an authentic carpet-bagger. While his publicity proclaimed he had spent 12 of his first 13 years in the state, he was still a son of his native Massachusetts. He waited, in fact, until the day before the Democratic National Convention opened in Atlantic City before he resigned as a member of the Massachusetts delegation. He was a registered voter in Barnstable, Mass., until October 15, when he removed his name from the voting lists. Bobby moved to New York too late to be eligible to vote there and so he did not vote at all in the 1964 election.* He had political ties to New York, of course. Bobby had worked in the state for his brother in 1960. Bobby had urged New York Democrats to nominate Morgenthau for governor in 1962, and he had kept in touch regularly with Democratic leaders and his brother-in-law Steve Smith during the years of the Kennedy Administration in Washington. But Bobby Kennedy had no more business running for the Senate in New York State than did, say, a Richard Nixon, who was eligible to vote in New York. Nevertheless, Bobby ran, with considerable risk. He ran because he wanted to continue his career, because he wanted to sustain and develop his political power and

---

* Thus, Bobby could not and did not vote for President Johnson and his Brother Teddy.

187

because New York's floundering Democrats could not find another candidate who looked like a winner.

At the time Bobby starred at the Democratic National Convention in Atlantic City, polls and form sheets showed him a runaway winner against incumbent Senator Kenneth B. Keating. The political rule of thumb holds that an incumbent Senator: 1. Is better known than his challenger. 2. Starts with a lead because of the benefits of past publicity and favors he has dispensed. 3. Disdains to attack; and instead places himself as the man with a solid record whose job must be taken from him. In the Keating-Kennedy race the pre-campaign situation was reversed. Kennedy was infinitely better known than Keating. He was 21 points ahead in Keating's own polls. It was Keating the incumbent who had to attack, because Kennedy, initially at least, could coast on his name.

Keating could not defeat Kennedy. Bobby could only lose to Keating. The Kennedy name; the heavy voting edge Democrats and Liberals enjoyed over Republicans; the fact that the budding Conservative Party threatened to siphon away 250,000 precious Republican votes from Keating with their own Senate candidate Professor Henry Paolucci; and the pall of the Goldwater candidacy in a state where the early polls showed Johnson winning two to one— all conspired to make many a Republican shake his head and say, "Poor old Ken. Boy, is he in for it."

Yet there would be a fight. No one knew it better than Bobby himself. All the indications were that he would win easily, but Bobby had been through enough campaigns to know that appearances cannot be trusted in politics. One of the great lessons the Kennedys learned in this respect was the Ohio campaign of 1960 where enormous crowds turned out for John Kennedy and where all the signs were for a Kennedy victory. Richard Nixon won Ohio by a wide margin.

Republicans in New York State were publicly outraged over the carpetbagger, Kennedy; and, of course, they were afraid a Kennedy victory might mean unification of the long-divided Democratic Party. The New York G.O.P. is known for its self-discipline and unity. The call went out that Keating must be saved, and rallying round were Senator Jacob Javits, Governor Rockefeller, Richard Nixon, Congressman John Lindsay and former President Eisenhower, former Governor Thomas E. Dewey, former Attorney General Herbert Brownell and Thomas Stephens, onetime presidential secretary. Walter Thayer, publisher of the New York *Herald Tribune*, came forth to raise $671,000. Republican professionals pressed labor leaders, spokesmen for racial and ethnic groups and whoever was friendly in the arts, to repay past favors to help "Keep Keating." The party was determined to throw everything it had against Bobby. Javits in particular could be counted on to wage total war because a Kennedy victory might mean a Javits eclipse.

The first Republican barrage was the cry, "Carpetbagger!" Keating welcomed Bobby to New York, said he would be "glad to furnish him with a guidebook, road map and other useful literature . . . which any sojourner would find helpful." Bobby, Keating cracked, "thinks the Gowanus Canal is part of the lower intestinal tract," and he reminded Kennedy that Montauk Point was on Long Island, not Cape Cod. As for Senator Rufus King, the Massachusetts resident who moved to New York and was elected to the U.S. Senate in 1789, it was romance, not politics which brought him to New York. G.O.P. State Campaign Director Michael Scelsi said Bobby "has thrown his diaper into the ring . . . into the wrong playpen."

There was an echo of the noise reform Democrats had made about Bobby coming to New York. And there was indignation. "I was so burned up over this Kennedy candidacy," said Herbert Brownell, who managed Keating's campaign, "that I got back into politics. If he is elected, it will establish that a rich man can come in, make a deal with bosses and change our whole constitutional system."

To this criticism, Kennedy retorted, "Let's assume I'm using this as a power base . . . Let's just assume the worst. I can't go any place in 1968; we have a President. He'll have my support. I'm going to have to do an outstanding job in the Senate, if the people all over the country demand that I be the [1972] candidate. So I don't see how New York suffers."

The campaign chart, which Kennedy men actually drew, showed Bobby with an early "convention halo" high and then rolling downhill through September as the carpetbagger charge was broadcast. The counterstrategy was for Bobby to immerse himself in great oceans of people to show them he wore not horns—just unruly hair, a sheepish smile, and dearly prized cuff links given him by his late brother. In his first week of campaigning, Bobby was seen by nearly 500,000 people.

He flew in the "Caroline" to Syracuse, where a fairground crowd of 20,000 heard him quip that he was rapidly becoming unemployed in Washington, that's why he came to New York. Furthermore, "I brought nine and a half other Kennedys with me to New York* I challenge any other candidate to make that statement."

Bobby seemed to be loved by everyone who turned out to see him. Nuns came running from their schoolrooms to see him. Old ladies wept. Dozens of girls, who managed to touch Bobby's hand, screamed deliriously, "I'll never wash it—he touched me." One girl actually ran around in circles and pulled at her hair. Some of the wild-eyed fans thrust books of memorabilia about John Kennedy and his assassination at Bobby for autographing. In downtown Syracuse, a middle-aged lady, caught in a swarm of people around Bobby's open, white convertible, cried out to a nun on the corner: "Oh, he's going to win just like Jack! Just like Jack!" A Democratic judge, watching from a safe distance, remarked, "When I see those people reaching for him excitedly, it makes me think they are really reaching for Jack. They want to get to Jack through Bobby."

On Sunday, September 6, there was panic on the beaches. The Kennedy troops were unprepared for the pubescent masses which ran from the sun-drenched sand on Long Island to the boardwalks, where Bobby was crushed. "There he is!" cried a teen-ager, "the one with the mussed-up, dirty blond hair." A girl in hysteria tugged at her bikini and screeched, "God, he's gorgeous." Bobby

---

* *The reference to Ethel's pregnancy was written by Gerald Gardner, one of the scriptwriters for the satirical TV program,* That Was the Week That Was. *Gardner constantly scurried about with "one liners" for Kennedy to use in the initial effort to project Bobby as warm, human and wonderful. Gardner told reporters that he was so devoted to the late President and Bobby that he volunteered to help him with his Senate campaign. Reporters were impressed with such sacrifice, particularly from the high-salaried Gardner, but the impression was erased after the campaign when the record books showed Gardner was paid $10,000 "for professional services"—eight weeks' work as joke writer.*

scrambled on top of the stairs at a bathhouse, waved and said, "Have a nice swim . . . I wish I was going with you. I'm glad we had a quiet time at the beach." The crowd became so frantic, Bobby ran like a trapped Beatle to the safety of a waiting car.

On September 9, Kennedy drew the largest crowds any candidate for the U.S. Senate has ever received in this country. Anyone following Bobby that day through upstate, Republican New York would have thought it was a presidential candidate who was campaigning. The reaction in Buffalo astounded the most jaded political reporters in Kennedy's party.

The "Caroline" landed two hours late that night. Downtown at the Buffalo Club, leading businessmen and community leaders were waiting for Bobby and were well into their highballs. The Kennedy motorcade started on the 10-mile trip from the airport down Genesee Avenue to downtown Buffalo. It took more than an hour because the streets were swarming with 150,000 excited people who screamed and waved signs, "We Love Bobby . . . Bobby for Senate . . . Bobby for President." People spilled onto the street, frustrating and angering scores of cops trying to keep order. Bobby's open convertible was stopped by a congestion of people. Desperate clawing hands tore the clothes of his aides. Bobby half waved, half smiled, and spent most of his time trying to stay upright in the back seat. Negro neighborhoods went wild. A Negro policeman momentarily stopped trying to hold back the crowd, applauded and cheered Kennedy as he passed by. The motorcade inched along in the red glare of railroad flares on curbstones. Finally someone made the decision to short-cut the route and speed down an unadvertised avenue.

Kennedy hurried into the Buffalo Club, hastily changed shirts and made a shy entry into the cocktail party nearly three hours late. The candidate was quickly introduced by John M. Galvin, chief executive officer of the Marine Trust Company of Western New York. Bobby brushed his hair back and said:

"I've been all over the state talking Medicare today and when I came into Buffalo tonight I thought I needed it myself. The Kennedys always felt Buffalo was a second home. My brother felt that way. President Kennedy ran on the idea of getting this country moving again. We are now in the longest period of prosperity this country ever enjoyed—42 months. People said we weren't the businessmen's friends. How in the hell could you have a better friend?

"My brother used to say when the market went down it was a Kennedy market. When it went up it was due to free enterprise. Well, we made an effort to get going in the past three and one-half years. We made a start. We must continue with other programs, health, education, too.

"I don't want to retire even though I'm getting old. I could retire on my daddy's money. But I'd rather work. I'd rather be in public service. I want to represent New York. I want to be Senator."

Bobby said this as though he meant it, and the men were charmed and thrilled. For men with ruffled feelings, they gave him good applause. Bobby thanked them and left for other waiting audiences, an overflow meeting of the Buffalo AFL-CIO, and then 4,000 cheering fans at the Erie County Democratic Committee meeting at Kleinhan's Music Hall.

It had been that way the whole 18-hour day. On Pulaski Street in Johnson City, Polish-Americans cheered and wished him long life. In Binghamton, he talked about unemployment and then admiringly quoted Theodore Dreiser, "It was a great town for girls." In downtown Jamestown, where the Republican vice-presidential candidate William Miller had attracted only 300 people, the streets were jammed with 4,000. When Bobby arrived at the Mark Twain Hotel in Elmira, the crowd wouldn't let him get out of the campaign car. There was a small crisis in Elmira, where Mark Twain is buried. Kennedy wanted a sampling of Twain wit, and jokeman Gardner didn't have any. A couple of quick phone calls produced some substitute lines by Will Rogers.

"I'm going to stay in New York," Bobby told the crowds. Wherever he went, he brought up his brother's name and 1960, and declared "a start was made and we must continue." There was lipstick on his cheeks, his hands and chin were scratched. His thumbs jerked upward as he talked. "Does it make any sense," he implored, "to have two Republican Senators from New York?" He smiled broadly when crowds roared "No." His attack on Keating was oblique. "If a man can't make up his mind about Goldwater," Bobby cried, "he should vote for me. I'm for Lyndon Johnson. I'm against

Barry Goldwater. I don't need a guidebook to know that. I am the only candidate who is against Barry Goldwater."

Between stops, Bobby was quickly briefed on the next locality, was handed three-by-five index cards. Some of these cards had literary quotations written on them, some contained a local fact designed to stir his audience or what might be called a "non sequitur statistic." An example of the latter was Bobby's earnest question: "Do you realize half the people in South America are under 25 years of age?"

In that three-day swing through 21 upstate cities, Bobby revived Democratic sentiment where Republicanism had been successful, though sedentary. Kennedy tapped the partisan feelings of Catholics and sparked the enthusiasm of others neglected by Republicans and appalled at the thought of Goldwater. Though Buffalo's crowd was the largest, Glens Falls' (a town of 21,000) was even more significant. Kennedy's plane arrived there at one a.m., five hours late, and yet there was a cheering throng of 4,000 waiting to see him, many of them in pajamas. The implications of this event made local Republican professionals shudder.

Yet when the "Caroline" was aloft, and Kennedy could meditate over soft-boiled eggs, roast beef and beer, he told his aides, and some reporters, too, that the crowds alone weren't convincing. Jack Kennedy had made similar observations in Ohio in 1960. He was blunting the carpetbagger charge, but he knew there was sympathy for Ken Keating. Bobby stared out of the window of the plane; and everybody sensed that he wanted to be alone. He would crook a finger and one of his staffers would come to give him an inhalator for a stuffy nose, a new batch of three-by-five cards, a list of the local Democrats whose names must be mentioned. Bobby was moving slowly from his experience of being the campaign manager to being the campaigner.

Kenneth B. Keating, though 64, was of postwar vintage in politics. In earlier years, he had been contented with the reputation of being "the best lawyer in Rochester." As is the case with many a contemporary public figure, however, Keating's wartime experiences made him restless. He became an Army volunteer shortly after Pearl Harbor, and spent most of World War II in the China-Burma-India theater of operations in intelligence work. When he was discharged as a major in 1945, he found life in Rochester a little too quiet and decided to run for Congress in 1946. He won in a "safe" Republican district and was re-elected five times. As a Congressman, Keating won himself credentials as a solid, middle-of-the-road Republican in the Eisenhower years. A graduate of Harvard Law School, he was an effective member of the Congressional Judiciary Committee. Keating vastly enjoyed life in Washington. He became very popular with his fellow Congressmen and Senators and was an accepted member of the Senate's "club," an organization which exists only in the minds of Senators, and whose membership is made up of those Senators who are considered "good guys" or "regular fellows." Because of his amiability and availability, Keating was sought out by Washington hostesses as a dinner guest.

In 1958, Keating was considered ready for the Senate by New York G.O.P. leaders. He had been a successful Congressman, and he would not have to campaign against incumbent Senator Herbert Lehman, because Lehman was retiring and a new Democratic candidate, New York District Attorney Frank Hogan, was the nominee. Keating had other qualities which help a candidate. He possessed a fine white mane of hair, twinkling blue eyes and the constant smile of a man saying "ah" for his dentist. His lateral vision was so acute he could spot a hand to shake off to the side while smiling at the person in front of him. He was and is a joiner in the Major Hoople tradition. He held memberships in the Moose, Elks, Eagles, Shriners, Kiwanis, American Legion, Veterans of Foreign Wars and Sons of the American Revolution. Among his citations are the Freedom Award of the American Committee for the Independence of Armenia and the Badischer Maennercher of B'nai B'rith. He had also been cited by the United Anti-Communist Action Committee, the Jewish Nazi Victims Organization of America, and the Polish Airborne Veterans Club.

But having a good record as a Congressman, being an amiable joiner and looking like a Senator were not enough. Keating squeaked to victory in 1958 by only 132,000 votes thanks to a coattail ride provided by a political upstart named Nelson A. Rockefeller.

Keating had a battle on his hands in 1964, Kennedy or no. Private polls taken for the Republican Party showed he could defeat either Mayor Wagner or Congressman Stratton, and it was essential that he should declare himself to be an Independent-Republican. Unless a Republican candidate, for state or national office, cracks the Democratic, Liberal and independent voting groups, he does not get elected in New York State. Keating was banking on his record as an accomplished Senator of liberal reputation and also on an amazingly low "antipathy quotient" of only six. "Antipathy quotient" means the number of people out of a sampling of 100 who express some form of major objection to a public person like the President, a Senator or a Congressman. The objection could be based on the man's views, his record, the cut of his suit, his manner of speaking, even the way he looks on television. The "antipathy quotient" system was developed by Cy Chaikin, partner in the New York City polling firm of Bennett-Chaikin. The lowest "antipathy quotient" recorded by Bennett-Chaikin before Keating's was that for President Eisenhower, who had an "A.Q." of only seven in 1956. A rating of 20 or more is considered dangerous in the game of politics. In 1964, President Johnson's was 17. Bobby Kennedy had 36, but the Bennett-Chaikin study showed that even those people who disliked Kennedy thought they might vote for him anyway. The studies also showed that nine out of ten Republicans in New York approved of Keating's Senate performance, that four out of five Democrats and Independents also approved. But study revealed another problem for Keating. While 44 percent of eligible, male voters in New York were for him, and 41 percent for Kennedy, only 37 percent of the eligible female voters favored Keating compared with the 46 percent who liked Bobby. And there are more women than men voters.

Even more perilous was Goldwater's high A.Q. of 47. Furthermore, a study conducted in August showed that only 33 percent of New York's Republicans had committed themselves to vote for Goldwater in 1964. The same study indicated the majority of New York Republicans opposed Goldwater on the five key issues of the campaign.

Keating had no choice. What his boosters called "bravery" was also political necessity. He had to refuse to support Goldwater. There was going to be an enormous vote for Johnson. Keating had to give Republicans, Democrats and independents cause to split their tickets. So on August 18, when he announced his candidacy, Keating's face turned grim as he told newsmen, "I cannot in good conscience conceal my convictions behind a façade of conformity disguised as unity. I seriously doubt that any voter in New York would be impressed by any lip service I might give Senator Goldwater."

His decision not to support the standard-bearer of his party brought immediate benefits. Many Democrats approached Keating during the early part of the campaign to shake his hand earnestly and promise their vote because "you had the courage to fight Goldwater." In not supporting the Republican presidential candidate, Keating took on an independent, underdog image. Then, when the dazzling Kennedy made his gigantic entrance, there was even more sympathy for the Republican Senator.

Keating lost votes on the Goldwater question too. In Ogdensburg one afternoon, two old ladies shook their fingers and demanded, "Why aren't you for Mr. Goldwater? We won't vote for you if you aren't for him." Keating quickly replied, "Well, if you want the other fellow, all right . . ." At a Republican rally at Bullshead picnic grounds on Staten Island, Keating clambered through the litter of beer cans and ice-cream wrappers onto a flat-bed truck which carried a large red-and-white banner reading: THE GOLDWATER TEAM. While a speaker lauded Goldwater, Keating pursed his mouth. At Republican meetings everywhere there was a mixture of Goldwater and Keating signs, and occasionally, some posters with photographs of Henry Paolucci, the Conservative Party candidate, who did support Goldwater. Kennedy forever reminded audiences he was the only candidate *against* Goldwater. Though he was needled by Kennedy and criticized from the right, Keating, on balance, was slightly ahead on the Goldwater issue.

When the September crowds dissolved, the "carpetbagger" and "bossism" tags remained pinned to Bobby. In New York City, Jews and Italian-Americans—who usually vote Democratic—voiced reservations about Kennedy. Many Democrats of liberal persuasion, not necessarily reformers either, thrashed over Bobby's controversial record on civil liberties, the McCarthy period, and easily revived memories of Old Joe. They also complained that Bobby was talking in generalities, was running on his brother's name, and wallowed in swarms of teen-agers—all *verboten* behavior for Pure Liberals.

Under the leadership of Gore Vidal and the late Lisa Howard, a blond television personality, a spirited group bearing the banner "Democrats for Keating" was mustered. Among the illustrious enlistees were Harvard Historian Arthur Schlesinger Sr.; Mrs. Marshall Field; Poet Archibald MacLeish; Carey McWilliams, editor of *The Nation;* Mrs. Agnes E. Meyer, widow of the late publisher of the Washington *Post;* David Susskind; Robert K. Bingham, managing editor of *The Reporter;* Barbara Tuchman, author of one of JFK's favorite books, *The Guns of August;* actor Paul Newman; Bill Todman of Goodson-Todman Productions; Mrs. Frederick Guggenheim; and Joseph Heller, author of *Catch 22.* Johnson-Keating buttons were circulated by the Democrats for Keating organization, and it became fashionable for certain liberals to wear them because the buttons were provocative and caused conversation.

The Keating campaign was building. Herbert Brownell, one of the shrewdest men in politics, stressed that it was an independent campaign, yet he was also able to recruit the best Republican troops in the state to work for Keating. He successfully coaxed several Republican county chairmen who were pro-Goldwater into tardy endorsements of Keating. The New York State Republican Party quickly raised a million dollars to be added to the independent campaign fund raised by Walter Thayer. In Washington, Keating even got quiet support from several Democratic colleagues on Capitol Hill, among them Alaska's Democratic Senator Ernest Gruening. Money from New York City Jewish voters, usually given to the Democratic National Committee in Washington, came in special gifts to Keating. The cry, "Let's Keep Keating," was loud by the first week in October.

In any other year, the size of Keating's crowds would have attracted no particular attention. But because of the thousands of people who swarmed around Bobby, the modest clusters which Keating attracted seemed significant. Newsmen could hardly avoid comparing the 30 placid Republicans who greeted Keating at Watertown, New York, with the 1,200 people who shouted for Bobby when he landed there. Keating bravely cried, "Glad to see you," to the straggling groups who met him, though his blue eyes betrayed his disappointment. Even in his hometown of Rochester, which had always given him good support, only 2,000 people turned out for him while Kennedy drew 20,000. When one of Keating's aides was informed that 150,000 people had jammed Buffalo's streets to see Bobby, he asked incredulously, "Were they all adults?"

Beset with adversity, Keating turned to humor. When his plane landed at the wrong airport in the Catskills, leaving his reception committee stranded elsewhere, Keating hurried to the control tower to salvage a few handshakes. When he roamed through a huge discount store upstate only to find a dozen hands to shake, he told one farmer, "I'm working on the theory cows are Republicans. That'll help." Often he looked out on a crowd of 40 earnest faces and said, "I am grateful for the nice showing of adults we have here tonight. . . . My opponent is putting on the biggest road show in this state since the Beatles." Once, at the Albany airport, newsmen surrounded him, but Keating's eye caught sight of a dozen people in the waiting room. He broke away, showed his wide smile over his shoulder and called out, "Do you think I am going to pass up an opportunity like this?"

There were other situations to make people feel sorry for Kenneth Keating. He went before the New York State AFL-CIO, cited his voting record, considered 80 percent "correct" by that labor organization's standards, and with sadness and humor in his voice, quipped, "I don't think any baseball team would get rid of a man who batted .800. That's better than Babe Ruth or Mickey Mantle." There were some cheers for Keating, but his long friendship with labor was ignored. Instead an endorsement for Kennedy was rammed through under the direction of Ray Corbett, president of the state organization. There was instantaneous pleasure expressed in Washington by AFL-CIO President George Meany, an old friend of Bobby's. But Meany's delight wasn't that spontaneous. He had urged Corbett and other New York State AFL-CIO officials to endorse Kennedy. The leaders of organized labor, with the exception of the Teamsters, were for Bobby because they figured him to be a winner and wanted to go where the power would ultimately be. But Keating persisted in his pursuit of labor, picked up the support of union

barbers and bartenders, who he said "really help, because they talk
to everybody."

Keating attended a longshoremen's banquet, took a bow,
and as he left, Joe Curran, president of the National Maritime
Union, grabbed him by the arm and said, "It was brave of you to
come here. They [the AFL-CIO] did a lousy thing to you. Bobby
never did a damned thing for labor."

Accounts of the daily reversals Keating experienced and the
overwhelming presence of a big name, Kennedy, stimulated interest
in the lesser-known Keating. As the underdog candidate, defending
himself against Bobby, Keating had unusual attention paid to him,
and he moved to explain why he should be kept as Senator.

"I seek no other reward," Keating said virtuously, "and
have no other ambition than to continue my service to the people of
the Empire State. . . . I've got this on my opponent, I can vote for
myself. It may seem immodest, but I'm going to vote for myself
because I think I'm better than him."

Keating, in his reversed role as challenger, attacked. Kennedy, he declared, "is a glamorous political hitchhiker . . . a Bobby-
come-lately." He couldn't figure out whether Bobby "is running for
President of the United States or is looking for some kind of new
federal job like Commissioner of the Northeast." As for Bobby
doing more for New York, Keating, in an effort to split Democrats,
said, "I know Lyndon Johnson. No freshman Senator is going down
to the White House and tell the President what he wants done. . . .
If my opponent isn't good enough for President Johnson, he's not
good enough for New York State. We should elect a man and not
a name. . . ."

"The only issue in this campaign," Keating declared indignantly, "is my record. My opponent won't attack my record, and I
agree with him. My record is good. If he can't find anything wrong
with my record, what's wrong with sending me back to the Senate
for six years?"

Indeed, Keating's record suited many political temperaments.
As a Congressman, he had supported Eisenhower 75 percent of the
time, as a Senator, 79 percent of the time. Additionally, he supported Presidents Kennedy and Johnson on 70 percent of their legis-

lative proposals. He opposed Goldwater on all 25 issues Republicans considered consistent with the 1960 platform. Keating had voted for the United Nations loan; the Nuclear Test-Ban Treaty; the 1964 Foreign Assistance Act; the National Defense Education Act of 1953; the Medical Education Construction and Student Loan program. He was in the mainstream of Republican thinking.

The longer he was in the Senate, the more liberal Keating became. He supported eight federal-aid programs for education between 1958 and 1964. He voted for the Federal Housing Acts of 1949, 1954, 1961 and 1964 and cosponsored, with Javits, a bill which would provide aid to middle-income housing projects. In the area of labor legislation, Keating voted for the Area Redevelopment Act, the Manpower Retraining Act, for extension of the Unemployment Compensation Act, for the establishment of vocational-training programs and aid to children of the unemployed. Twice—in 1962 and in 1964—he voted for Medicare programs which included financing under the Social Security System. In 1964, he cosponsored, again with Javits, an amendment to the Medicare bill which would have broadened its coverage and also allowed older people to participate, on a voluntary basis, in private insurance programs, with the Government making payments to the people. Keating also voted for anti-poverty measures, youth programs and the Food Stamp Plan, which provided for the distribution of surplus food to people in depressed areas.

Keating had an excellent record in civil-rights legislation dating back to the time he was a Congressman. His name was one of several on the 1957 Civil Rights Bill. He wrote the provisions in the 1960 bill which gave the Justice Department and the FBI the power to apprehend those who bombed homes or churches to intimidate people. Keating also helped write the voting-rights provision of the 1964 Civil Rights Act.

In his 18 years on the Hill, Keating had compiled a first-rate voting and attendance record. He had also uttered enough words —on both the House and Senate floors—to fill a closet full of Congressional Directories. If he was lacking in any way, it was in not having his name alone on a piece of major legislation. Keating had coauthored, in the House, and cosponsored, in the Senate, many major bills as well as amendments. Indeed, Keating was in the top

10 percent with respect to the volume of legislation he advanced; but somehow, Keating's bills often wound up bearing the names of several legislators and therefore he never got full credit. He does have the distinction, however, of being one of only two living Senators who authored an amendment to the Constitution—the amendment giving the residents of the District of Columbia the right to vote in national elections.

By 1964 Keating had a reputation as a good Senator, a Liberal Republican whom right-wing organizations condemned. He was an unquestioned liberal on civil rights, and his friendship for minority groups was proven. And he had achieved some success, and had gained considerable favorable publicity, through his efforts to alert the American people about the placement of Soviet missiles in Communist Cuba in 1962. Keating was effective in revealing information about the missile buildup which the Kennedy Administration had either denied or concealed. Yet despite his record and the publicity he had enjoyed, Keating needed considerable help in his campaign against Bobby.

No man in New York could punch Kennedy around more than Senator Jacob Javits. Javits is New York's best vote getter, and Keating was eager to follow Javits' suggestions. One afternoon, in a station wagon rattling over Manhattan's streets, Javits coached Keating.

"There are three or four Jewish delicatessens," Javits explained, "which are very, very important. Back in 1954 when I ran against Roosevelt [F.D.R. Jr.], he was mobbed. People hysterically pulled his clothes. There was almost a riot. Everyone said I was behind three to one. But I did fine at those delicatessens. I beat Roosevelt by 173,000 votes."

"Is that so?" Keating said, looking at the Senator who had carried New York by 960,000 votes in 1962. Keating was listening to the campaigner who had also defeated Bob Wagner in 1956. Kennedy was respectful of the senior Senator and often asked reporters what Javits was likely to be up to next. Because when Javits talked, Jews and Liberals listened. On statewide television and in public appearances, Javits questioned Kennedy's qualifications as a "liberal," the magic word in New York.

Javits was "troubled" with Kennedy's performance on civil

rights. He said Bobby, as Attorney General, was "seemingly insensitive" for 30 months to appeals for civil-rights legislation, an attitude which Negro leaders found difficult to understand. Javits had described one part of Kennedy's testimony on pending civil-rights legislation as a "tragic retreat" even "before the battle has begun." Furthermore, Javits declared, Bobby had authorized the appointment of federal judges in the South who had "strong segregationist views," including Judge William H. Cox of Mississippi, who had referred to Negro plaintiffs in a voting case as "a bunch of niggers."

Javits was also "troubled" about Bobby's allowing FBI agents to rouse newsmen in the middle of the night at the time of the steel-company crisis in 1962; about "his failure . . . to fight for liberalized immigration legislation which Senator Keating and I had introduced . . ."; about "his sponsorship of wiretapping legislation without judicial safeguards." He also noted that Kennedy had allied himself with New York's Democratic bosses rather than the reform movement "founded by Herbert Lehman and Eleanor Roosevelt." Javits said he was appalled by Bobby's "cynicism" in coming to New York to "use it as a political springboard, and resigning as Attorney General at the eleventh hour" to displace a fine man like Keating.

All these were stiff punches indeed. But Javits' most powerful blow was his statement that "Robert Kennedy owes the liberals in our state an explanation of why he chose to make his start in public life by joining the staff of Senator Joseph McCarthy's investigations subcommittee in January, 1953, at a time when Senator McCarthy's record on civil liberties and reckless charges was already too clear."

Joseph McCarthy suggests Hitler to most New York Jews. Any association with McCarthy, fairly or unfairly drawn, makes Jews draw back, whether they are Democrats or not. Javits, and to a greater degree the Reform Democrats, talked up Bobby's affiliation with McCarthy to hold off the nominally Jewish (and liberal) commitment to the Democratic candidate. The rumor that one of Bobby's eight children had, as a godfather, the late Senator Joe McCarthy, was circulated in New York City. And Lisa Howard, who was suspended from her job at the American Broadcasting

Company for her political activities, was showing a letter around which she described as proof.

The letter was from a prominent New York attorney who is a Republican and who served as Assistant U.S. Attorney in the Eisenhower Administration. He had written the letter to Gore Vidal, whose dislike of Bobby had been publicly and widely expressed. In the letter, the New York attorney recounted a conversation he had with Bobby in 1956 when the two men discussed politics. Bobby, according to the attorney, told him the Republicans had eliminated a man Bobby considered their very best—Senator Joseph McCarthy. The attorney said he expressed great surprise with Bobby's statement, and was startled when Bobby emphasized his point by telling the attorney he thought so well of McCarthy that he made him godfather to one of his children.

Herb Brownell did not plan to discourage the Vidal-Howard group from using the letter in the campaign against Kennedy. As it turned out, the letter was mentioned in only one news story during the campaign and was never published in its entirety. But the rumor was spread among many Reform Democrats that Joe McCarthy was indeed godfather to one of Bobby's children and Gore Vidal had a letter to prove it.

Senator Joe McCarthy's widow, Mrs. G. Joseph Minetti, energetically denied the godfather rumor, and yelled to a reporter, "They are trying to smear Bobby, whom I love, and my dead husband." Her present husband, a member of the Civil Aeronautics Board, spent some time helping in Bobby's Senate campaign office.

Another McCarthy story circulated by Vidal and some reformers concerned Paul Newman, the actor. Bobby wanted Newman to play himself—Kennedy—in the movie based on Bobby's best-selling book, *The Enemy Within.* Newman told Vidal that he tried to persuade Bobby the movie wouldn't work out because the "villain," Jimmy Hoffa, was still a free citizen. In the conversation, Newman told Bobby he was planning to narrate a film, *Point of Order,* based on the Army-McCarthy hearings. Newman said Bobby became angry on hearing this, and told Newman he should not be part of such a project. Newman quarreled with Kennedy over this suggestion. As it turned out, the producers of *Point of Order* decided to do without a narration by Newman. A few months after the episode involving Bobby and Newman, the actor joined Vidal in criticizing Bobby as a senatorial candidate and became a member of the Democrats for Keating organization.

There was a certain logic in the attack on Kennedy. Javits' two-fisted assault was to soften him; associating Bobby's name with McCarthy was to be the punch which sent Bobby reeling; the charges concerning the General Aniline case were to send him down for the count. But as the former light-heavyweight champion of the world, venerable Archie Moore, once said, "There are punches which knock you out, and there are punches which knock you *to*."*

The punch intended for the knockout was thrown under the expert guidance of Herbert Brownell. But the blow only served to knock Kennedy "to" and gave him the hoped-for opportunity to hit back. Brownell, as Attorney General, had dealt with the sale of the General Aniline and Film Corporation, a multimillion-dollar corporation, seized from the giant German chemical cartel, I. G. Farben, during World War II. Brownell and six other Attorneys General had wrestled with suits filed by Interhandel, a Swiss holding company, which claimed it owned 89 percent of Aniline's stock. The United States argued that Interhandel was a "front" for I. G. Farben, which had exploited Jewish slave labor. There were suits and countersuits, claims and counterclaims, from 1948 to 1962. The U.S. Department of Justice was just plain weary of the Aniline case. It was late in Bobby's administration of the department that a settlement was agreed on, and at that time neither Senator Keating nor Senator Javits offered any noticeable protest with the terms of settlement. The arrangement was that the U.S. would sell 89 percent of the stock on the open market, splitting the proceeds 50-50 with Interhandel. The U.S. got the entire amount from the sale of the remaining 11 percent. Thus Aniline was once again a privately owned and operated concern. Interhandel was satisfied with its cash settlement. And the U.S. Government had rid itself of a snaggly, protracted problem.

---

* *Uttered by Archie after his sensational championship fight with the Canadian slugger, Yvon Durelle, in 1958. Archie was knocked down four times before he revived and flattened Durelle in the 11th round.*

But there were suspicions about the deal, largely among Jewish groups. Shortly before the Keating-Kennedy campaign opened, Abraham Kraditor, former national commander of the Jewish War Veterans, wanted to know the precise details and voiced suspicion about the Aniline settlement. Keating's managers felt a strong statement by the Senator on the Aniline case would be useful in the campaign.

With Brownell coaching, Keating issued a lengthy position paper which charged, in effect, that Attorney General Kennedy had made a deal with a "huge Nazi cartel." Keating said later he wasn't questioning Kennedy's motives, only his procedures, and certainly his opponent wasn't guilty of any "heinous crime." But the implication was that Bobby had thoughtlessly risked the return of money to former Nazis.

At this point in late September, according to his political enemies, Bobby Kennedy was a carpetbagger, a foot-dragger on civil rights, basking in his martyred brother's glory, a onetime associate and pal of Joe McCarthy, a would-be wiretapper, and now, a benefactor of former Nazis. And there was poor Ken Keating, liberal, victimized, the accomplished Senator, underdog, courageous resister of Goldwater and Goldwaterism, the kindly, white-haired New Yorker.

If there was one point in the campaign when Keating was ahead, it was during the first week in October. Kennedy's private poll showed Keating with 40 percent of the vote, Kennedy with 39, and 21 percent "not sure." Keating's own poll showed Kennedy leading with 44 percent, Keating at 41, and the remaining 15 percent "undecided." But Keating's poll showed a trend manifesting itself for the Republican Senator. Offsetting this, however, was another study taken by the Keating organization which showed a discouraging fatalism among those who said they would vote for the Senator. Three out of four voters who said they were for Keating also stated they thought he would *lose* to Kennedy. "We needed a shot of confidence," Keating explained later. "We tried to get the bandwagon going that first week in October. That's why I announced that if the election were held then, I'd win."

Kennedy had anticipated this low. One month before, he had told Ethel, "The first week in October will be our worst time."

Samuel Lubell, the self proclaimed unscientific pollster, wrote, "Robert Kennedy is running well behind Senator Kenneth Keating," and attributed this to a break "against Kennedy among normally Democratic voters in New York City."

The Kennedy staff conferences at the Carlyle Hotel livened up. Debs Myers, a crafty Kansan who served as Mayor Wagner's press secretary, had argued all through the campaign for Kennedy to identify himself with Johnson for one simple reason: Johnson would win New York in a landslide, so Kennedy should go with the big winner. The early strategy had been to present Bobby as a friendly, nice guy, not the overbearing fellow his enemies said he was. Kennedy was not to attack the white-haired Senator, because this would provoke charges of "ruthlessness." The slogan was "Let's Put Bob Kennedy to Work for New York," and the candidate was shown in shirtsleeves, all set to go. Kennedy would be *better* for New York and give it the Democratic representation it deserved.

But now the strategy was changed so that Kennedy would be in a fighting position. Bobby straddled a turned-around chair, asked for ideas and viewpoints. There was a variety of advice from Steve Smith, Ed Guthman, Peter Straus, Bernard Ruggieri (Wagner's legislative adviser), Justin Feldman, John W. Douglas, Bill vanden Heuvel and Myers. Some thought any assault on the "kindly, moderate, objective" Keating, to use one staffer's description, would only intensify sympathy for him. But Myers, Steve Smith and others insisted the only way you beat any strong incumbent is to attack him. Bobby agreed, and researchers went to work on the previously privileged Keating record, looking for flaws which would dismay liberals.

Other strategy revisions were made. Shirtsleeves were out and coattails in. The new slogan was "Get on the Johnson, Humphrey, Kennedy Team." The campaign photograph of Kennedy with his sleeves rolled up was discarded and a new photo, with Bobby in full-faced friendliness, took its place. Seasoned Democratic generals and troops were called in to bring the Jews and Italian-Americans—now disproportionately in Keating's column— back to Democracy.

Bobby quickly became more of a Democrat. Early in the

campaign he had stressed the Kennedy legacy and invoked his brother's name. Now, with the New York polls showing a mounting landslide for Lyndon Johnson, Bobby emphasized the fact that he too was a Democrat. The most reliable poll in the state of New York is that conducted by the New York Daily *News*. As of October 15, the *News* poll showed Johnson with 76.4 percent of the New York State vote, Goldwater getting only 23.6 percent. The *News* also showed Bobby clearly ahead of Keating by 20 percentage points. This poll proved to be a few points too generous to both Johnson and Kennedy, but when it was first published in mid-October, the Kennedy men were thankful they had changed the theme of the campaign 10 days before.

When Johnson campaigned in New York, he raised Bobby's arm in comradeship and told crowds the United States needs a "young, dynamic compassionate, fighting liberal Senator from New York." Despite the fine words, Johnson's close friends confided that the President would not be unduly grieved if Bobby lost to Keating. But the Johnson-Humphrey-Kennedy team rolled on. Hubert Humphrey, full of delightful exuberance, toured the streets of New York City, Bobby at his side, and both men waved as enthusiastic Democrats should. Humphrey can't help bubbling over when he campaigns, and his fervor affected Bobby, who is usually reserved around crowds.

Bobby showed, in one outburst, that he was capable of punching Keating around. "It's about as low as you can get," he snapped, as he discussed Keating's charges on the Aniline case. "The charge that I made a deal with Nazis can't help but have an adverse effect on how Jewish people feel about me. . . . If this kind of charge were true, I wouldn't deserve to be elected to any public office. The charge isn't true. My family, too, has suffered from the Nazis. I lost my brother and my brother-in-law to the Germans. The idea that I would turn over money to the Nazis is ridiculous."

Kennedy struck back at Javits, too, describing his charges as "distortions and untruths." He claimed Keating, as a member of the Senate Judiciary Committee, had not objected to his appointments of southern judges, and furthermore, not one civil-rights case had been brought in Mississippi under Eisenhower. Finally, in addressing himself to each of Javits' charges, Kennedy explained he quit the McCarthy committee only to return later (on Democratic request) to write a report critical of McCarthy.

Traditional Democrats wanted to come back to their party, and Kennedy's soft campaign of September had not given them cause. Though the Jewish vote usually runs 80 percent Democratic in New York, a private poll taken at Keating's request showed that on October 6 Kennedy had 46 percent of the Jewish vote, Keating had 37 percent, and the rest of the Jewish voters were undecided. The Italian-American vote, which nominally runs 65 percent Democratic, was only 48 percent for Kennedy.

One of the least distinguished features of the Keating-Kennedy campaign was the pursuit of the ethnic vote. Even though it was his grandfather who emigrated, say, from Italy, the grandson might still consider himself an "Italian." Therefore, he will be appealed to as "Italian." In the vocabulary of politicians an ethnic voter simply is a person who considers himself one. Thus, two thirds of the votes cast in New York State are "ethnic," and the largest blocs are the Jews and Italians.

Keating played on the traditional suspicions some Jews had of the Kennedys by referring to the Aniline business, McCarthy and civil liberties. Furthermore, Keating had been adopted by many Jewish groups, was referred to by Jewish leaders as "our good friend," and had even had an Israeli forest named in his honor. When he toured the Lower East Side along with Javits and New York Attorney General Louis Lefkowitz, Keating ate blintzes and hot-pastrami sandwiches, called out "A Bi Geszundt!" (good health) to the beaming crowds, and embraced the man who carried a sign reading: "Keating: Nasser's Number One Enemy . . . Israel's Number One Friend." When Kennedy was asked if he favored continued shipments of food to Nasser's Egypt, he answered "yes," thus leaving himself open to charges of being pro-Nasser. Keating's managers predicted he would get 50 percent of the Jewish vote.

Bobby was perplexed over this problem. In Catskill resorts he drew the crowds, but Keating got the affection. One night, in Grossinger's, Bobby stood on a chair and painfully remarked, "My father spent a lot of time in Hollywood in the thirties and got to

know many Jewish families. He knew the Warner brothers and Sam
Goldwyn, and he admired the way they taught their children respect for their parents and love for each other. My father liked that
and decided to bring his own up that way. That's the way we were
brought up."

Only a few diners responded to this earnest attempt by
Bobby to show a Kennedy bond with the Jewish community; most
of the guests kept right on eating. Newsmen who were present
winced at Bobby's frank but awkward effort to win his audience's
good will.

Kennedy and Keating both went through the ritual of calling
for more aid to Israel and protesting Soviet anti-Semitism. As a
Catholic, Bobby was also able to publicly support the proposal, before the Vatican Council, to exonerate all Jews of responsibility for
the crucifixion of Christ. Bobby neglected no opportunity to tell
how, as a newspaper correspondent, he rode a tank from Tel Aviv
to Jerusalem during the Israeli-Arab war. "I predicted Israel would
win," Bobby said, "and I was only 22 at the time." Kennedy was
moved, as were scores of candidates in New York before him, to
wear a *yamilke* (the Jewish skullcap) and sit solemnly with a
Hasidic rabbi while photographers clicked away. When Keating
proposed that Israel be included in the North Atlantic Treaty Organization, Bobby responded as though he had a proprietary, previ-
ous interest, and declared Israel did not want to be part of NATO,
thank you. The fight for the "Jewish vote" continued shamelessly.

Javits told Jewish audiences Keating was his "teammate."
And Javits knew the neighborhoods, the right and wrong things to
say to Jewish groups and when to show up. Keating, invited along
with Kennedy, attended the convention of the Manhattan region of
the Zionist Organization in America. Kennedy was absent, and the
chairman pointedly referred to Keating: "We are not neutral to our
dear friend, and he is our friend."

At first, Bobby relied on "name" Jews for help. Harry
Golden arrived from South Carolina, wrote a long letter to *The New
York Times* on behalf of Bobby, delivered speeches and made tapes
for Yiddish radio broadcasts. But Jews believe more in a Javits
than a Golden, for the latter is a prosperous author who homes
toward power centers, and only four years before had been strongly

anti-Kennedy. More impressive was Connecticut's Senator Abraham Ribicoff, who had been a salesman for J.F.K. in 1960. Ribicoff spoke to influential Jewish groups in behalf of Bobby, but told him he looked out and saw the same disbelieving faces which had been skeptical of Jack Kennedy in 1960.

The struggle for Jewish favor became so intense that humor had to result. In the middle of the Keating-Kennedy race, if an enterprising fellow had a few unemployed Arabs around, he could have made a quick buck renting them out as pickets. Keating's headquarters was delighted that it was the first to be picketed by real, live Arabs. The Action Committee on American-Arab Relations finally decided to picket *both* headquarters, to the great relief of Kennedymen, and sent the following telegrams:

Senator Kenneth B. Keating   *October 14, 1964*
Campaign Headquarters
521 Fifth Avenue
New York City

We resent your disrespect for the rights and feelings of American Arabs and some 80% non-Jewish citizens of New York State, in your bid for the so-called "Jewish" vote. Accordingly, we shall picket your headquarters October 15. The Action Committee will support Kennedy. If Zionist Jews believe that you are the best servant of Israeli interest, may they vote for you and send you to the Knesset.

Dr. M. T. Mehdi
Secretary-General, ACAAR
441 Lexington Avenue, NYC

Mr. Robert F. Kennedy   *October 14, 1964*
Campaign Headquarters
9 E 42nd
New York City

We are deeply disappointed in your anti-Arab and pro-Israel remarks. Accordingly we shall picket your headquarters October Fifteenth. However, as Keating is the master of the dexterous politics, and as we believe you are a fair-minded person who considers American interest above factional and minority pressure groups, we have de-

cided to support you by calling upon our members, friends and supporters, estimated between 50,000 and 75,000, to vote for you. The Zionist Jews who may vote against you in favor of Israel are free to go to Israel with Keating.

> *Dr. M. T. Mehdi*
> *Secretary-General, ACAAR*
> *441 Lexington, New York City*

The telegram to Kennedy caused consternation in his press office, and his press director, Debs Myers, furiously chewed on his cigar, as he quickly composed a statement of repudiation, released with terribly deliberate speed to the Associated Press and United Press International and all the ships at sea. Myers' fast wire to Doctor Mehdi read:

I HAVE MADE MY POSITION CLEAR IN SUPPORT OF THE AMERICAN COMMITMENT TO SECURITY AND PROGRESS OF THE STATE OF ISRAEL AND IN OPPOSITION TO THOSE ARAB COUNTRIES WHICH ARE ENGAGED IN WAR-LIKE ACTIVITIES IN THE MIDDLE EAST. I DO NOT SEEK, DO NOT WANT, AND DO NOT ACCEPT SUPPORT FROM ANY PERSONS OR ORGANIZATIONS WHO DISAGREE WITH MY STAND. I AM SURE MR. KEATING WOULD TAKE THE SAME POSITION AS I ON THIS MATTER.

> *(Signed)*
> ROBERT F. KENNEDY

The "Italian vote" which Kennedy hoped to get wavered awhile longer because Keating was thumping for liberalization of the immigration laws and bragging about how he got a bill through Congress to make Columbus Day a national holiday. He also criticized Kennedy's part in the Cosa Nostra hearings and charged that the hearings, which featured an endless listing of hoodlums with Italian names, were a "publicity stunt" and "needlessly reflected adversely on the good name of the Italian-American community." Keating got instant support from Mario Biaggi, president of the Grand Council of Columbia Associations in Civil Service, who described the hearings as an ". . . anti-Italian smear . . . a one-man show produced, staged, directed and prompted by Mr. Kennedy" when he was Attorney General.

To these charges, Kennedy angrily replied he had asked Valachi to voluntarily leave the federal penitentiary at Atlanta to testify before the Senate committee, and that Valachi had come willingly.

He accused Keating of "attempting to prejudice Italian-American voters against me." If he had wanted to, Kennedy could also have cited the long devotion and service of two of his closest associates: Angie Novello, his personal secretary; and Carmine Bellino, who had been with him since early Teamster investigation days as a careful accountant.

Nevertheless, there was talk in Italian neighborhoods about how Kennedy "made every Italian look like a gangster." The summer had been torn with racial disturbances, and many Italian-Americans lived in proximity to Negroes. In a bar in one such area, a knot of men viewed a Kennedy television speech with disdain. One complained, "He hurt every Italian you know. All he talks about is niggers and spics." But the overriding truth was that when Bobby campaigned in Italian neighborhoods he was mobbed by huge, enthusiastic crowds. The women cried and kissed Bobby's face and hands.

The Kennedy name got automatic support from other voting "blocs" who had come to love the late President in 1960. Many Negro leaders, for example, felt Keating deserved Negro voter support, but couldn't say so for two reasons: 1. Negro leaders are expected to pay total allegiance to the Democratic Party; 2. Negro leaders these days must follow the Negro rank and file; and on October 6, a poll showed them to be 75 percent for Kennedy, with 17 percent undecided.

Keating's difficulty was manifest when he appeared before the state NAACP convention in Buffalo, just as it had been when he was turned down by the AFL-CIO weeks before. In fact, Keating went into a dither. His prepared text for the NAACP speech criticized Kennedy for abandoning the Justice Department "with an unfinished task in front of him," *i.e.,* civil rights. But when Keating actually delivered the speech, he softened the remark to wishing Kennedy "would have continued his work in civil rights as Attorney General at this juncture. . . ."

The next day, Kennedy spoke to the same convention,

pounced on Keating, was loudly cheered when he accused him of inciting "the very prejudices which all of you and many other persons have been the victims." When Keating announced himself as being for Puerto Rican statehood, Kennedy, with the enthusiastic support of New York's Puerto Rican leaders, snapped back that the Puerto Rican people didn't want statehood.

Kennedy flaunted his possession of the Polish-American vote by marching, without official invitation, in the Pulaski Day Parade. Keating and the President of the Polish-American Congress (a Republican) fumed. The ethnic and voting-bloc situation was confusing that Sunday, October 4. In addition to the parade there was a breakfast at the Jewish Center in Manhattan, a rally of Chinese-Americans, a protest meeting of Brooklyn Navy Yard workers, and an Interfaith Rally Day meeting at Central Park Mall. Between scampering from one ethnic event to another, Keating went on *Meet the Press* and piously proclaimed he was "disturbed" with Kennedy's appeals to voters on a racial and religious basis.

Now that Bobby had his dukes up and could pose as the underdog, he was in his favorite role of being the attacker. Once Kennedy unloaded his criticisms, Keating was left floundering and puffing indignantly. The more Keating protested, the less he looked like a high-minded, decent, mature Senator. And the more Kennedy attacked and discredited Keating's "liberalism" the quicker apostate Democrats came back to the fold.

Keating was charged with voting against federal aid to education, with cutting funds for the Manpower Retraining Bill, as voting repeatedly against housing measures, as being against Medicare (another magic word in New York) and with voting against legislation for youth.

Bobby's attack on Keating's "liberalism" was relentless and Mayor Wagner backed him up with some especially severe attacks on Keating's record. He said Keating had no right to be called a liberal, and ticked off what he said were the Senator's "against votes" concerning distribution of surplus food, free school lunches, inclusion of retail and service industry employees in minimum-wage categories. He also accused Keating of being against Senator Kefauver's efforts to spotlight abuses in the drug industry and correct excessive profits in drug sales. Then Congressman Emanuel Celler, with Bobby at his side in a Carlyle Hotel suite, told reporters Keating had voted with Goldwater 99 times on 106 key issues, and concluded, "The unshakable, undeviating and irrevocable partnership has been that of Goldwater-Keating-Thurmond." This was a little strong, even from a crusty local liberal, and Kennedy was asked if he agreed. To Celler's embarrassment, Kennedy honestly answered, "I wouldn't have expressed it that way."

By mid-October the assault on Keating was fully mounted. Each day a new ad, demolishing his record, ran full-page in New York City papers. Wherever he campaigned in the city, Bobby cried, "My opponent would like you to think he is a liberal—but his record is clear. What was the position of this liberal Senator on public housing and public power questions, on scholarships for young people? He was against them. He would like you to think he is a liberal. But in your heart you know he is on the right." Kennedy also informed the public that Keating, as a Congressman, accepted the approval of the "Americans for Constitutional Action," the right-wing counterpart of the Americans for Democratic Action. The word was getting around to those three or four Jewish delicatessens Javits had mentioned that Keating wasn't so liberal after all, and Kennedy sure had *chutzpah!* Bobby's legislative researchers were baggy-eyed from looking for weak spots in Keating's 18-year record.

One of these, they thought, was his position in regard to the Nuclear Test-Ban Treaty. On October 20, in Syracuse, Bobby cut loose, said Keating had "ridiculed" the treaty and spoken out for it only after its passage was certain. Kennedy also said that statements Keating had made in early 1963 had actually "jeopardized" the treaty, that President Kennedy was forced into asking Defense Secretary McNamara to go on television and explain what had happened in Cuba in order to allay public apprehension about the treaty.

Keating was outraged and said he had always been for the treaty. Kennedy's statement was "preposterous and unprincipled . . . a complete and utter distortion . . . a falsehood." He wrote Bruce L. Felknor, executive-director of the Fair Campaign Practices Committee, a private organization supported by donations from the public. Keating asked for an investigation of Kennedy's tactics. Kennedy was incorrect, Keating charged, in saying that he had opposed federal aid to education and that he had "ridiculed" the Test-Ban Treaty. Keating also complained Kennedy was using the same techniques to "distort my progressive record" in other fields.

What followed looked like comedy. Felknor wrote Kennedy indicating the committee felt he was distorting the Keating record. Keating's office got wind of the letter and prepared a statement declaring the committee was "shocked and angered" with Kennedy's actions. In the confusion a committee staffer unintentionally gave a copy of the Felknor letter to a reporter of the *New York Herald Tribune*, which promptly printed it. The letter said Kennedy's description of Keating's position on the Test-Ban Treaty "is not only false and distorted, but also appears to be either a deliberate and cynical misrepresentation or the result of incredible carelessness, touched with luck."

Kennedy's headquarters demanded an apology from Felknor for the improper release of the letter. Felknor was so embarrassed by this dreadful mishap that he had already prepared a letter of apology. There was great thrashing about, with Kennedy staffers visiting Felknor's office. One committee member, Ralph McGill, a friend of Bobby's, and publisher of the Atlanta *Constitution*, resigned after a conference at Kennedy's headquarters. (Another member, Cardinal Cushing of Boston, resigned later.) It was clear the committee had handled the matter badly. The letter was withdrawn, and Felknor apologized, saying, "It should never have been written."

"This is a good example of taking the lemon," chirped Debs Myers, "and making lemonade."

Former G.O.P. National Chairman Meade Alcorn was less good-natured about the Felknor letter episode. He charged Kennedy with a "ruthless and unconscionable attack" on the committee and claimed he applied "brutal pressure" to get the letter withdrawn.

The battle was now just where Kennedy wanted it to be—in

New York City, where he had suffered the greatest defections. For many, Bobby's horns were now shorn, and for those deeply stirred by the memory of President John Kennedy, there was Bobby taking John, the late President's three-year-old son, by the hand as he campaigned in the Bronx.

His sisters—Pat, Jean and Eunice—traveled around the state giving speeches for Bobby and evoking feeling for the Kennedy name. Rose Kennedy also campaigned for her son. She told audiences that she once had to use a hairbrush in punishing Bobby, but that he grew into a fine man and she was proud of him. Kennedy's advisers discussed the possibility of Jackie Kennedy's appearing or speaking for Bobby, but he wisely ruled against this idea.

Other speakers worked to stir up Democratic feeling. Arthur Schlesinger Jr. debated Gore Vidal on the question of whether Bobby was a nice guy. The debate seemed to wind up a tie. John Kennedy's special counsel and speechwriter, Ted Sorensen, arrived to assure intellectual audiences that Bobby was good for New York. One liberal endorsement of Bobby backfired. A thoughtlessly prepared advertisement proclaimed that Adlai Stevenson was voting for Robert F. Kennedy. The Fair Campaign Practices Committee dutifully pointed out Adlai had already voted by absentee ballot in Illinois.

Arthur Schlesinger, Sr. concurred with the Committee for an Effective Congress as it endorsed Keating. *The New York Times* and the *Herald Tribune*, along with all other New York City papers —the *Post* excepted—came out for Keating. The liberal magazine, *The Reporter*, published an article documenting how Kennedy had unfairly criticized Keating's record. Both *Time* and *Newsweek* did cover stories on Keating. Kennedy and Keating continued to blare out how low the other fellow's tactics were. The charges slopped over into the news columns and occupied too much radio and television time.

As could be expected, Jimmy Hoffa got dragged into the campaign when one of his intrepid henchmen had 100,000 leaflets distributed in Harlem claiming Bobby was a fake on civil rights. As usual, the Teamsters got a "zero" rating for political effectiveness; Harlem was all Bobby's.

The New York Times, weeks before, had carefully interviewed both candidates, studied the answers, printed them in full, and concluded that Keating and Kennedy "are in substantial agreement on a wide range of controversial state and local issues . . . but they differ sharply on some politically potent issues . . . as the desirability of tax relief for commuters and the method of reapportioning the legislature." The *Times* was being unduly fussy here on the latter issue because New York voters *really* concerned with issues in the Keating-Kennedy race did not rank commuting and reapportionment very high in their considerations.

Kennedy, in criticizing Keating's record, used the old trick of picking his opponent's selected votes and identifying them as the rule rather than the exception. A legislator will occasionally vote against a bill he favors in principle because it is insufficient or has an objectionable "rider" or amendment attached. As Javits pointed out quietly, his own record or that of Hubert Humphrey could be plucked in this fashion to make it appear pro-Goldwater. But the fact Kennedy had stirred up the record gave the campaign a sharp and lively turn.

After swapping charges of who was distorting who's record, they squabbled for days over how and when to debate. Each repeated charges that the other was ducking a face-to-face meeting. On October 24, CBS wired both candidates, inviting them to debate on television on October 27, from 7:30 to 8:30 p.m. Keating accepted immediately. Kennedy, then well ahead of Keating in the race, did not respond. On October 27, CBS wired Kennedy in the morning, informing him he had until 3:30 that afternoon to accept. He didn't accept because the question of format had not been settled. Keating then bought the 7:30 to 8 time slot to debate an empty chair. He would tape the program at 5:30. Meanwhile Kennedy's advertising agency bought the 8 to 8:30 time for a Kennedy rebuttal. Keating's schedule was delayed so he had to go on "live" at 7:30. He prepared to go on the air assuming that Kennedy would appear in the studio a few moments before his *own* program, set for 8 p.m.

At one minute before airtime, Kennedy and several aides, followed by two-score newsmen, marched into CBS and hurried to Keating's studio. Kennedy poked his finger at a Keating staffer and barked, "Kindly inform Senator Keating I am here and ready to go on the air." A CBS official blocked him, as he had blocked others earlier, and told Kennedy the time was Keating's. After an angry exchange of words, and some pushing, Kennedy declared, "This is dishonest," and went to his own studio where he complained, on his half-hour program, of "political trickery."

Kennedy's blitz of the studio unsettled Keating, and the Senator, who had debated an empty chair, lost his poise as he left the building. Keating was so befuddled, he refused to talk to reporters, and his aides scattered chairs and artificial palms in the way of pursuing newsmen. He vanished into a cab, but the scramble was all caught on television film by cameramen from other stations. When Kennedy finished *his* half hour he came out and discussed the "debate" episode at a press conference. His own camera crew filmed the press conference. Clips that showed Kennedy to advantage were sent to upstate television stations. Thus the whole state was exposed to the Keating debacle. Kennedy spent the rest of the evening telling audiences how Keating's people had barred him from the studio. Actually, Kennedy was blocked by WCBS-TV Producer Norman Kramer. Kennedy later admitted that he had given CBS no notice he was going to arrive and that he had no special reason for showing up at the last minute.

Kennedy's campaign was masterful now. He had stripped Keating of his underdog mantle and had cast doubt on Keating's liberalism. There was no question that Keating was *Republican* and Kennedy *Democrat*, the brother of a beloved Democratic President, and the teammate of President Lyndon Johnson. Kennedy's principal adviser was LeMoyne Billings, the late President's personal friend. Billings felt that the initial advertising effort succeeded only in enhancing the unpleasant image of Bobby as ruthless and arrogant. Billings decided that a friendlier Bobby should be shown, one who looked you straight in the eye. One advertising memo for the campaign read: "Human-interest stuff should be included—Bob with all the children, something perhaps with Jackie, even material without Bob—Ethel doing things, in fact, anything at all that a good smart politically savvy public-relations man can think up."

The new Bobby image was brilliantly executed in the television campaign. The TV spots and programs were unrehearsed and impromptu. Kennedy answered questions, simply put by ordinary citizens, and handled them so naturally that he looked like a warm, sincere and able man. Kennedy's television campaign alone removed many of the fears the "ethnic" voters had about him. Keating's television and radio commercials, on the other hand, were hollow and repetitious (Carpetbagger! . . . Carpetbagger!). Forever, there was Javits patting Keating on the back as though the Senator were his nephew from Rochester. The million dollars Kennedy spent on television in one month—October—had far more impact than the million Keating spent in the two-month period, September and October.

According to the Kennedy campaign chart, Bobby would run away from Keating in "Phase IV," and that he did. The charges of "Carpetbagger" had been diminished. Kennedy seemed more liberal than Keating now, and Democrats of Jewish and Italian descent were coming home in the sunset. Liberals were satisfied that Bobby could be substantive and not just a stimulant to juvenile glands. And there was Lyndon Johnson with a showing of 74 percent of the vote in the New York *Daily News* poll. No candidate had a larger, more comfortable coattail to ride than Robert Kennedy in 1964. His own private polls showed him leading Keating 53 to 45 percent, with the Conservative candidate getting two percent. Even Sam Lubell reversed his earlier findings and now predicted a Kennedy victory.

Keating became desperate. He had always been twice as fast on his feet as Kennedy, and now he scampered after voters in order to shake their hands. Crowds were modest and responded sincerely, often giving the impression they *hoped* Keating would win but doubted he would. Keating implored his audiences to reject Kennedy's "tissues of falsehoods and distortions." He talked darkly of million-dollar speech writers and hatchetmen from Massachusetts. He spoke bitterly:

"Lyndon didn't want him. He went to Lyndon and said he'd like to run for the vice-presidency with him. Lyndon said, 'Not you, Bobby.' He asked to become Ambassador to Vietnam. Lyndon said, 'Not you, Bobby.' He asked for another Cabinet job.

Lyndon said, 'Not you, Bobby.' So Bobby looked over the country and lit onto New York."

Keating said Bobby believes New York is a place where you change planes for Hyannis Port, that he didn't know what it is to be a Senator, "to bring home a mother from the old country so she can join her family . . . to bring home a soldier to visit a dying parent." Keating said, with supplication, "My only desire is to serve and not to rule."

Keating again called for a debate and even bought another $10,000 worth of TV time. But there would be no debate. Kennedy was comfortably ahead, so why debate? Keating could only hope for millions of split tickets.

With the election 10 days off, Kennedy knew he had it won. He cut down his schedule, sat in his hotel suite and watched himself on television. He joked publicly about the debate fiasco. He talked as though the campaign were all over, and he spoofed Keating. One night, at a shopping center in Ossining, Bobby raised his right thumb aggressively. With a smile which mocked indignation, he cried:

"Who grew up in Westchester County? I did. Keating didn't. Does Ken Keating know the problems of Westchester County? No. BOO-BOO Ken Keating! BOO-BOO. Did he go to Bronxville schools as I did? No. Keating is the carpetbagger. He says keep New York's own. Imagine that. BOO-BOO, Ken Keating. BOO-BOO. Do you want a local boy in the U.S. Senate? That's me! There's even some talk about Keating dumping garbage in the Hudson River."

A few days before the election, Kennedy talked with a visitor in a car while three of his youngsters jostled around. "There were some surprises in the campaign," Bobby said. "I didn't expect the personal attacks. I didn't expect the Nazi stuff. I didn't think Keating would do that. I was also surprised by the degree of bitterness from the liberals. But I think they actually helped me. Those people are impossible. We went through the 1960 stuff all over again—my father, Senator McCarthy and so on. *The New York Times* gave us trouble. Jack Javits was plenty tough. He gave me hell."

But the game was over and he had won it. Kennedy stepped out of the car at Rockefeller Center and put his hands in his overcoat pockets. As he entered the revolving door of the RCA Building, he paused and said, "You know, I risked more in entering this race than most people realized. It could have been very bad for me."

X

NEW BASE OF POWER

ON THE FACE OF IT, there was nothing remarkable about Kennedy's win. Indeed, it would have been remarkable had he *lost*. Lyndon Johnson swamped Barry Goldwater in New York by 2,669,597 votes, carried all 62 counties in a state in which the majority of counties are Republican. Bobby won by 719,693 votes, carried 19 counties and notched a modest victory. The President won by 1,949,904 more votes than Bobby did.

Yet his situation was entirely different from Johnson's. The President ran against a candidate disapproved by his own party in New York. Keating had the support of most of his party and a fair share of independents and Democrats besides. There was little attack on Johnson. There was full attack on Bobby, much of it vehement. Bobby is inherently controversial and didn't have to be a carpetbagger to attract the crackle of political fire. On the presidential line, people were just *against* Goldwater. Bobby protected himself with the Kennedy name, his own personal appeal and his late strategy change. He could also shelter himself behind the normal Democratic and Liberal majorities. What insured his rescue, of course, was the free ride on the Johnson coattail.

All through the campaign, Brownell told Keating, "We can survive a million and a half at the top, but nothing beyond that." Brownell and Keating were prepared for an enormous Johnson win, but nothing like the colossal 2.7 million it was. In defeat, Keating could claim the distinction of setting a national record for running ahead of his ticket. His fine showing was even more impressive because the Conservative Party candidate, Henry A. Paolucci, siphoned away 212,216 nominally Republican votes. For many months afterward, Keating, his smile just as broad, got heartening applause and handshakes wherever he went. The campaign gave him an identification he never enjoyed before, particularly in New York City where, all things considered, he did exceptionally well.

Kennedy was particularly glad when it was over. He spent the early hours election night with his family, dropped by to see Jackie Kennedy and her children, then had a late dinner at Steve Smith's with Ethel and his mother. He was gracious in receiving Keating's concession of defeat. But Bobby did not mention Lyndon Johnson in his victory statement. He declared, "We started something in 1960, and the vote today is an overwhelming mandate to continue."

There were many ironies. It was Bobby Kennedy who stirred up the Democrats in upstate New York, but when the swirls subsided, it was Lyndon Johnson who benefited most. Lyndon won upstate by 1.3 million votes, Bobby by only 8,644. Yet despite the mitigative quality of his win, Bobby received more votes than his late brother did in New York in 1960.

Moreover, Bobby showed even greater strength among Catholic voters than J.F.K. did. Seventy percent of the Republicans who defected to Bobby were Catholics. He ran especially well in Catholic neighborhoods, and overall, got twice the Catholic votes Keating did. Kennedy won solid majorities among Polish-Americans, Puerto Ricans and Negroes. Fears that Italian-Americans might defect turned out to be foolish. Kennedy's attack on Keating's "liberalism" brought a significant number of doubting Jews to his side, so Bobby, while not recovering the normal Jewish Democratic vote, did get respectable support. There were a couple of soft areas for Bobby. Even with the Johnson landslide, he got a smaller percentage of the New York City vote than his brother did in 1960. And Bobby was unable to crack the three heavily populated counties surrounding New York City—Westchester, Nassau and Suffolk. Johnson carried them all; so did Keating.

Had the campaign gone on two more weeks, Bobby's margin would have been bigger. He already had the "gut Democratic" vote and was satisfying the more educated with position papers on housing, civil liberties, higher education, air pollution, narcotics, the United Nations and mental health. These papers were given only modest attention in the press, but they served Bobby in that voters who were serious about issues now had something solid from Kennedy on his views. Bobby's attack on Keating's record got much more press notice and was also less admirable than the position-paper effort. Five months after the election, a special subcommittee of the Fair Campaign Practices Committee concluded "that Senator Kennedy's remarks in Syracuse about the Keating record were such as to lead to a substantial distortion in the public's mind as to Keating's position, especially as regards his support of the Nuclear Test-Ban Treaty." The committee, which had badly handled the affair, tried to smooth things out by saying, "All sides were hurt in this matter," Keating, Kennedy and the committee itself.

It was a bad contest. Debate of genuine issues was scant. Neither man successfully made a case against his opponent. Money was lavishly and wastefully spent (each campaign cost an estimated $2 million). Logistics were often confused. Hardly a day went by that Kennedy didn't decide to cancel an appearance, and his tardiness became chronic. Neither man delivered what could be called an eloquent speech. In the beginning, Bobby's speeches were disjointed, and at the end, only a little improved. Both men were unfairly caricatured; Bobby as a ruthless ogre, and Keating as an ineffectual, insincere hack. The campaign brought only slight change to their images. Keating's "antipathy quotient" was upped a little. But Kennedy did not shed the charge that he was unprincipled. When it was suggested that his advertising and campaigning had erased the "ruthless" image forever, Bobby cracked mischievously, "Yeah. Now I can go back to being ruthless."

The bunting was still up and the last vote barely counted when newsmen and Kennedy fans revived talk about Bobby Kennedy for President someday. Bobby was diffident. "If it comes, all right," he said. "If it doesn't come, that's all right too." National Committeeman Edwin Weisl Sr., President Johnson's chief spear carrier in New York, dismissed such notions. "Kennedy for President?" asked Weisl, "He'll have to prove himself as a Senator."

Whatever the character of his victory, Bobby was the first Democratic Senator since Lehman and a cause for joy to the party. His win, the Johnson sweep, and the fact that Democrats won all over the state where, in a non-Goldwater year they wouldn't have, gave the frustrated party great relief. The second most Republican state in the nation—in terms of elected officials—was no longer Republican. The Democratic Party in New York State, torn for years by factional fighting, saw an opportunity, fresh and bright.

New York is as national as any state can be. It has the nation's largest city; a network of other big cities; an extensive, rich agriculture and industry; beaches, mountains and plains; a population of 18 million which includes generous doses of many nationalities and races; and a history of big, important government which has responded to people's demands for social reform. Seven of the 13 Democrats named for the presidency since the Civil War were New Yorkers. Until 1960, each presidential election in this century had a New Yorker as one of the nominees.* Three times a New York Democrat and a New York Republican faced each other in presidential races. No governorship in the republic carries more prestige than that in New York. Accordingly, the state has produced a line of strong, first-rate governors, including the present occupant of the Albany statehouse.

On paper, New York should be nearly as Democratic as it became in the Johnson sweep of 1964. The Democratic Party has a substantial margin in voter registration; a majority of its citizens are those who usually vote Democratic—Catholics, Jews, the foreign-born, Negroes and Puerto Ricans; and 88 percent of its people live in cities, towns or suburbs. But it doesn't work out that way. The primary reason lies in the suspicion which people who live outside New York City have of the "wicked" Democrats who rule it. People live in four kinds of areas in New York: in New York City; in its suburbs; in the upstate cities and their suburbs; and in the truly rural areas. The last three have voted Republican for many years in New York.

If Dwight Eisenhower, who lived in New York from 1945 on, can be considered a New Yorker.

Republicans gave them good reason to do so. Besides their fear of the "wicked" Democrats, the people "outside" New York City have been offered a Republicanism which advanced progressive programs and good government—often ahead of the Democrats in social legislation. The progressives—Dewey, the late Irving Ives, Brownell, Javits and Rockefeller—controlled the G.O.P. beginning in the late '30's. The Dewey and Rockefeller administrations executed advanced programs which the Democrats were hard put to match. Under Dewey, the nation's first law barring discrimination in employment was passed; the state's first thruway was built; and a pioneer system was established wherein workers, disabled in sickness not connected with their jobs, received benefits. During the Rockefeller years, a program of rent subsidy (later copied by the Federal Government) was established; discrimination in the rental and sale of private housing was prohibited; commuter railroads received considerable state aid; and scholarships and tuition grants for college students were tripled. The Republicans managed, therefore, to maintain broad voter appeal and always offered a good ethnic mix of candidates.

Given these two facts—the aversion upstaters and suburbanites felt toward Democrats in the city and the enlightened programs Republicans pushed—the New York G.O.P. split the Democrats and won election after election, though being a minority party. They won a significant victory in 1942 according to this formula: Present one anti-boss gubernatorial candidate (racketbusting Dewey), put him on a progressive platform which included public development of water power and a state Fair Employment Practices Commission, and combine with a divided Democratic Party (Farley and Lehman factions warred in the Democratic Party that year). The formula worked again in 1958. That year was a good one for Democrats all across the country, but in New York, the party had split between reformers led by Lehman and Mrs. Roosevelt, and Tammany Democrats led by Carmine De Sapio. The result: Anti-boss candidates (Rockefeller and Keating) ran on a progressive platform against De Sapio's candidates (Averell Harriman and New York District Attorney Frank Hogan) and won. New York Republicans came out of the 1958 election with both U.S. Senators; the governor and his entire cabinet (with one exception); control

of both houses of the legislature; a majority of the U.S. Representatives in Washington; and 57 of the 62 county boards of supervisors. The 1958 setback, and the endless Reform vs. Tammany
wrangle, dismayed all Democrats, particularly upstate Democratic
leaders.

Their morale was improved in 1960, however, when John F.
Kennedy carried New York State and especially excited upstate
New York. In Erie County, where Buffalo is located, Stevenson
got only 37 percent of the vote in 1956; J.F.K. got 57 percent. In
Oneida County, where Utica and Rome are the principal cities,
Stevenson got 31 percent of the vote in 1956; Kennedy got 52.2
percent in 1960. Kennedy's performance was repeated in other
upstate counties.

Much of this good showing was a result of the return to the
Democratic Party of Catholic voters whom Eisenhower had won
away in 1956. The trend continued in 1964, with Bobby's candidacy providing additional stimulus. So strong was the return of
Catholics to the Democratic Party that even the popular Republican leader of the State Senate, Walter Mahoney, an Irish Catholic,
was rudely deposed in Buffalo. Catholic Democrats who had here-
tofore split their tickets for Mahoney abandoned him in the 1964
landslide.

The Johnson sweep was so total in New York that even in
the suburban counties around New York City, which have been
overwhelmingly Republican, Democrats were elected to the U.S.
Congress and to the New York Legislature. Some Democrats even
won in the thinly populated rural areas.

With the Democratic Party winning in all 62 New York
counties—and thus cracking the Republican hold on the population areas outside New York City—it was evident that this bonanza
required consolidation. The first opportunity would present itself
in January, 1965, when the state legislature convened in Albany,
with the Democrats in the majority for the first time in 30 years.
Democratic chieftains rubbed their hands in anticipation of the
golden days ahead. Nearly all of them, except the Wagner lieutenants from New York City, talked about how Bobby would eventually
become the One Great Democrat.

The nominal leader of the New York Democratic Party

was Wagner. He had survived New York City's Democratic jungle for 12 years. But Wagner, in 1964, controlled only an urban piece of a divided party. He did not have the allegiance of the Democratic leaders of two of the city's five boroughs: Brooklyn, led by Assemblyman Stanley Steingut; and the Bronx, led by Charley Buckley. While Wagner had run for mayor as a reformer in 1961, the reform clubs gave him only tentative support, and indeed, one leading reformer, Congressman William Fitts Ryan, actively opposed him in late 1964. Clearly Wagner's power in New York City was shrinking. Moreover, the city's power in state Democratic politics had greatly diminished since 1958, when Harriman became the first Democrat in the history of the state to get more votes *outside* the city than inside. This was due to ascending power of the Democrats upstate and also to the fact that Negroes and Puerto Ricans—who are rapidly displacing the white and non-Spanish middle class in New York City—do not have good voting performances.*

Bobby Kennedy knew these political facts about New York quite well. He had traveled the state for his brother in 1960, and by this time he was an experienced campaigner in his own right. He understood the need to unify the Democratic Party, but he decided to stay out of the struggle for leadership of his party in the state legislature. He was too busy, anyway, organizing his own staff and office in Washington.

In Albany, the Wagner forces were outnumbered by a coalition of upstate and suburban Democratic bosses who were determined to elect their men to the leadership of the New York Assembly and Senate. The anti-Wagner group was led by State Chairman William McKeon and Nassau County leader John English, both Kennedy men. They were pugnacious because they felt that Bobby, wherever he was or how little he said, stood behind them approvingly. There was no need for Kennedy to intervene, because the anti-Wagner group was doing his work.

The coalition would not exclude from its list of leadership candidates a legislator from New York City so long as he was

---

* *In Harlem, only 42 percent of those eligible to vote in 1964 did so. In Puerto Rican neighborhoods, the figure is only 20 percent.*

authentically anti-Wagner. Thus, they finally settled on Stanley Steingut, Wagner's old political enemy from Brooklyn, for Assembly leader, and Jack Bronston, the bright legislator from Queens, for Senate leader. The anti-Wagner group mustered 53 of the 76 votes needed to elect Steingut, and 18 of the 30 needed to name Bronston. Wagner, and his supporters in the state legislature, wanted to elect Joseph Zaretski, who had been Senate minority leader for many years, and Anthony Travia, who was his counterpart in the Assembly for an equal length of time. Zaretski and Travia were best known as steady second-placers. The anti-Wagner coalition was determined to elect fresh leadership to go with a fresh, state-wide victory.

But Wagner would not release his votes, which were necessary for the upstate and suburban leaders to get a majority to install new leadership. The fight between pro-Wagner and anti-Wagner forces polarized the Democrats, which had comfortable majorities in both houses. The people of New York witnessed a comic spectacle of a party showing no capacity to govern. The quarrel became acrimonious. Pro-Wagner legislators stood up and accused the anti-Wagner crowd of trying to elect a Senator, Julian B. Erway, whom they charged held anti-Negro and anti-Semitic views. The debate became more irrational, with both sides feeling threatened with the loss of the control of state jobs, which totaled $4 million. The faction which controls a payroll of this size also holds considerable political power, hence the struggle between anti- and pro-Wagner groups. At first Republicans were gleeful, then impatient, and finally acted righteous, especially after the episode concerning an Albany phenomenon named "Lulu" and her evil sister, "double-Lulu."

New York State Senators and Assemblymen are paid $10,000 annually, a salary among the highest in the nation for state legislators. Legislative committee chairmen are given an additional $5,000 "in lieu of expenses," and this allowance is popularly known as a "Lulu." Chairmen of prestigious committees are sometimes allowed a "double-Lulu," meaning $10,000, an attractive extra indeed.

As the leadership fight dragged into late January, to the huge embarrassment of the Democratic Party, Wagner dispatched one of his most effective political lieutenants, J. Raymond (The Fox) Jones, to Albany to confer with his political opponents. Jones, a seasoned Harlem politician and leader of the Manhattan Democratic organization, was to try to work out one of those intricate political compromises which keep government going everywhere.

Jones' companions on this trip were New York City Election Commissioner Maurice O'Rourke and Queens Assemblyman Moses Weinstein, both political associates of Wagner. The three men met in an Albany hotel with State Chairman McKeon, John English of Nassau County and two of their associates. To this day, it is not precisely clear what transpired in that meeting. It is known that McKeon discussed committee chairmanships and expense accounts. The meeting resolved no problems. When Jones returned to New York City, he reported to Wagner who, in turn, charged McKeon with offering what was "tantamount to a bribe," a "double-Lulu" for Zaretski, who would become chairman of the Senate Codes Committee. This plum for Zaretski, according to Jones, would be exchanged in return for Wagner giving his votes to the McKeon-English group. This charge was followed with another, this by Julius Edelstein, Wagner's executive assistant, accusing a "Kennedy bloc" in Albany of making the proposal to swap the "double-Lulu" for the necessary votes. Edelstein used the term "Kennedy bloc" in talking with a reporter, and it was the first mention of Bobby in the welter of charges which grew out of the Albany meeting. Wagner had not authorized Edelstein to issue such a statement, and quickly called a press conference to disavow the statement.

With the Democratic dirty wash now visible to all, and with bills piled up by the hundreds in the legislature, Republicans demanded a state investigation. It was quickly called by the State Investigation Commission and held in a hearing room in Manhattan. Into this room strode the Democratic chieftains, nervously adjusting their ties and straightening their suits. They hardly looked like the noble lieutenants who, during the 1964 campaign, proclaimed they would lead the people of New York into Lyndon Johnson's Great Society. They protested mightily. They denied charges and asserted their high principles. They affirmed their affection for one another, Wagner included. They wanted only unity and leadership. To the man, they claimed not to know what the mayor meant when he talked of "bribe" and "double-Lulu," no matter how earnest and pious he was in testifying before the investigating commission. Even two witnesses, favorable to the mayor, testified they had not heard the word "bribe" or the expression "double-Lulu" in that mysterious meeting.

Election Commissioner O'Rourke's face reddened when he was questioned about bribe offers. He had heard none, he protested, and explained, "If I thought there was a bribe, I'd go to the District Attorney's office. I'm not going to wait until I take a shower and eat my dinner before I tell somebody that somebody is being raped. I will run and get a cop."

It all boiled down to Wagner, the reputed state leader of his party, calling State Chairman McKeon a liar. Many state legislators and political reporters, accustomed to the deals made in Albany, got a laugh out of the hearings, because they were sure an attempt had been made for a deal between the Wagner and anti-Wagner forces. The anti-Wagner bosses and McKeon, because of Kennedy's challenge to Wagner's leadership, had pushed too hard to consolidate their strength in Albany. They underestimated the fighting qualities of Wagner, and never dreamed he would retaliate by breaking the rules of backroom politics by making public what went on in the backroom.

For the most part, Kennedy had wisely stayed out of this mess, intervening just once with a suggestion that a secret ballot be conducted among Democratic legislators to elect their leaders. Tawdry as the whole "Lulu" episode was, the State Investigating Commission somehow made no recommendations for prosecution. But the effect was that the anti-Wagner bosses now looked seamy, and Wagner had portrayed himself as virtue itself.

McKeon and his Kennedy men had not suffered their last from Wagner. A few days later, Republican State Senator John Hughes rose to resolve that Zaretski (Wagner's man) be named President therefore Speaker, of the Senate. A shock wave resounded through the chamber. Totally surprised, senators hurried into conferences, the anti-Wagner senators angry because they realized a deal had been made between Wagner and the Republicans. Another ballot was taken—the 28th on the leadership question—and

Republicans accomplished what floundering Democrats had failed to do—name a new Senate leader. Twenty-five Republicans joined 15 Wagner Democrats to elect Zaretski. The next day, 46 Republican Assemblymen joined 35 Wagner Democrats to elect Travia. There were cries of outrage by the anti-Wagner Democrats. One compared the situation with Hitler's burning of the Reichstag. Steingut refused to congratulate Travia. McKeon fumed that "Wagner-fellers" and "Rocky-crats" conspired.

It was clear that emissaries of Wagner and Rockefeller had made arrangements. The mayor compromised to save his political skin. Rockefeller also went halfway by doing Wagner's bidding in exchange for a tacit understanding that Zaretski and Travia—two fairly tame fellows—would move the governor's legislative program. Republican morale was lifted. The spirit of the energized Democrats was darkened. The Kennedy men had been stopped. Bob Wagner had again demonstrated his political adroitness.

Bobby professed to be gloomy over the outcome. It was unfortunate, he said, that Democratic leadership was decided by Republicans. "The situation has deteriorated as far as the Democratic Party is concerned," he lamented and adding that the party had failed the people who gave it such a clear mandate. Bobby's disappointment turned to cool indignation on the question of state patronage. After three days' deliberation Kennedy took his first public action in the Democratic family fight by writing Zaretski and Travia to let them know of "my opposition to filling jobs without paying careful attention to the ability of the men selected for the jobs . . . dealing the jobs out like so many cards off the top of the deck is intolerable. . . ."

The letter was without warmth or congratulation for the newly elected leaders, was directive in tone, and got right to the point. Kennedy recommended that a talent hunt for staff be conducted in the successful fashion his late brother employed in 1960. "This operation," Bobby wrote, "in which I participated along with Sargent Shriver and others brought such distinguished men as David Bell, Douglas Dillon, and Robert McNamara to the Government." Kennedy's other suggestion was that "full disclosure" be made of all jobs involved, with listing of duties, pay and expenses, and that jobs "not in the public interest" be eliminated.

So there he was, challenging. Bobby was also reprimanding the "bad guys." The sharp tongue many Democratic politicians had heard in 1960 was at work again. Zaretski was incensed. He phoned his friend, Julius Edelstein, and asked for advice. Edelstein, who writes Wagner's speeches and advises him on political matters, conferred with the mayor and it was decided Edelstein should draft a reply for Zaretski. The new Senate leader agreed to the plan, and Edelstein put his skill to work. The "Zaretski reply" was frosty.

"You already know from your brief experience in the legislative branch," the letter opened didactically, "that there is a difference between legislative staff positions and positions of administrative duties in the executive branch. . . ." Zaretski "wrote" that he wasn't aware that Kennedy's recommended procedure for hiring had ever been used in the U.S. Congress "or even by you. . . ."

There was only one snag in the execution of the "Zaretski letter." In his haste to get mimeographed copies to New York City morning newspapers, Zaretski unthinkingly stuffed the statements into envelopes bearing the return address of the mayor's office. One newspaper noted the odd combination of letter and envelope and printed a jumbo picture of them on the front page. Thus Bobby learned what Edelstein and Zaretski had been up to, and once again Mayor Wagner was embarrassed.

Zaretski, meanwhile, decided to say something on his own about the matter. He told newsmen Bobby's letter was "unwarranted, uncalled for and unfactual." He described Kennedy as "presumptuous" and added, "I didn't tell him how to choose *his* staff, did I?" He charged Kennedy with trying to take over the legislature and snapped, "That's not his job. I would like to see him conduct himself like other United States Senators, attending to his business in Washington and not the business in Albany. I didn't think he was the Democratic State Chairman. I thought he was just elected to the Senate."

Speaker Travia's resentment toward Kennedy was expressed in milder form. He noted that Vice President Humphrey had congratulated him on being named Speaker, but Bobby hadn't. Travia said he thought Kennedy was "misinformed" and wanted to assure Bobby that all appointments would be made on merit and ability.

Wagner tried to smooth out matters by stating that political appointments in themselves weren't necessarily bad (as Kennedy indicated) and he was sure Kennedy's letter was well intentioned. But the criticism continued. Democrats called the Kennedy letter "bad taste." Republicans reminded Bobby he made many political appointments as Attorney General. Rockefeller saw an opportunity to slam Bobby, and acidly remarked, "His boss-controlled candidates lost. He obviously is sore and is carrying on his fight by writing this letter."

Bobby had been snared in the never-ending cat-fight which characterizes his party in New York. All eyes were on him. No matter what his actual role in the Democrats' favorite pastime was, it would be magnified. Republicans responded quickly, too, for anything they could do to cut Bobby down would forestall that day they feared—the day Bobby would unify his party and end Republican successes.

Kennedy's goal of becoming the No. 1 Democrat in New York involves a tactic which can only hurt Republicans. In order to unify Democrats behind him, he attacks Republicanism. And if he successfully unites Democrats, he will remove the ploy by which New York Republicans succeeded for nearly a generation—that is, capitalizing on the split Democratic Party.

Bobby's first objective is to be identified as the Democrat who is the prime mover in deciding who will run for the highest offices in the state. Thus his name figured large in newspaper accounts of the intricate and uneasy maneuvering for the mayoralty nomination after Mayor Wagner startled everyone by announcing he would not run again. And thus Bobby must indulge in constant and detailed criticism of Rockefeller and his administration. He wants to make Rockefeller, already suffering from unpopularity, even more unpopular in order to soften him for the Democratic gubernatorial candidate in 1966.

Indeed, Kennedy's maiden speech in the Senate amounted to an attack on Rockefeller, and a side effect was to catch Senator Javits offguard. The incident illustrated Bobby's ambivalent behavior. Where, in December, 1964, he told upstate New Yorkers they should solve their problems locally, he was now offering an amendment to the Appalachia (anti-poverty) bill and charging

Rockefeller with being "short-sighted" in not requesting that New York be included. Javits quickly had to defend the governor. Rockefeller retorted that Kennedy could serve the affected area of New York—a group of 13 counties, only one of which was listed as "depressed"—by pushing for a federal expressway through the section.

The assault on Rockefeller continued with other statements from Kennedy's Washington office. He charged that the Rockefeller Administration had failed in its handling of the problems of the chronically troubled New Haven Railroad, a principal commuting line for New Yorkers. Kennedy was severe in criticizing the state's treatment of narcotics addicts, said the emphasis was on a "publicity program," and that New York was "derelict" compared with California's effort. (Bobby favors comparisons with California, governed by a Democrat, Pat Brown.) Kennedy also hit Rockefeller for what he called the deterioration of the Hudson River Valley area, for the governor's proposed state sales tax, and on yet another state matter—a bill, which Rockefeller opposed, to raise the state minimum wage to $1.50 an hour, which would exceed the federal minimum of $1.25 an hour. Kennedy noted that he had nine children and needled Rockefeller on something he has in common with him—namely, wealth. Bobby said, "I know I couldn't get by on $1.50 an hour and I doubt if Mr. Rockefeller could."

For seven years, Rockefeller-baiting has been a popular sport with New York's Democrats. Mayor Wagner engaged in a running battle with the Republican governor since 1958, largely over the question of state aid to New York City. Each year Rockefeller would announce, in munificent tones, how state aid to New York City was being increased. And each year, Wagner would moan about how the city was being short-changed. But Wagner's perennial criticisms became tiresome and repetitious, and were even less credible after the resolution of the Albany leadership mess.

Kennedy's attacks on Rockefeller, therefore, were fresh, and were welcomed by Democrats. They served to make Bobby more of a regular in the New York State Democratic Party. Now that Wagner has left the mayoralty race—and with it what political power he had left in New York City—Bobby's credentials as commander-in-chief in the war against Rockefeller are solid.

The crucial battle in that war, of course, will be conducted in 1966 when Rockefeller is up for re-election. In the summer of 1965, Rockefeller was at an all-time popularity low in his state. Kennedy and other Democrats do not underestimate him, however. Rockefeller is a tough, courageous campaigner and does not lack wherewithal. He spent $125,000 of his own money in 1965 to produce *Executive Chamber*, which starred him in a series of television programs about the state's problems. Nor did he shrink from controversial vetoes. He correctly turned down one bill which would enable the City of New York to receive $9 million in federal poverty funds on the grounds the bill was so badly written it allowed the Federal Government to usurp state laws. Later Rockefeller okayed the bill but only after the language was changed. And he spent considerable time in 1965 trying to picture the Democrats as the bumblers and obstructionists they proved to be in the New York Legislature. This, in the face of severe criticism of Rockefeller for the huge, $4 billion budget he called for and for his insistence on a statewide sales tax.

Rockefeller is generally regarded by Democrats as politically damaged and maybe even a sitting pigeon for their candidate to oppose him in 1966. This presents a difficult situation for Bobby, who tends to be a perfectionist when it is up to him to decide who the best candidate would be. The problem for Kennedy is that he might be presented unattractive choices. The name most often mentioned as Rockefeller's opponent in 1966 is that of Franklin D. Roosevelt Jr., chairman of the U.S. Equal Opportunity Commission, and voting resident of Dutchess County, New York. Roosevelt's name is enough to enthuse Democratic voters of middle-age or older vintage, but party professionals do not consider him a suitable candidate. His campaign performance in 1954, when Javits upset him in the Attorney General's race, was considered mediocre, and Roosevelt really is unacquainted with current New York State problems. Those three initials, F.D.R., however, are still potent at the polls, and "young Roosevelt," as he is still called (he is a 50-year-old grandfather), has expressed an interest in running for governor in 1966.

There are others who want to take on Rockefeller in 1966. Nassau County Democratic leader John English has a candidate in

Eugene Nickerson, who, while enjoying a political reputation largely confined to Nassau County, is a bright and ambitious man quite anxious to become governor. Then there's Howard Samuels, a Syracuse industrialist, who has long argued that the future strength of the Democratic Party in New York lies upstate. Congressman Sam Stratton is still trying to rise out of and beyond his congressional district. Robert Wagner, while leaving the Mayoralty, has indicated he would like to stay in public life. Finally, there is the star of the 1965 Democratic Mayoralty primary, Queens District Attorney Frank O'Connor. Though he ran for City Council President in the primary, he got more votes than any of the Mayoralty candidates, and admitted he would like to run against Rockefeller in 1966.

Kennedy dearly wants to name the man to run against Rockefeller. He wasn't so sure he wanted to state a preference for a Democrat to run against Republican Congressman John Lindsay in the New York City mayoralty race. He said he was prepared to campaign for Bob Wagner, and like all other Democrats, was shocked with Wagner's withdrawal. Kennedy took the position he would work for whomever Democrats nominated in the mayoralty primary, and that the candidate could easily defeat Lindsay.

This stance kept Bobby out of the Democratic infighting in New York City, but sustained his reputation of loyalty to the party. "Why should Bobby get into that primary mess?" one of his aides asked. "It can do nothing but get him in trouble."

Whenever Democrats gather in New York City, say, at a cocktail party, and talk about party matters such as the mayoralty situation, Kennedy's name is almost immediately injected. He is looked to as a source of power, as a prime mover, and this is testimony of the fact that he is close to acquiring most of the Democratic political power in New York State. By the spring of 1965, there were three principal groups in the Democratic Party which are inclined to oppose Bobby: The Lyndon-Johnson-forever wing led by Edwin Weisl Sr.; the Wagner forces in New York City; and a scattering of Democrats still unhappy over Bobby's invasion of the state.

Weisl is a 69-year-old Wall Street lawyer of gentlemanly mien and substantial wealth. For years he was a quiet figure in

New York politics. In 1960 he was one of a small group in New York City who supported Lyndon Johnson for the presidency. Soon after the assassination, President Johnson was on the phone with Weisl, asking his old friend for advice and counsel. He is Johnson's man in New York State and serves that role through his position as National Committeeman. He has not exercised his influence in federal patronage matters, but Democrats respect the fact he could, because of his close relationship with the President. Weisl is soft-spoken and amiable, but has a quick memory for favors owed and old antagonisms.

He is a man of the '30's in several ways. Weisl was a good friend of President Roosevelt. In 1937 F.D.R. introduced him to a gangling young Texas Congressman named Lyndon Baines Johnson. A friendship developed and with it a loyalty seasoned by the years. It was also in the thirties that Weisl met and had business transactions with Joseph P. Kennedy. Weisl was associated with John Hertz, then an officer of Paramount Pictures, and Hertz hired Kennedy to make a study of the corporation. According to Weisl, Kennedy and Hertz differed over Kennedy's findings, and Kennedy was unpleasant in his dealings both with Hertz and Weisl. Joe Kennedy's buccaneer manner and hot temper were not forgotten by Weisl.

As long as Johnson is President and Weisl is National Committeeman, Bobby will not have absolute power in New York's Democratic Party.

And as long as Wagner was mayor and held patronage rights over city jobs and also the loyalty of the majority of the city's organizational Democrats, he was a deterrent to Kennedy's power in New York City. But with Wagner leaving City Hall, pro-Wagner Democrats are looking for another leader. Many hoped to find that leader in former City Council President Paul Screvane, whom Wagner favored to succeed him. But Screvane, even with Wagner's public support, was defeated in the mayoralty primary, and Wagner's political strength was further diminished. An anti-Wagner candidate, City Comptroller Abraham Beame, who had the support of Charley Buckley and other old line leaders, won the primary, and thus a new political alignment in the New York City Democratic party was effected.

There is also a group of Democrats who don't like Kennedy because of old grievances and current frictions. Upstate, Congressman Stratton feels he was twice denied higher office by Kennedy. In 1962 Stratton wanted to run for governor, but Bobby used his influence to persuade New York Democratic leaders to select U.S. Attorney Robert Morgenthau as the nominee. Stratton still smarts from the setback he received in trying for the senatorial nomination. In June, 1965, when Kennedy asked the House Appropriations Committee for funds to start work on two upstate New York dams, Stratton opposed the move. The committee, heeding the wishes of the Congressman who represented the area, turned down the Kennedy request and Stratton was delighted.

Nor was Bobby able to make peace with New York Senate leader Joseph Zaretski. A few weeks after the exchange of acrimonious letters, Kennedy visited Albany, spotted Zaretski outside his chambers and shouted—so newsmen would hear—"Hi, Joe!" in a most friendly way. Zaretski, warmed by the greeting, took Kennedy to the Senate floor, got unanimous consent for him to speak. Bobby charmed the legislators with his banter, and brought a hearty laugh when he said, "I thought for a while I might write all of you a letter."

However, the work which the legislature did under the leadership of Zaretski and Tony Travia disappointed Kennedy, and he found it difficult to hold his tongue. In late May he spoke at a Brooklyn Democratic dinner, and in rather biting terms declared Democrats in the legislature had reneged on their campaign promises about nonpartisan redistricting and constitutional reform. "The business of parties is not just to win elections," Kennedy lectured. "It is to govern. And a party cannot govern if it is disunited. . . . We have so far failed our test. We have failed because we have forgotten the lessons of the campaign. We have allowed our campaign unity to dissolve in quarrels within the party." The Brooklyn dinner was boycotted by Mayor Wagner, 13 of Brooklyn's 22 Democratic leaders and by another eminent citizen of Brooklyn, Assembly Speaker·Travia. They stayed away because they were political enemies of Brooklyn's top Democrat, Stanley Steingut, who was being honored at the dinner. Kennedy took notice of their absence.

"Some of the leading Democrats of this area and the state are not present," he chided. "A man who did so much for me, Tony Travia, is not here. It's unfortunate. If there were a dinner for Tony Travia, I would attend."

Kennedy's criticism of the Democratic leadership in the legislature stung Zaretski and he hit right back at Bobby. He said Kennedy's attitude was "divisive," that Kennedy had done nothing to heal the division in the party, and that Kennedy had swallowed "hook, line and sinker" the Republican notion that upstaters must dominate the legislature to prevent New York City from winning control. Kennedy replied wryly that "the way things are developing at the moment, the Republicans don't need very much help in keeping the Democrats split."

A few years ago Bobby avoided, when he could, formal party gatherings, but since becoming Senator, he has been a good sport about attending such Democratic rituals in New York. He does not particularly enjoy taking part in the symbolic fellowship of political dinners and the other gatherings all politicians must attend, but he is always good-natured at these events. Invariably, even at testimonial dinners for other Democrats, Bobby is the center of attention. Dozens of people crowd onto the dais to be photographed with him or to get his autograph. He is pawed over, and bravely smiles through his shyness. He has even been able to master the necessary political art of telling total strangers, "It is good to see you." Kennedy would rather sit in intense conversation with university people, labor leaders, social workers, businessmen who willingly feed him ideas.

Naturally, Bobby takes seriously his position of being head of the Kennedy family at ceremonial functions honoring his late brother. On Memorial Day, he spoke at the unveiling of a marble monument and bronze bust of John F. Kennedy in Brooklyn. A crowd of 20,000 pressed around him, and some of the people, on seeing Bobby, became hysterical. During the ceremony, his eyes filled with tears at mention of his brother. He told the audience his brother would not have approved of such a ceremony because he wanted people to be concerned with the future, not the past. Then Bobby quoted from Alfred Lord Tennyson's *Ulysses*: " 'Tis not too late to seek a newer world."

The public image of Senator Robert Kennedy is generally a favorable one in New York. There is evidence that the Jewish community, which held some suspicions of Bobby, is more comfortable with him now. The Zionist Organization of America presented him with a volume of writings by his brother entitled "John F. Kennedy on Israel, Zionism and Jewish Issues." He is invited to countless Jewish functions. The Jewish Nazi Victims Organizations of America invited Bobby to be their principal speaker when they commemorated the 20th anniversary of the end of World War II. In his speech he referred to the suffering of the Jews during the war, and he restated his total support for the State of Israel. But on an occasion when the mention of "Germany" could revive deep feelings, Kennedy also noted the "intelligent policy" of the present Federal Republic of West Germany toward Israel. Kennedy has a quality of frankness which comes through on occasions like this, and his advisers feel this frankness will serve to reduce suspicions of him.

Another event that captured the attention of New York's Jewish community was the grant of $1,450,000 from the Joseph P. Kennedy Jr. Foundation for establishment of a mental retardation research center at Yeshiva University. Bobby, his mother, and his brother-in-law, Sargent Shriver, attended a luncheon to mark the occasion and happily noted the new installation would be named the "Rose Fitzgerald Kennedy Center" and would be built right alongside the Albert Einstein College of Medicine.

Kennedy is still aware of the difficulty he initially had with the Jewish community in the senatorial campaign. The importance of this community to a politician is readily understood by an appreciation of the fact that there are 2,517,330 Jews in the state of New York, and that 85 percent of those eligible to vote do so. Senator Keating won the confidence of many Jewish voters by sponsoring and supporting legislation they favored and also by faithfully attending Bar Mitzvahs and other Jewish social events. Kennedy feels it is best for him to avoid an awkward show of deferential treatment, and he is seldom seen on the Bar Mitzvah circuit. It would seem Kennedy is right in refraining from making gratuitous gestures toward the Jewish community and in performing, as a Senator, in a way which will win its confidence and respect.

As for voter appeal, Bobby has a good situation in the state of New York. He is very popular among the Poles, the Italians, and the Irish. The Democratic Party traditionally has the overwhelming support of Catholics and Jews, who form the majority of New York State's population. One member of the Kennedy family even cracked: "Bobby is much better off here than in Massachusetts. New York has proportionately fewer Protestants." And when Bobby goes to Harlem or Spanish-Harlem in New York City, crowds swarm around him. With a few exceptions, the heads of the state's labor organizations are enthusiastic supporters of Bobby. The Democrats who originally backed him when he came to New York are still for him, and nearly all the reformers have come around too. Suburban and upstate Democratic leaders are solidly behind Bobby. When State Chairman McKeon resigned in late summer of 1965, he was replaced by another Kennedy man, John J. Burns, mayor of Binghamton and father of 12.

The locus for Bobby's New York operation is the remodeled six-room suite of offices in the Post Office Building near Grand Central Station in Manhattan. There, an extraordinarily gracious receptionist, a former actress, engages visitors in lively conversation about the contemporary paintings, on loan from Buffalo, which hang in the waiting room. Inside, Philip J. Ryan, a former assistant U.S. Attorney, heads a paid staff of eight and 12 volunteers who often work 12 hours a day answering countless phone calls and an average of 150 daily letters. One floor up, Senator Javits' New York staff of three regulars, assisted by as many as 10 unpaid political-science students, carries on as though they work for *the* New York Senator. There is a tone of smooth competence in the Javits office, like that of an established firm.

A Macy's-Gimbels' kind of competition is developing between the New York offices of the two Senators. Ryan sees the function of his office not only to receive requests and complaints—as is customary in any Congressman's office—but to "initiate business." Thus a total of 16 projects has been developed. They include poverty, housing, education, conservation and narcotics, all substantial problems in New York State. Kennedy staffers sometimes go into the field like neighborhood social workers as they gather information on any of the aforementioned subjects. As part of an education project, Kennedy's office wrote to principals of special schools for difficult children in New York City, advising them of benefits they could apply for under the 1965 Education Act and earlier education acts. Staffers go into the field and consult on poverty operations, advising this neighborhood or that agency on what grants they are eligible for.

The mail pours in, most of it containing requests. A member of the "Committee of Outraged Parents" wants to discuss narcotics problems with the Senator. A meeting on the Hebrew Special School for Children is arranged. The Senator is invited to speak at a seminar on the Political Future of Puerto Ricans in New York City. He is asked to appear on the "Irish Hour" radio program. The American Water Color Society wants R.F.K. to attend an exhibit. A businessman has questions on a monorail project. Many of these requests are routine and come to every Senator's home office. The majority of letters Bobby receives in New York City deals with the poverty program, narcotics, education and other subjects Kennedy identifies himself with. Ryan says he is confident the volume of mail and calls will surpass anything Javits might get, and that Kennedy will emerge, though junior in seniority, as the better-known Senator in New York.

Kennedy has managed to poke into other state problems which have attracted considerable interest in the press. He ventured into a strictly local matter when he addressed an educators' meeting and criticized those teachers who refused to teach in Negro neighborhoods. On another occasion, in the spring, Kennedy visited the west shore of the Hudson River in the metropolitan New York City area, and surveyed the garbage dumps, junked cars, dead rats and general atrophy along the river. He shook his head and told reporters, "It all seems dirty to me. Something must be done." At that time, he had just cosponsored, with Senator Javits, a bill to create a "riverway," a park bordering both shores of the Hudson in that area. Any New York politician worth his salt must concern himself with the proposed closing of the Brooklyn Navy Yard. Shortly after his election, Bobby made a *pro forma* visit to Defense Secretary McNamara's office on behalf of the ancient yard—

directed for extinction by McNamara—and got the same negative answers Keating had received months before. Some local problems require special handling. When the anti-poverty program in New York City was charged with scandal and maladministration, Kennedy and his staff quietly conducted its own investigation. He was particularly careful not to criticize the anti-poverty program in Harlem, which is controlled in large part by Congressman Adam Clayton Powell—probably because Powell is chairman of the House Labor Committee, which Kennedy will eventually deal with as he advances labor, welfare and education legislation in the Senate.

One of Bobby's more sensational adventures into state problems occurred in late summer when he made two unannounced visits to two overcrowded state-operated schools for mentally retarded children. What Kennedy reported after these visits amounted to a shaming of the Rockefeller Administration, though Bobby was careful to disclaim any partisan attack. He told the New York State Joint Legislative Committee for Mental Retardation, which somehow had quickly convened in a Bronx hotel, that many children at the two schools "just rock back and forth. They grunt and gibber and soil themselves. They struggle and quarrel—though great doses of tranquilizers usually keep them quiet and passive." He declared "there are no civil liberties for those put in the cells of Willowbrook [one of the two schools in question]—living amidst brutality and human excrement and intestinal disease."

Newspapers, radio and television stations had been alerted that Kennedy was going to make news at the committee meeting, and there was considerable coverage of his criticisms. The story made the front page of *The New York Times* and other papers and also appeared during prime time on television. Kennedy's words carried additional impact because of the fact that the Kennedy family had suffered the experience of having one of its own in a school for the retarded.

Kennedy had spent 80 minutes at one school, 90 at the other, and had not informed the directors of the schools that he was coming. The director of the Willowbrook School, Dr. Jack Hammond, was annoyed with Kennedy's sudden visit, and said he was afraid the charges he made would "devastate the morale of my employes." Dr. Hammond added: "You can't take things out of context and paint a flash picture, either verbally or with camera, and present it as a whole. To understand the operation at all and be fair you have to stay a couple of days. He didn't have enough time here to make the statements he did."

It was revealed later that Kennedy had access to information which described overcrowding and other shortcomings at the two schools. His remarks were based, in part, on two reports which had not been publicly released, but were to be presented to the State Legislature for consideration. In point of fact, the State of New York has generally excellent facilities for the mentally defective and retarded, and the New York State Acting Commissioner of Mental Hygiene, Dr. Christopher F. Terrence, protested that Kennedy had "distorted out of all perspective" the deficient conditions at the two schools. Governor Rockefeller, caught in the heat of the bad publicity, quickly summarized the improvements his administration had made in the State's facilities for the retarded and reviewed his efforts to persuade the Democratically controlled Legislature to increase appropriations for the care of the mentally retarded. He claimed New York's master plan for treatment of mental disabilities "was so outstanding, that it served as the blueprint for the federal program presented to Congress by the late President Kennedy." Rockefeller also stated: "No other state—in fact, no nation—can cite a comparable record of achievement in dealing with mental disability."

Despite the Rockefeller Administration's credible defense against Kennedy's charges, the overall impression the public had of the episode was that Bobby Kennedy had found the unfortunate children living in deplorable conditions in the schools. It was an embarrassing, almost impossible, situation for Rockefeller, Dr. Terrence, and the school directors. Kennedy had indeed spotlighted the worst conditions in an otherwise admirable system of care for these children. Staff members at any such school, however, live with the truth that inmates do rock back and forth, grunt and gibber, and are unable to control their excretory functions.

Kennedy's statement included a disclaimer of partisanship. "Our shortcomings," he said, "are due to no one man and no single administration." But whatever the merits of Kennedy's criticisms of the state's care of the retarded, he had made another successful political assault on Rockefeller.

Bobby caught politicians in both parties off guard shortly after he was elected by showing a remarkable interest in Upstate New York. Traditionally, New York has had one senator oriented toward New York City and the other toward upstate. Kennedy's credentials all pointed him toward an interest in New York City. In the period between his election and the day he was sworn in, Bobby visited 12 upstate cities in a series of "fact-finding" tours, as he calls them. He met with mayors, city councils, boards of supervisors, businessmen, labor leaders and farmers. Some of the old upstate railroad and factory towns have suffered economically from the decline of railroads, the movement of industry to other states and the reduced manpower needed to maintain agriculture. Kennedy did not deport himself as an optimist who had all the answers. He was serious, intent, laconic and even sad as he listened to the recitation of problems.

Where in the fall he had talked of bright tomorrows, now, in the gray of winter, he told people he brought "no magic wand or a briefcase full of solutions." In a discussion of how the area's economy could be improved, an elderly businessman asked, "Isn't it true, Senator, that we *can't* depend on the Government?" Kennedy's reply was not quite appropriate to the thinking of the Great Society. He merely answered "Yes." Wherever he went, he talked of the value of self-help, while assuring his audiences he would see what federal help was available. "I don't think your answer is in Washington," he told Binghamton's city councilmen in their chamber. "Your answer is here." Barry Goldwater could not have spoken these words any better.

The important result, though, was that Kennedy collected and catalogued the list of ills which beset the small town and rural areas of Upstate New York. He made another dozen such fact-finding tours, and had his staff prepare recommendations on how a community with, say, an unemployment problem could be helped. Kennedy encountered such local worries as pulpwood scum on Lake Champlain, the presence of pesticides in milk, the closing of Veterans Hospitals, the proposed shutdown of an airport, even the gathering rockpile on the American side of Niagara Falls. "I was elected Senator for the entire state," he told Upstate New Yorkers, "not just to represent New York City."

Accordingly, he announced plans to open an upstate office in Syracuse. Javits quickly countered by opening *his* upstate office in Buffalo and got it into operation several months before Kennedy was able to select a man to manage his Syracuse office.

The Kennedy penchant to "work" the Republican territory continues and is probably one of the smartest pieces of political effort a Democratic figure of any stature has undertaken in New York in decades. The Democrats have New York City. Their vote builds in other cities. It is the towns, villages and countryside that wait to be wooed. And Kennedy, by being serious, a good listener, and restrained in his pronouncements, has already acquired respect and support in areas long neglected by Republicans. It also removes from Bobby's credentials the onus of being a New York City Democrat. But the remarkable truth is that Bobby, while aware of the political benefit of such upstate attention, actually has developed a protective feeling about these forgotten areas of small-town America, often referred to contemptuously as the "bushes." He watches over them like so many animal pets in need of help and husbandry.

There is already considerable evidence Kennedy will innovate even more in serving his constituency. A man capable of climbing a mountain to make sure he is the first Kennedy to reach the top; a man who will tell a predominantly Jewish audience that U.S. food should not be barred from Nasser's Egypt; a man who would presume to instruct state Democrats publicly how to dispense jobs—here is a man with many future surprises for New York.

After only one year in the state, Bobby is fully inside New York's Democratic political house and no one owns more of it than he does. He is probably the most powerful freshman politician in the state's history. He draws huge crowds. His words, and movements, overcome all competition for attention. His title, "Senator Kennedy," fits him already. Some of the boyishness is gone. He stands a little stooped, his big bony hands ready to be thrust up to make a point. And wherever he goes, there are cries around him, "There's Kennedy . . . There's Bobby Kennedy. . . ." His response is still an awkward half-wave of the hand, and perhaps a remark in humor which tends toward wry.

Even before Wagner's surprising exit from the mayoralty, Bobby was replacing the mayor as the favorite whipping boy of New York State Republicans. The fact that Republicans know who their real political threat is amounts to a tribute to Kennedy's own political strength and also serves to consolidate it. Another sign that his political position is firmer in New York is the feeling of resignation about Kennedy by many Democrats who had misgivings about him when he came to the state as a carpetbagger. Their protests, heard before and during his Senate campaign, that he was ruthless and was using New York as a power base for future ambitions, have subsided—for the present at least—and even the reformers seem to have worked out a truce in their minds.

There are two elective offices in New York which, if occupied by Democrats, could be used to block Bobby from total control of the state's Democratic Party. They are the office of governor and the office of the mayor of the city of New York. In mid-1965, however, Democratic aspirants for those offices were looking *to* Bobby for blessing and support, not away from him. It would be remarkable, indeed, if a Democrat was elected to either of these offices who did not have Bobby's approval. The conclusion must be that it is unlikely Bobby will have any serious trouble from a Democratic governor or Democratic mayor. His Democratic political opposition remains small and in diminished form—from New York State National Committeeman Edwin Weisl Sr., and from a scattering of political figures who feel they have old scores to settle. Mayor Wagner is no longer even modest opposition to Kennedy. If Wagner wants to run for governor in 1966, he will first have to get Kennedy's support.

The true certification of Bobby's ultimate power in the New York State Democratic Party could come at the 1968 Democratic National Convention. It would be that instant when television cameramen will focus on the leader of the New York delegation as he stands up to announce for his state. If Bobby Kennedy has anything to do with it, those cameras and lights will focus on him.

XI
THE BEGINNINGS OF
A SENATOR

□□
□□

THERE IS FEELING OF BEING PART OF HISTORY
that wells deep in the men elected U.S. Senators as they gather for
swearing-in ceremonies on the opening day of a new session. The
Senate Chamber itself, with its cream and dark red marble, its gold
silk damask walls, and the mahogany desks, the snuffboxes and the
anachronistic little bottles of sand used for blotting ink, are reminders of the rich crust of tradition that characterizes this delib-
erative body. The Senate has never felt secondary to the Executive
and Judicial branches of Government, and has often asserted its
position with a show of thundering power. It functions with relatively few rules, and cares not to add many. It tolerates all manner
of outrageous remarks, as long as individual Senators are not im-
punged by these remarks. Indeed, after many months of extravagant
accusation and bellowing rhetoric, the late Senator Joseph Mc-
Carthy was condemned for what amounted to bad manners. The
Senate is hard put to judge its members formally or publicly; rather,
it would prefer to form private judgments. Though the existence
and role of the Senate's "Inner Club" is more talked about than
real, U.S. Senators ultimately act like club members. The initiate
is almost always cordially received, but seldom is any special fuss
made over him. Many a governor, upon becoming a U.S. Senator,
had a painful time in his early months in the Senate because there
was no one around to defer to him and stand in awe of his guber-

natorial power. The new Senator can only let time pass and judgments be formed about him. "The U.S. Senate," the late Sam Rayburn once said from his vantage position as leader of the House, "is the fairest jury before which a man can be tried. In 99 percent of the cases, it renders the right verdict."

Bobby Kennedy took his first step toward that senatorial judgment on January 4, 1965, when the clerk's voice, alphabetically summoning groups of Senators for the oath, called out: "Messrs. Kennedy of Massachusetts and Kennedy of New York . . ." The Senate Chamber seemed like the setting for a graduation exercise. Above, in the galleries, were eight more Kennedys: Ethel and her four oldest children; Joan Kennedy, Teddy's wife; Patricia Lawford and Jean Smith. As many people in the galleries gawked at the Kennedy women as at the brothers walking slowly down the center aisle below.

Teddy's face, usually full to the point of being jowly, was drawn and thin. He walked stiffly, leaning heavily on a cane. For five months he had lain flat on his back, his spine immobilized. Bobby, his shoulders stooped, offered a small smile, and his walk seemed soft. He looked like a man who was thinking, "I shared the greatest office, and now I am among 100. Do I really belong here?" Carl Hayden, Senate President Pro Tempore, his 87 years giving him the appearance of a desert turtle, breathed out the oath to the Kennedy brothers. The galleries cheered long and loud. When the ceremonies were over, many Senators walked to the back of the Chamber where the Kennedys were sitting and congratulated Teddy on his recovery and re-election. They said hello to Bobby, but were reserved.

Bobby drew the press of course. "It will be a totally new life," he told a reporter. "I wouldn't be here unless I had wanted to come, and I'm deeply committed. I expect my manners to be good. I have no complaints." After half a moment he added, "I was remembering and regretting the situation that gave rise to my being here."

Two days later, Bobby was introduced to a duty all freshmen Senators must perform, that of presiding over the Senate when the Vice-President is absent. The freshmen take turns in this duty which becomes tedious and tiresome when there are dull sessions in progress. He was also reminded of his beginner status when he was assigned to a minimum of office space. There were no privileges evident here. Bobby, who had brought from the Attorney General's office a long, fierce-looking stuffed tiger—a gift from Indonesia—had to have it carted home because it took up too much space.

The long arm of Lyndon Johnson circles the U.S. Senate just as it had reached around many a Senator's shoulders in years gone by. For that reason, many observers thought the President would, in effect oversee the assignment of committee posts to Bobby. Johnson knows the mind of the Senate about prerogatives too well to have interfered that way. He is satisfied to get what he wants from his former colleagues without ultimatums or directed orders. As one Senator remarked, "Lyndon won't bypass his own chances of success with his legislative program to get Kennedy. He just won't do it." Another commented, "Lyndon is too smart to rough him up."

Accordingly, Bobby did pretty well with his committee assignments. It used to be that a freshman senator usually wound up with three minor committees and directions on how to find the Senate dining room. But several years ago, then Senate Majority Leader Lyndon B. Johnson worked it out so each freshman Senator got one major committee assignment. The Democratic Steering Committee, which considers committee assignment requests from freshmen Senators, neither feared nor favored Kennedy in its deliberations. His committee assignments were fair and caused no special stir in the Senate.

Bobby's real first choice was the Foreign Relations Committee. "I knew I wouldn't get it," he said later, "so I went for Labor." Teddy was already a member of the Labor and Public Welfare Committee and wasn't overly delighted to have Bobby come aboard too. Bobby could cast a long Kennedy shadow here. "Labor," as it is known in short form, deals with education, health and welfare legislation. Inasmuch as Labor would be important to the advancement of aid-to-education legislation—a subject which greatly interests Bobby—this assignment was ideal for him. Furthermore, Labor would also give him the opportunity to wage modest combat with Senator Javits, his New York colleague who is the ranking minority member of the committee. It is rare to find both New

York Senators on the same committee, and it is apparent there will be occasions when Javits and Kennedy will get in each other's way.

Kennedy's second committee assignment was Government Operations. He is quick to declare he is not a member of that committee's subcommittee on Investigations. He had been counsel and staff director for the investigative subcommittee for several years, and all he needed to revive his image of the relentless investigator was an assignment to it as a member. At that, some Senators think Bobby will use the Government Operations Committee to his advantage one day. "There are opportunities on that committee," explained a Republican Senator, "for plenty of publicity. If you're nationally ambitious, and I think he is, you need publicity."

Bobby has a fondness for the Government Operations Committee and its chairman, Senator John L. McClellan of Arkansas, who took a fatherly interest in him during the labor-investigation days. Bobby knows the committee's work well. Again he confronts Javits, who is also on Government Operations.

Bobby was personally drawn to his third choice, the District of Columbia Committee, though it is not considered a prestige committee. When he was Attorney General, he took a serious interest in the problems of youth in the District, particularly Negro youth, and helped with school and playground projects. There is a transference value for Kennedy with this committee. Many problems of the District, the population of which is 54 percent Negro, are also found in New York City neighborhoods.

Altogether, these committee assignments are appropriate for Bobby. They can be used to develop, to build, and to present new ideas in education, welfare, labor, juvenile delinquency. Kennedy was eager for a special subcommittee on youth to be formed, but the existing subcommittee on unemployment and manpower stood in the way. Whatever Kennedy's ambitions for assignment to prestigious committees may be, however, he is balked by the seniority system. Bobby must wait in line for appointments to the more desirable committees. He is number 99 of 100 senators. His good friend, Joseph D. Tydings Jr. of Maryland, is No. 100 and thus the lowest ranking Senator. Tenure is still the greatest factor in acquiring solid power in the Senate. As a Democratic colleague explained, "Unfortunately from Bobby's standpoint, we operate under the seniority system, not a system of blood relatives."

Bobby Kennedy's arrival in the Senate caused many Senators to pretend he wasn't there, that he was just another freshman. One sourpuss said, "There's not much talk about him. The only attention he'll get is from the press." Bobby's face certainly wasn't new. He had been around the halls of the Senate office buildings for a dozen years, and one old Democrat remarked, "He wasn't friendly with Senators before. He'd go by one of us a dozen times without speaking. He always seemed absorbed in something."

A thoughtful midwestern Democrat who likes Kennedy offered a detached, if realistic appraisal, "Bobby doesn't need the Senate, and the Senate doesn't especially need him. Both are aware of this fact. Bobby will go his own way, and might even form his own group."

A senior Republican Senator pointedly noted that Bobby made two trips to his brother's grave on the anniversary of John Kennedy's inauguration as President, and acidly observed the second trip was necessary because photographers weren't around for the first trip. "This is a pretty sophisticated and hard-boiled crowd," the Senator said of his colleagues. "They notice stuff like that."

Similarly, Bobby's mountain-climbing episode was described by one Senator as "unnecessary showing off . . . just for advertising." Another said, "We all admired him from a physical standpoint, but the whole thing was a publicity gimmick." A midwestern Republican lectured, "Mountain climbing is fine when Congress is not in session, but New York's legislation is important and he should have been here." But this kind of reaction was described by Connecticut's Senator Abraham Ribicoff as a "smear." Ribicoff, who was close to the late President and knows Bobby quite well, said the climb up the mountain named in his brother's memory was "the last catharsis for him. It was necessary for him to salvage himself as a human being. When his brother died, some of him died with him. He had to get it all out by climbing the mountain."

It is customary for freshmen Senators to pay courtesy calls on various Senators soon after arrival on Capitol Hill. Bobby followed the custom, but his candor and shyness do not serve him well in such rituals. Immediately there were comparisons with Teddy's highly successful tour of the Senate offices two years before. "It's painful when Bobby comes in the dining room," a Democratic Senator explained. "We try not to look. Nobody likes him yet. Somehow you don't mind Teddy. He's so outgoing." It is Teddy most Senators get to when they discuss Bobby. "If I'm here fifteen more years," said one veteran, "I'll never develop rapport with Bobby. Teddy is the likable one."

Of course, Teddy has been around long enough to acquire a few privileges of seniority, and more importantly, possesses the capacity to indulge in fellowship. Once, he paid a courtesy call on Mississippi Senator James Eastland, whose votes and views are the antithesis of his Democratic colleagues in the Northeast. Though it was mid-morning, Eastland, warming to Teddy's charm, broke out a bottle of bourbon and poured drinks for his guest and himself. Teddy took a swig, and when his host's attention was diverted, emptied the rest into a wastebasket. Eastland poured again, and again, and was pleased with Teddy's apparently good drinking manners. The situation grew more mellow and Eastland's wastebasket more pungent. The Mississippi Senator is fond of Teddy—he's a real good fellow who would take a drink at 10:30 a.m. with a southern Senator.

Teddy has advantages other than natural conviviality. He was spared the liabilities of working as Senate investigator, political stalker and trouble shooter for his brother, and eventually, the nation's No. 1 cop. Bobby was all these, and his reputation was well known. The different temperaments of the Brothers Kennedy prompted this apprasial from an otherwise sympathetic Democratic Senator, "Teddy talks to you and wants to know what he can do for you. There's no warmth in Bobby. He looks like he's ready to cut someone's gizzard out."

Bobby's reputation for abrasiveness also makes him a man to be reckoned with. "He has more guts in his stomach," said one liberal Republican Senator, "than a lot of people in the Senate have." A corollary observation on Captitol Hill is that Bobby will succeed because of the lethargic condition of the Senate, and the presumptions of many Senators that the venerable institution will never change. The fact is, however, that in 1965, the U.S. Senate was ripe for change, and Bobby's actions as a freshman Senator, while not flamboyant, showed a zest for innovation which prompted predictions that Bobby would go places.

There were other Senators, however, who agreed with one respected Republican who warned, "Bobby will blow his stack before he gets his big chance in the Senate. He has too much impatience, and this is a patient place." Another Senator remarked, "Remember, Bobby could stub his toe the way he handles New York. He's in there with a smart one in Javits." A Republican Senator, far removed from Javits' liberal views, chortled that "Javits made a fool out of Bobby on the Appalachia amendment."

The occasion for the now celebrated Kennedy amendment was a session on February 1, heavy with discussion and debate on the Administration's Aid-to-Appalachia Bill. Senator after Senator got up, in the best tradition of pork-barreling, and described what measures should be taken in his state to alleviate poverty. The "War on Poverty," as it is called, had actually begun under President Kennedy, but now was very prominent in President Johnson's plans for the Great Society. There had been much to do about the impoverished Appalachia region, and the program to help that area had become a bellweather of President Johnson's poverty effort. All winter, various Government agencies and bureaus had urged newsmen and television crews to hurry to the back hills of Appalachia and report on the living conditions there. The stories and programs which resulted showed rural hollows of poverty, the rise of smoke from coal stoves, and the faces of skinny, dirty-faced youngsters in their shack homes. Since most Americans live in circumstances far better than these and think something should be done for the people in Appalachia, the issue has considerable political appeal. A Senator must be *against* poverty just as he must be *for* the flag, motherhood and wide roads.

When the Appalachia bill is coldly analyzed, it turns out to be a tough-minded program, with roadbuilding getting $840 million of the $1.1 billion appropriated. The rest of the appropriations go for water conservation, sewage projects, economic planning and vocational training for the people who live in the multi-state region roughly called Appalachia.

When the Aid to Appalachia Plan was originally proposed in 1963, "Appalachia" was to cover large portions of 11 states, and its northern edge was to be the Pennsylvania-New York border. However, New York's Governor Nelson Rockefeller did not choose to make New York State a participant in the plan when it was first proposed. Rockefeller held that the original concept was to help people in the coal-mining areas which had been chronically depressed. He couldn't see how New York's Southern tier of counties really fitted the description of Appalachia because there was thriving industry in many towns and cities in the area. Rockefeller argued that what the Southern New York counties really needed was completion of intra-state Route 17, the cost of which would be shared by the State and Federal Government. The State of New York and the Federal Bureau of Public Roads had cooperated on the Route 17 project since 1949, when it was first proposed by the Dewey Administration. Sections of this highway had been built, but the project had been tied up in bureacratic red tape in Washington, a situation which vexed both Democrats and Republicans in New York. So, in 1962, Rockefeller wrote Secretary of Commerce Luther Hodges in an attempt to get a speed-up order for Route 17. Rockefeller felt the federal response wasn't satisfactory, and added this to his list of reasons why New York should not be included in the Appalachia program. Another reason for Rockefeller's reluctance to put the 13 counties into the Appalachia program was the fact he was running for the Republican presidential nomination during this period, and did not want the Federal Government designating any section of his state as a poverty area. He was supported in this attitude by several county boards of supervisors who also wanted to avoid the shame of wearing the poverty-area label.

Shortly after being elected, Bobby made several trips to the southern-tier counties in New York which border on Pennsylvania. He came back with a report that in several of these counties, about 15 percent of the families had annual incomes of less than $2,000. Kennedy decided the 13 counties belonged in the Appalachia bill, even though only one county was classified as "depressed" at the time.

He was not alone in the Senate in finding areas outside

Appalachia which might deserve inclusion. Teddy Kennedy had a plan for New England. Arkansas's John McClellan came up with one for the Ozarks. Michigan's Patrick McNamara cited depressed counties on his state's Upper Peninsula as sorely needing help. But Majority Leader Mike Mansfield, fearing that the Appalachia bill would be hopelessly delayed by the elastic notions of his colleagues, dissuaded these Senators from offering their amendments. The only Senator not dissuaded was Bobby. He made the point that the southern-tier counties were contiguous to the area in Pennsylvania already designated to be included in the bill. And he saw a lovely opportunity to embarrass Rockefeller.

But the most Kennedy could do was to offer an amendment directing the Appalachian Regional Commission—which would administer the aid—to *consider* including the 13 counties. Since this commission acted only after consultation with and the approval of the governors of the affected states, Governor Rockefeller would still have the final say for any such program for New York. Kennedy pressed ahead, however, and was adroit enough to give Senator Javits about an hour's advance word that he was going to offer an amendment to the Appalachia bill. Thus Javits was caught on the Senate floor with scant time to prepare a defense for his Republican governor's position.

The Appalachia amendment speech was Bobby's debut on the floor; some newsmen called it his maiden speech. Whichever, it began embarrassingly. The presiding officer, Democratic Senator Joseph M. Montoya, of New Mexico, opened by recognizing "the Senator from Massachusetts." When the laughter died down, Bobby asked that the *Congressional Record* show it was the Senator from New York. That point cleared up, Bobby cited his long interest in Appalachia, going back to West Virginia primary days, and declared Governor Rockefeller had been "short-sighted" in failing to include New York in the program, was guilty of a "grievous error." Therefore, he was proposing an amendment to make possible the inclusion of the 13 southern-tier counties, pointing out they were no better off than the adjoining counties in Pennsylvania. Kennedy was making his points satisfactorily when he was asked to yield back eight of his ten minutes. Without thinking, Kennedy said, "I shall," but Senator Javits, the old pro, called across the floor to advise Kennedy, "Don't yield it back. Reserve it." Kennedy quickly said, "I reserve it." In a moment, Javits was on his feet, neatly instructing Bobby that his amendment was so phrased that "it may take us all the way to the Canadian border." Kennedy had not specified the names of the counties. Furthermore, Javits lectured, the bill specified that New York, like other states, would have to have a program requiring consultation with the governor, and indeed, his approval. So Javits proposed an amendment to Bobby's amendment so that the phrase, "in consultation with the governor of the State of New York," would be included. After this fatherly talk, Bobby agreed to the Javits changes, and his amendment passed by voice vote. *The Congressional Record* was changed that night on Kennedy's request, to expurgate any unflattering references to Rockefeller. Kennedy's Administrative Assistant, Joseph Dolan, told Javits' Administrative Assistant, Richard Auerelio, that Kennedy regretted several of the remarks he made about Rockefeller and had them stricken from the record. This, of course, is every Senator's privilege. And in a statement Kennedy released after his floor appearance on the Appalachia bill, he described some cities in the 13-county area as "relatively prosperous."

The news accounts of the proceedings left the reader with the impression Kennedy indeed had scored a modest victory in getting his amendment passed. Javits was depicted as being nimble in his defense of Rockefeller and adept at handling the Kennedy challenge. So much for the public impression. In the days which immediately followed, however, most Senators remembered the essentials: Bobby defied protocol in giving Javits such short notice; the value of the amendment was really slight because all it did was enable the commission to consider the 13 counties in question; and Rockefeller could continue to argue that one good, modern highway through the area—as projected by New York and the Federal Government many years before—would provide a stimulus to the area's economy.

The exchange between Kennedy and Javits on the Senate floor on February 1 was to be the first in a series of incidents between the two Senators. A pattern emerged, where Bobby would do nothing totally disrespectful of the senior Senator, but neither would he feel inhibited in his position as junior Senator. The more

Bobby shows his mettle and strength in the Senate, the more his rank, "junior Senator," is heard from those suffering affront. For a junior Senator is expected to defer to the senior Senator from his state, even if the senior Senator is of the opposite party. This is the case in Massachusetts, where Teddy Kennedy conforms to protocol, and joins Republican Senator Leverett Saltonstall to announce federal projects and plans for their state. Similarly, the senior Senator is consulted on appointments, including the raft of postmasterships dispensed every year. Bobby's relationship with Javits will be one of the yardsticks fellow Senators use in deciding what Bobby's senatorial manners are.

On the day after the Appalachia episode, the Office of Economic Opportunity, whose director is Sargent Shriver, gave Javits and Kennedy 45 minutes' advance notice about a $390,000 grant to restore a slum block in Harlem. Kennedy's office had been studying the Harlem situation, and when the word came, Bobby could order Legislative Assistant Adam Walinsky to drop everything and turn out a release at once. That Walinsky did in 20 minutes, and the statement was hurried to Bobby at the news conference. Javits arrived without a statement. Kennedy got the publicity advantage in the press. Javits was miffed and suspected Kennedy had advance inside information. Bobby's office was gleeful over the one-upmanship.

Two weeks later, Kennedy flew to Syracuse on a previously scheduled trip. He and his staffers knew an announcement on Syracuse would come from Shriver's office that day, but didn't know the exact timing or the details. While Bobby's plane was in the air, Javits' office—acting on a Capitol Hill tip—phoned Shriver's office and the White House to complain that Kennedy was going to make another surprise announcement of a grant. As soon as Kennedy's plane landed, a staffer phoned Bobby's Washington office and got the information he expected. The White House, mindful that Javits is ranking minority member of the Labor and Public Welfare Committee, had hurried the details to both Javits' and Kennedy's offices of a $483,610 grant for Syracuse. Javits and Bobby vied to get the announcement out first. Kennedy, however, again got the publicity advantage because he was able to make the announcement in the benefited city.

Bobby, through his own actions and through the aggressiveness of his New York and Washington staffs, was giving Javits the fits. There was more to come. Though New York Republicans get only a dribbling of Puerto Rican votes, Javits, to maintain his liberal reputation, champions the cause of the many Puerto Ricans in New York. The Kennedys have always been popular with Spanish-speaking people, and Bobby wanted to arrange for an amendment to change state literacy requirements for voting to help them. Bobby showed his proposal to Javits who found it constitutionally defective. So Bobby took it to Teddy, who serves with Javits on the Judiciary Committee. The senior Senator was furious and protested to Teddy, who persuaded his brother to agree to Javits' modifications for the proposal, whereupon a joint announcement was made. Javits had additional reason to be angry because he had co-sponsored a similar bill in 1962, which had not moved, and he did not want Kennedy to upstage him.

Only a few weeks later Bobby was at it again, this time attacking the New York State program on narcotics users. He characterized the Republican approach by commenting, "I don't think they've gotten off their tail yet." As Attorney General of New York in the mid-'50's, Javits had helped start the very program Bobby was criticizing. Javits also thought he had made a gentleman's agreement with Kennedy that they would work together on a federal narcotics program which would benefit New York and that no announcements would be made without consultation. Moreover, Bobby had embarrassed Javits once more by suddenly putting him in the position of having to offer a quick defense of the Rockefeller Administration. This Javits did rather heatedly at a press conference. When the matter was resolved, Bobby said there had been a misunderstanding.

Despite public handshakes and disavowals of bad feelings, Javits and Kennedy are now on guard with each other, and Javits does not like the unfamiliar feeling of being on the defensive. His staff is pleased when staffers of other Democratic Senators call up and provide tips on what Bobby is up to. And Kennedy's office delights in ferreting out information about federal activity in New York—information which Bobby can use to upstage the senior Senator.

A few well-wishers hoped Bobby would follow Teddy's lead in the Senate and remain fairly inconspicuous in his first year or two. But while Bobby is shy, he is seldom silent on subjects he feels deeply about. In February, he said he was bothered by the fact that more and more money was being spent on aid-to-education and that children, particularly slum children, were falling farther and farther behind. "Our educational system," he lectured a teachers' group, "has operated on the premise that we have no need to change. . . ." Kennedy said if he had to mark schools and teachers, "a good number of school systems would flunk."

He recommended that the records of pupils in school systems benefited by federal aid be checked regularly to determine if those pupils were progressing satisfactorily. Several leading educators, including Lynn M. Bartlett, Superintendent of Public Instruction for the State of Michigan, agreed with Kennedy and also recommended that such a checking system be built into the $1.2 billion federal education program so that its effectiveness could be measured. Though this could lead to charges of federal interference in the educational process, Kennedy got his way. An amendment providing for the checking system was incorporated in the 1965 bill which would give financial aid to elementary and secondary schools.

Again, in April, Kennedy spoke so convincingly on the Senate floor on the disproportionate contribution which New York taxpayers make for federal aid to education that Senator Wayne Morse, never a Kennedy fan, rose to say, "Only self-restraint prevents my shouting Hallelujah, Hallelujah, Amen." Kennedy's presentation was superior. He stressed the fact that New York is burdened with the highest taxes in the nation, spends much more per capita on education than the states most benefited by the proposed aid-to-education bill. He also pointed out that the state of New York also provided education for the enormous numbers of poverty-stricken migrants who enter the state each year. Kennedy's plea for balance in the aid-to-education formula prevented a loss of $17 million to New York State.

Bobby's proclivity for speaking up in situations where freshman Senators usually defer to their elders was not confined to the Senate floor. A few days after the violence and murder at Selma,

Alabama, in early March, a bipartisan group of civil-rights-minded Senators met with Attorney General Nicholas Katzenbach to discuss voting-rights legislation. Senators Paul Douglas and Javits were exercised and wanted action. Bobby, who is knowledgeable about registration problems for Negroes in the South, spoke up and cautioned against haste. He reminded his fellow Senators that even in areas in the South where Negroes could register without difficulty, many did not because they were illiterate or uninterested. Kennedy wanted the Senators to consider these two factors. Javits, an old civil-rights warrior, was irked with this attitude and remonstrated Kennedy. He said any new legislation should be "optimum," and said, "Let's keep our eye on the ball, Senator Kennedy. This is a bill to help guarantee Negroes in the South the right to vote." The meeting was private, but somehow word was leaked to the press about what had transpired. Senators who attended the meeting regretted that a report about the exchange between Kennedy and Javits had gotten into print.

Bobby had another lively inning in the spring after being accused in a Senate subcommittee hearing of finagling a *Life* magazine article which reflected badly on Teamster President James R. Hoffa at a time when he was under indictment. It was claimed that Bobby had provided the magazine with Sam Baron, a disgruntled Teamster who would tell all about Hoffa in an exposé article. Such an article was published in *Life* under Baron's by-line.

The charge against Bobby was made by Thomas A. Bolan, a New York lawyer, who, while defending Roy Cohn in a separate case, came across a memo from a *Life* correspondent which described Bobby's involvement in the article. It would be hard to find a man of the law who would consider it ethical for the Attorney General of the United States to work behind the scenes to discredit a citizen under federal indictment.

The day following the sensational accusation, Bobby asked to be heard by the Senate subcommittee, chaired by Senator Edward V. Long, Missouri Democrat, who had remarked he was "shocked" with the charges against Kennedy. In anger, Bobby declared, "There was an implication across this country that I acted improperly and I resent it." Senator Long said, "I can understand that you would."

In the exchange which followed between Kennedy and the subcommittee counsel, Bernard Fensterwald Jr., Baron was described by Fensterwald as a "fink," a derogatory term unionists apply to anyone who is disloyal to the trade-union movement. Bobby heatedly declared he was "shocked" that Fensterwald would so describe a person who provided information to his government. Bobby went on to testify that the Department of Justice never provided evidence or information to any magazine—including *Life* —on the Baron case; he also testified the *Life* memo which described Bobby's interest in the article, was true. Thus, the matter was left unsettled, and in rather ambiguous form. While Bobby angrily proclaimed his innocence, many newsmen and observers familiar with the workings of journalism in Washington suspected that Bobby, as Attorney General, had promoted and assisted in an editorial effort which damaged Hoffa at a time he was under indictment.

Bobby, who had berated countless witnesses before Senate committees, expressed strong indignation over the conduct of Senator Long's subcommittee. He said if the subcommittee really wanted to reveal finagling and snooping in Government, ". . . the practices of the committee might be studied as well." This barb, aimed at this committee, did not ruffle Senator Long, who replied, "I do regret that the Senator feels that he has not been extended every courtesy by this committee."

Kennedy's display of outrage over the way he had been treated provided critics of his own work on subcommittees with an opportunity they had long waited for. *The Toledo Blade* ran a bristling editorial which stated, in part:

> Isn't it rather late for Bobby Kennedy, of all people, to be complaining about implications and insinuations, which were his chief stock in trade when he was often employing the investigating powers of Congress for political advantage?

Provocative as these incidents were, they only sustained Bobby's reputation for feistiness. His actions on the civil-rights-voting-bill package and his statements about President Johnson's foreign policy were premonitions that Bobby was going to take on heavier matters. They gave cause for senators to elbow each other and say, "Look what Bobby's doing."

In the closed meeting of the civil-rights-minded senators, Kennedy had taken a legalistic line on voting-rights legislation, and indicated support for the Administration approach as outlined by Katzenbach. As the weeks wore on, however, and as Teddy Kennedy sought support for his amendment to outlaw poll taxes in state and local elections, Bobby was ready to go along with his brother. Then a story broke in a Washington paper claiming that it was the Kennedy Brothers vs. Lyndon Johnson on voting-rights legislation. Neither brother wanted any of that, so Bobby did not become a co-sponsor of Teddy's amendment.

There were some odd turns on Teddy's amendment. While the Administration, as represented by Attorney General Katzenbach, opposed the amendment on constitutional grounds, Bobby got Katzenbach and Burke Marshall, who formerly headed the Civil Rights Division of the Justice Department, to coach Teddy on how he could best phrase his amendment to make it constitutional. By mid-April, Bobby declared Congress did have the power to end *all* poll taxes. Thus, he was now fully allied with his brother. But the brothers agreed it would serve no purpose for Bobby to help gather votes in support of Teddy's amendment. Indeed, Bobby's involvement might even have turned away votes.

Teddy faced formidable opposition from Senate Democratic Leader Mike Mansfield and Minority Leader Dirksen, both anxious to get on with the business of passing the voting-rights bill. Teddy, however, from his Judiciary Committee post, brought his charm and influence to bear on civil-rights-minded Senators. The Administration pointed out that it wasn't the controversial poll tax which kept Negroes from voting so much as the fact that Negroes were denied the right to register in the first place. Nevertheless, Teddy was able to muster support because of one single, persistent fact: The poll tax was long a symbol of Negro oppression, and many Senators wanted to eliminate it by legislation and let the Supreme Court decide the constitutionality afterward. Thus the lines were drawn between Teddy's bloc of Senators and those who favored the Administration's position as laid down by Leader Mansfield.

The confrontation between Teddy's group and the Administration forces was dramatic. Three Kennedy women sat in the galleries: Teddy's wife, Joan; Ethel Kennedy; and Mrs. Eunice Shriver. Chance made it even more dramatic for, as the debate began, Bobby again presided from the Vice President's rostrum. Senator Everett Dirksen, speaking in his rolling, mellow voice, asked, "If Congress can tell the states by statute this afternoon that they cannot impose a poll tax, why not tell them they cannot impose a cigarette tax or any other tax?"

Mansfield opposed the amendment on practical grounds: "The choice," he said, "is between the course of risk and the course of sureness." To him, "risk" was the constitutional test Teddy's amendment would have to pass, and "sureness" was the soundness of the Administration bill.

Teddy rose from a seat in the front row next to Mansfield and defended his amendment although, by early count, he already knew he did not have enough votes for passage. "It is a settled constitutional doctrine," Teddy declared, "that where Congress finds an evil to exist, such as the economic burden in this case, it can apply a remedy which may affect people outside the evil." This was Teddy's best argument, but it wasn't strong enough.

Even so, there was expectancy and tension when the roll call was taken. Teddy lost, 49-45, but among the majority of 49 were a number of southern Democrats and northern Republicans whom the Administration had to recruit to defeat Teddy's amendment. By gathering 45 votes to his point of view, Teddy had made an impressive show of strength, and after the roll call many Senators who voted against him came to his seat and patted him on the back. It was an honorable defeat for the Kennedys.

Nevertheless, the voting-rights bill was to provide a measure of victory for the Kennedys, and for Bobby. There are about 500,000 Puerto Ricans in New York City of voting age who have fulfilled the residency requirements to vote. Less than half of them are registered, largely because Puerto Ricans are slow to learn English and New York State's simple literacy test is too much for them. About 90 percent of the Puerto Ricans vote Democratic, and they are especially fond of the Kennedy family.

Bobby had been enthused all spring about the idea of pushing for an amendment to the civil-rights voting-rights bill which would provide that no person should be denied the right to vote because of inability to speak, understand, read or write English, so long as the person has a sixth-grade education. After his earlier tiff with Javits on this proposal—a spat mediated and settled by Teddy Kennedy—Javits agreed to co-sponsor Bobby's bill to amend the voting-rights legislation. Again, there was opposition from the constitutionalists, who said the Federal Government had no right to tell the states how to conduct their elections. Bobby sounded out a majority of the Senators on his amendment, and to his delight, learned he had enough votes to win.

In the middle of all this, however, Republican Congressman John V. Lindsay of New York City caused a major surprise by announcing he would run for mayor of New York City. In a tight race, the thousands of Puerto Ricans who could be added to election rolls by Bobby's amendments would be the difference between victory or loss for Lindsay. Senator Javits was on the spot. He dearly wanted Lindsay to upset Mayor Wagner and show the nation that the New York brand of liberal Republicanism is successful. But he wouldn't back off the amendment, said he was "proud of it . . . because it is right." Furthermore, Javits said, Congressman Lindsay was also for it, "without hesitation."

The debate over the Javits-Kennedy amendment was minimal, although Republican Senator Thurston Morton of Kentucky needled his New York colleagues. "New York has a Republican governor and a Democratic legislature and has been preaching for years to the rest of us around the country how to run things," Morton said. "Don't you think they could work this out in Albany?"

The amendment passed easily, 48-19, and Bobby even got the satisfaction of support from Florida and Louisiana as well as from the Senate Leader Mike Mansfield. Though the House voted the amendment down, 217-202, it was restored in conference between the Senate and House and Kennedy's plan prevailed. The constitutional question about the amendment remains, however. In any case, New York's Democrats now look for a harvest of an additional 100,000 Puerto Rican votes. Republicans grind their teeth.

The amendments which Bobby was able to get passed on education, voting rights and, the Appalachia program were estimable accomplishments. But his most significant action, as a freshman Senator, were his major criticisms of the Johnson Administration's foreign policy and his statement on American nuclear policy. When Kennedy spoke on these matters, he spoke as a man who had not long ago served as assistant President of the United States. In the spring of 1965, the nation was increasingly concerned with the serious problems in Vietnam, in the Caribbean and with the major Communist powers. In the minds of most Americans, Bobby Kennedy is strongly identified with the memory of President Kennedy and how he had dealt with foreign relations and nuclear policy. As early as June of 1964, Bobby had suggested in his speech at the California Institute of Technology that military actions alone were not enough to win a lasting victory in Asia. In the spring of 1965, Bobby was even more convinced that the Johnson Administration was counting too heavily on military operations in Vietnam and should concentrate more on the political and economic aspects of our difficulties there. Kennedy's views were hardly original, for most critics of the Administration used the same line.

He refrained from making his thoughts on Vietnam public until May 6, when the Senate debated President Johnson's request for a special $700 million appropriation to continue the war in Vietnam. A half-dozen Senators had spoken, but most of the time was used by Senators Ernest Gruening, Wayne Morse and Gaylord Nelson, who opposed the President's request, and who cast the only Senate votes against it. When Bobby spoke, he first stated his generalized support of the Administration on Vietnam and also on the question of the Dominican Republic. But he offered support which was tentative with the understanding there would be no "blank check" for American activities in Vietnam. Kennedy stressed that the Administration should work for "honorable negotiation" between the warring Viet Cong and the South Vietnamese. Then he added, "I believe that we have erred for some time in regarding Vietnam as purely a military problem when in its essential aspects it is also a political and diplomatic problem. I would wish, for example, that the request for appropriations today had made provisions for programs to better the lives of the people of South Vietnam. . . ."

This amounted to support, with a rather strong note of reservation. Bobby's remarks on the revolution in the Dominican Republic, however, all but amounted to a break with Administration policy. He agreed with President Johnson's determination to keep Communism out of this hemisphere. "But this cannot mean," said Bobby, "that we plan to act on our own without regard to our friends and allies in the Organization of American States." Thus he criticized the unilateral character of U.S. intervention, and praised the O.A.S. for its role in the cease-fire negotiations in the Dominican Republic. "This seems to be a record deserving commendation, not criticism," Bobby noted. And he lectured about our future course in Latin America:

"Our determination to stop Communist revolution in the hemisphere must not be construed as opposition to popular uprisings against injustice and oppression just because the targets of such popular uprisings say they are Communist inspired or Communist led, or even because known Communists take part in them."

In the case of the Dominican Republic, Kennedy acknowledged the presence of professional Communist operators, but asked that the matter be kept in perspective and reminded his audience that "the revolutionary forces include also many non-Communist democrats."

Naturally this speech stimulated a number of newspaper and magazine interviews with Kennedy and his staff. In one speculative article, he was described as saying that President Kennedy would have acted differently from President Johnson on the Dominican Republic problem. This article angered Bobby, and he quickly denied he ever speculated in this fashion. Nevertheless, Bobby had given the impression that he had indeed broken with President Johnson, in a modest way perhaps, on foreign policy. His remarks on the matter became more vehement. "It is not a question of intervening or not intervening," he explained, "but rather of doing it legally or illegally."

This seemed to be statement enough from Kennedy, but he was to deliver two more startling speeches within a matter of weeks. On June 23 he spoke again from the Senate floor on the proliferation of nuclear weapons among nations, and urged President Johnson to halt the spread of these weapons. This speech also stimulated comment from the press and caused pain to the White House. Kennedy had declared that five nations could now explode nuclear bombs, and that "a dozen, perhaps a score of other nations" could develop nuclear bombs in the next three years. A situation could soon develop, he had warned, where the actions of an irresponsible leader ("the head of one of the innumerable two-month governments that plague so many countries . . .") could lead to a chain of reprisals and even the utter destruction of the world. While Kennedy acknowledged President Johnson's concern with the spread of nuclear weapons, he laced his speech with references to President Kennedy's foresight in his policies on the control of nuclear weapons. Then he quoted his brother as having said in 1963, "I ask you to stop and think what it would mean to have nuclear weapons in so many hands, in the hands of countries large and small, stable and unstable, responsible and irresponsible . . . There would be no rest for anyone then, no stability, no real security and no chance of effective disarmament."

Bobby asked for President Johnson to initiate negotiations "at once" with all nations having nuclear weapons, including Communist China. Without directly connecting this urging with a suggestion that the United States be more moderate, perhaps conciliatory, in its negotiations with other nations on nuclear matters, Bobby pointedly quoted President Kennedy in the closing portion of his speech. We must remember, Bobby stated, "as President Kennedy said, that 'no government or social system is so evil that its people must be considered as lacking in virtue.' . . . In the final analysis, our most basic common link is that we all inhabit this small planet. We all breathe the same air. We all cherish our children's future. And we are all mortal.' "

Senate Majority Leader Mike Mansfield was the first Senator to compliment Bobby about his speech. Mansfield had long questioned the American conduct of the war in Vietnam, and he told Bobby, "It is a speech that should have been given because as long as we accept the status quo, the more we will continue to move backward." Senator Gale McGee of Wyoming also praised the speech and added that it would be "criminally irresponsible" to use the war in Vietnam as an excuse for delay of nuclear disarmament. Senator George McGovern of South Dakota called Bobby's speech "one of the most significant statements made in this session of Congress." Senator Phillip Hart of Michigan said the speech was "magnificent." All told, 16 Senators commended Bobby for his speech.

He had sent a copy of the speech to the White House one day before he delivered it and had offered not to give it if there were objections. The White House did not reply. Vice President Hubert Humphrey read the speech just before Bobby delivered it in the Senate chamber and told him he believed it was "thoughtful and constructive."

What Bobby had actually done was to hit the Johnson Administration in a vulnerable area, and he even acknowledged that it was difficult to negotiate new treaties on nuclear-weapons control while a war was being waged in Vietnam. President Johnson had appointed a committee to study the world-wide spread of nuclear weapons, and that committee, headed by former Deputy Defense Secretary Roswell L. Gilpatric, had delivered its report to the President in January of 1965. The Gilpatric report was classified "top secret" and sent to the Defense and State departments and the Atomic Energy Commission for study. It was not sent to the Joint Congressional Committee on Atomic Energy, or to the Armed Services Committee; and when Bobby was later asked by newsmen why these committees had been "left out," he replied, "You better ask the Executive Department." The only comment from the Executive Department came from White House Press Secretary George Reedy, who noted that the Gilpatric report was being studied. He added rather coolly, "Of course, we are glad Senator Kennedy is also interested in this field."

There was and is no question that the development of nuclear weapons by an increasing number of nations is of great concern to the United States. That concern was manifest in the Test Ban Treaty negotiated by the Kennedy Administration in 1963. It is also true that President Johnson, in 1965, was in the painful throes of dealing with difficult foreign questions, the most vexing of which was Vietnam. For Kennedy to speak out on the need for new treaties on nuclear weapons—however laudable that goal is—was, in effect, to provide just one more harassment for the Johnson Administration. While 16 Senators and many important newspapers lauded Kennedy's speech, most of the other 83 Senators and many officials in the State and Defense departments concluded that Bobby once again had acted with audacity.

Brother of the late President or not, Bobby was still a freshman Senator, and though his nuclear speech had been strong and thoughtful, there were other Senators whose seniority made it more appropriate for them to talk up on the question. New Mexico Senator Clinton Anderson or Rhode Island Senator John Pastore— veteran members of the prestigious Joint Atomic Energy Committee—had chosen other occasions, when the U.S. was not involved in hostilities, to speak on the nuclear-weapon question. Bobby's speech clearly marked his independence in the Senate, and his explanation for delivering it was, "These are matters about which I've had strong feelings for some time, so I spoke out on them."

Kennedy could have said the same about his next speech, delivered on the morning of July 9, not on the Senate floor, but in a converted streetcar barn in Washington, where 149 police officials from 22 foreign nations were being graduated from the International Police Academy. He began by saying he wanted to discuss the question of revolutionary wars, the kind of police officers might have to deal with in their own countries. The Academy, an adjunct of the Agency for International Development, specialized in teaching methods for combatting Communist infiltration by guerrilla forces.

Bobby had worked on the speech for several days with his legislative assistant Adam Walinsky. About 3:30 p.m. the day before he was to deliver it, copies of the text of the speech were sent to the news media in Washington. Within the hour, reporters were phoning Kennedy's office to ask if the Senator was going to begin an extensive attack on the Administration's Vietnam policies. Newsmen, familiar with Kennedy's earlier speeches on foreign and nuclear affairs, spotted several passages which seemed sharply critical of the Johnson Administration's conduct of the war in Vietnam. Among the passages were these:

If all a government can promise its people, in response to insurgent activity, is ten years of napalm and heavy artillery, it would not
be a government for long. . .

Victory in a revolutionary war is won not by escalation, but by
de-escalation. . .

Air attacks by a government on its own villages are likely to be
far more dangerous and costly to the people than is the individual
and selective terrorism of an insurgent movement. . .

In the early evening, Kennedy decided to have the provocative passages deleted from the text which he would deliver the
following morning. The original text of any speech, however, once
it is distributed, can be used *as is* by the press. So on July 8, newsmen filed their stories about the speech they had received from
Bobby's office. The next day, Bobby did not actually criticize the
President when he spoke to the graduating policemen, but the story
which newspapers and broadcasters carried was that Kennedy had
again attacked the Johnson Administration on Vietnam. The real
theme of the speech was that the American approach to revolutionary wars should be primarily political, not military—which was
the way President Kennedy would have seen the situation too.

Bobby argued that military action alone cannot succeed in
nations where social revolutions are taking place. He cited the example of the Philippine Republic, where Communist insurgents
were stopped in the '50's by a combination of military force and
effective social reform. After he delivered the speech, received by
a fairly impassive audience, Kennedy met with reporters and emphasized that his criticism was about United States policies during
the last 20 years, including his own brother's Administration. "We
can all do better," he told newsmen. But for all the fine words and
later explanations, the truth was that the deleted passages were a
severe criticism of the Johnson Administration's policies in Vietnam
and came at a time when President Johnson had indicated the Viet-
namese war would be escalated. Bobby had again displayed his
unerring tendency to get into controversy, to stir up the air and
attract attention.

Robert F. Kennedy, in mid-1965, was no ordinary freshman
senator. A decade earlier, any freshman who aggressively amended
major bills, questioned his elders (sharply at times), and rebuked

his own Administration would have been considered a brash whip-persnapper. There are Senators who do consider Bobby just that—a brash whippersnapper. But the majority of Senators *do not* because they realize that the United States Senate, in 1965, is going through a major transitional period.

Many of the great southerners are gone—men like Senator Walter George of Georgia, Carter Glass of Virginia, Olin Johnston of South Carolina. Other southern Senators who were always in the forefront for constitutionality don't show as much fighting spirit anymore, or are elderly or ailing—Senator Richard Russell of Georgia; Harry Byrd of Virginia; Spessard L. Holland of Florida; James O. Eastland of Mississippi; and Samuel J. Ervin of North Carolina.

Even the liberal Senators who fought from the heart have declined in number and influence. Hubert Humphrey has gone on to the vice-presidency. The voice of Paul Douglas of Illinois is heard less frequently. New York's Herbert Lehman left the Senate in 1957. Michigan's Pat McNamara, a former pipefitter with a social conscience, is in his seventies, and may not be a candidate for re-election in 1966. The "middle men" of the Senate, those who usually favor the moderate course, as exemplified by Mansfield, are bland and lack stature. And on the Republican side, an ailing but increasingly respected Senator Dirksen presides over a feeble and divided minority opposition.

The new ferment in the U.S. Senate, the "new boil," is being generated by the band of recently elected "secular liberals," as one of their colleagues calls them. These are totally pragmatic men moved more by charts, polls and averages than by fiery conviction. Their number includes Senators Birch Bayh Jr. of Indiana; George McGovern, South Dakota; Thomas J. McIntyre, New Hampshire; Walter F. Mondale, Minnesota; William Proxmire and Gaylord Nelson of Wisconsin; Gale McGee, Wyoming; and of course, the brothers Kennedy. The new breed is less constrained by constitutional considerations, they are more inclined to pass laws and let the Supreme Court decide afterward on the constitutionality. They have no leader at the present, and perhaps they never will have one, for the Senate remains a collection of individualists. But the Kennedy brothers could be the rallying force for this new breed.

Both Teddy and Bobby provide an excitement the Senate hasn't experienced in some time. When they enter or leave a Senate committee hearing room together there is the inevitable cluster of teen-agers crowding close to them for autographs. When the Senate is in session, and the walnut doors open to let them enter—Teddy leaning on a black teakwood cane, Bobby somber-appearing and slightly stooped—there is buzzing from the people in the galleries. If either brother looks up to the gallery, there is a ripple of gasps or giggles from the young girls sitting there.

The motions and manner of the brothers differ greatly, however. Bobby, because of his low seniority, has to sit in the absolute last row of seats in the Senate Chamber, a rump tier of four places for freshman Democrats. Teddy sits closer to the front because of his seniority. When there is business which concerns Bobby, as the Puerto Rican voting-rights amendment did, he moves about the floor nervously, putting his hand to his mouth, looking like a worried basketball coach. Teddy is more composed, and partly because of his physical disability, remains near his seat. He is quicker to smile and scrupulously courteous when he addresses the presiding officer of the Senate. He is unquestionably more popular with his fellow Senators than Bobby is. One Democratic Senator, noting Bobby's outspokenness, observed, "If I had to pick between the two, Bobby appears to be more diligent. But Teddy seems to have the makings of becoming a Senator's Senator." A friend of both Bobby and Teddy, a man of Irish extraction, describes their personality differences by saying, "Teddy is smiling Irish. Bobby is black Irish, moody and morose."

When Bobby congratulates another Senator on the Senate floor—that great pit of elephantine bowing and trumpeting—the felicitation is quick, almost abrupt. Teddy is more inclined toward glad-handing and back-thumping. He coaches Bobby on how to get along in the Senate, even talked him into attending the breakfast prayer meetings put on by Mississippi Senator John Stennis. Teddy and Bobby both realize the need for Bobby to gain understanding and develop friendships with many Senators who now eye him coolly. Those Senators who know and like Bobby try to explain to their colleagues that the longer you know Bobby, the more you will like him. Bobby's membership in the Senate Democratic Campaign

Committee will provide him with a schedule of speaking dates for fund-raising dinners. This kind of party duty has won friends for many a Senator, and in Bobby's case, it could also serve to help erase old doubts about him. "By traveling around the country, helping other Senators raise campaign money, by learning how to accomplish things peacefully here in the Senate," said one Democratic Senator of Bobby's relations with his colleagues, "that's how Bobby will win the lasting chips you need around here."

The Kennedy brothers do a lot of talking back and forth on the phone. They also exchange needling notes, reminding one another who is overshadowing whom. When they are in kidding moods, Teddy calls Bobby "Robbie Boy" and Bobby calls his brother "Eddie." Six years separate them in age; eight years separated the late President and Bobby. The pressures on Bobby and Teddy in the Senate are not so intense as those Jack and Bobby felt in the Kennedy Administration. Therefore, there is less reason for Bobby and Teddy to become so close to each other. But they are close, and as they work together in the Senate, they will probably become closer.

Yet they have had a few senatorial differences. They split on a total of three votes in the first six months of 1965, the most significant being on a bill to label cigarettes as a potential health hazard. Bobby stood up on the Senate floor and argued that cigarette advertising should carry warnings that smoking endangers health. Teddy was politeness itself as he rose and grilled Bobby on the validity of his argument. Bobby responded with statistical evidence on the dangers of cigarette smoking. Bobby smiled as he realized he was losing the debate, and Teddy voted with 74 of his colleagues against Bobby, who had the support of only three other Senators. On another occasion, the brothers were attending a meeting of the Veterans Affairs Subcommittee when the question of closing certain veterans hospitals in New York State came up. Teddy was presiding at the meeting. Bobby questioned, at considerable length, the witnesses who testified that the New York hospitals in question were indeed in good condition and should not be closed down. Bobby got a bit carried away with his probing and Teddy interrupted, saying, "If the Senator from New York will yield . . ." Bobby yielded, and Teddy questioned another witness about hospitals in Massachusetts. Bobby was annoyed and doodled impatiently on a pad. When he was permitted to resume his own questioning, he turned to his brother and said caustically, "I am glad we got that clarified for Massachusetts, Senator. Now, to get back to New York . . ."

But this was only a mild, even good-humored tiff, and the essential truth is the Kennedy brothers constantly confer with each other, trade information, usually vote liberal on legislation, and help each other in every way. Bobby says of their relationship, "I think we have, as I did with my older brother, the same general interests. Our philosophies are the same. And as brothers we obviously talk more together. But you can't put us in any categories."

Of the two brothers, however, it is Bobby who is geared to do things in a big way. It is Bobby who uses "The Caroline," the Kennedy airplane which is now a legend. It is Bobby, who, through the Kennedy family offices in New York City, makes the most use of the research, polling and organizational facilities available there. Like Teddy, he has the family money and wherewithal to get things done which many Senators simply cannot afford. Despite his seniority in the Senate, Teddy, thus far, has deferred to Bobby on the matter of speaking out on major issues. It is Bobby to whom the press, the politicians and ultimately the public, will look for major political moves, indeed, a new "Kennedy leadership."

All Kennedys attract, recruit, and try to hire the best people. Bobby has a staff which compares in quality with any on Capitol Hill, built around five of his former aides at the Justice Department.

There are 100 men on the Hill who are indispensable to their employers, United States Senators. These men are called "Administrative Assistants" and though they are, in effect, executive officers, their duties are not standardized. An "A.A." can be political liaison man, speechwriter, or mere coat carrier or No. 1 adviser. Bobby's A.A. is Joseph F. Dolan, who served three and one-half years as Assistant Deputy Attorney General under Bobby, and whose association with the Kennedys goes back to 1956, when he was Legislative Assistant to Senator John F. Kennedy.

Dolan, a 44-year old lawyer, was born in New York City, but has spent most of his adult life in Washington and in Denver, where he was a member of the Colorado House of Representatives.

He is long on legislative experience, much of it investigative, and at the Department of Justice he screened candidates for judgeships and worked on legislative programs within the Deputy Attorney General's purview. On Capitol Hill, Dolan is considered capable, politically professional, and he has a good sense of humor. An associate describes Dolan as "a completely disguised intellectual. The further you push, the more you realize there is, and the more you realize you will never hit bottom."

Kennedy's Legislative Assistants look like twins and are among the youngest in such jobs on the Hill. Four years ago they were greenhorn law-school graduates, and now they are drafting amendments and bills which will help form Bobby's senatorial reputation. They are Peter Edelman, 27, Harvard Law School ('61, *magna cum laude*) and Adam Walinsky, Yale Law School ('61, Order of the Coif). Both are dark-haired, spectacled, intense, and cause confusion among secretaries because they are look-alikes. They first met in mid-1963 when they became special assistants at the Justice Department. Both had worked as clerks for federal judges, Edelman having served U.S. Supreme Court Justice Arthur Goldberg. When Bobby resigned as Attorney General, Edelman and Walinsky joined his campaign staff as legislative researchers and speechwriters.

On Capitol Hill they are already known as the precocious and occasionally irritating Kennedy aides who supply their boss with detailed briefings. At this stage in his Senate career, Bobby is mostly confined to offering legislative amendments. "How could it be otherwise," Walinsky asks, "when the Great Society has a program for everything?" However, he has equipped Kennedy with information and proposals on aid to education, the Appalachia program, Hudson River conservation, and police brutality in the South. Edelman has drafted Bobby's programs and legislation on narcotics addiction, cigarette advertising, voting rights for Puerto Ricans, the New Haven Railroad commuter service. Edelman and Walinsky are like two phenomenal halfbacks on the freshmen squad who you just know will be All-Americans by the time they are juniors. A year or so from now, Kennedy will probably be offering major bills drafted by these young lawyers.

A transitional figure in Bobby's Senate office was Edwin

O. Guthman who, for three years as press secretary to Bobby at the Justice Department, was chief custodian of his public image. Guthman fended off charges of "ruthless" and countered with background briefings for reporters during which he described the "authentic Robert Kennedy," the Attorney General who warred on crime, helped the nation's youth, advanced rights for Negroes, and served as principal adviser to his brother in the White House.

Guthman had been through the Teamster days; the 1960 Presidential campaign, the dramatic events which surrounded Bobby's career in the Justice Department, including the violence at Oxford, Mississippi; Bobby's world travels; the assassination, and the New York Senate campaign. He knew the entire Washington press corps and a good part of the press outside of Washington, and was respected by newsmen. He joined Bobby in body-slamming touch football, fetched Bobby's inhalator when his sinuses clogged up, suffered through his sadness following the assassination, and helped hold back overeager crowds from the open convertible during the senatorial campaign.

During the Senate campaign a number of opportunities for increased income came Guthman's way; and reluctantly, in March, he broke the news to Bobby that he would accept an offer by the Los Angeles *Times* to become its National News Editor in May of 1965.

Guthman's successor, Wes Barthelmes, a former Washington *Post* reporter, who had been serving as Administrative Assistant to Congresswoman Edith Green of Oregon, was selected after extensive interviewing by Kennedy, Dolan and Guthman. His chores will not be simple. Newsmen and writers from all over the world present hundreds of inquiries about Bobby, and he is always surrounded by the rumors, intrigue, talk and speculation Washington newsmen thrive on. Bobby Kennedy is the kind of public figure whose words and actions are always magnified and wrapped with weighty significance by journalists.

Bobby also needs a personal secretary of monumental endurance and abiding devotion. He has one in Miss Angela M. Novello, best known as "Angie," who has been with him since 1955. Angie can be seen at 9 a.m. behind a mountain of mail on her desk, and often can be found in the same situation 12 hours later. She has a sense of who's *for* and who's *against* Bobby Kennedy and conducts her business accordingly. One observer, who understandably wants to remain anonymous, says Kennedy staffers regularly gulp "loyalty pills." Angie acts as the sorority mother to the dozen or so girls who type, file, receive visitors and otherwise perform an enormous number of tasks.

The Kennedy offices are small and poorly laid out, a bit worse than those usually assigned to junior Senators. The main suite is in the New Senate Office Building and consists of three tiny rooms and a large office which is Bobby's. In these rooms, as many as 18 aides work in all the comfort of two people in a telephone booth. Desks are piled high with Senate documents, research, periodicals, and the endless correspondence. The mail comes in like wheat into a bin, a thousand letters a day, a total of 183,000 letters the first six months. At last count, several thousand letters remained unopened. Bobby's mail is the largest received by any Senator on Capitol Hill, twice as large as that addressed to Teddy. It is rich with emotion, a sense of communion, lavish praise, cheering and supplication; more than one third of it comes from outside New York State.

Bobby's staff in his Washington office works 10- and 12-hour days, and though Bobby is often away, it seems as though he is always there because his taskmaster presence looms. Everyone works as though the next hour were a deadline. His office seems to be the last one on Capitol Hill to take a coffee break, and the first one where the typewriter ribbons need changing. Secretaries who felt they couldn't survive the Kennedy marathon have left, admiring Bobby for what he is trying to do but weary from doing it for him. And one critic complained that Bobby too often returns from long weekends of vacationing to criticize the staff for being behind in its work.

The Kennedy fans who daily troop into the cramped waiting area of his ground-floor offices know none of this, of course. Most of them ask to see Bobby, know that they won't be able to and then leave happily anyway when the receptionist smiles and tells them that the Senator will be told about their calls. The visitors usually linger for a moment to look over the collection of photographs, taken of Bobby during Kennedy Administration years, which line the walls of the waiting room.

This collection of photographs is only a sample of what is in Bobby's office, a blue-carpeted room that looks out on the corner of Constitution Avenue and First Street, Northeast. The visitor is at once reminded of the importance of the Kennedy family to Bobby. A large oil portrait of Lt. Joseph Jr. hangs over the couch opposite Bobby's desk. It hung in the President's office until November 22, 1963. The memory of Joseph Jr. is further commemorated by a picture of the Navy destroyer which bears his name and on which Bobby served as a seaman. There is a formal photographic study of Mr. and Mrs. Joseph Kennedy Sr. and their children and spouses. There is a picture of Bobby's children in prayer. There is another of him, in color, as he stands atop a ski slope.

The family's political history is there. President William Howard Taft stands rotund and jolly with Boston Mayor "Honey Fitz" at Beverly, Massachusetts, in 1912. A portrait of the members of the Hoover Commission, including Joseph Kennedy Sr., is inscribed to Joe by his friend, Herbert Hoover. There is a photograph of Harry S Truman with Teddy, and one of Bobby talking to Astronaut John Glenn and Robert Frost.

In one corner, over a table, is a collection of photographs and memorabilia of John F. Kennedy which amounts to a shrine. Most prominent are the striking photographs which bear quotations from his speeches and books. An impressionistic painting depicts the late President standing before a joint session of Congress. A sheet of ruled, yellow legal paper with the doodlings and notes President Kennedy made at his last Cabinet meeting, October 29, 1963, is framed in black and inscribed: "For Robert Kennedy, from Jackie." And there is a photograph of Bobby's eldest son, Joseph, sitting by the White House fountain. It is inscribed: "A Future President Inspects His Property—(signed) John F. Kennedy."

Bobby's desk is almost clear of paper. A folder, "Calls to Make," seems urgent. Marked copies of magazines lie nearby. A four-inch statue of St. Patrick presides over the pencils and pens. There is a plaque from the Harlem & Stuyvesant Lawyers Association, honoring Bobby for his work on "The Rights of Minorities." When Bobby is at his desk, he sits in the huge, red-leather swivel chair which he had at the Department of Justice and which was given him by the department's employees when he resigned.

When Bobby is in his office, he moves quietly about, walking from one room into another as though he were a stranger out of place. If he makes small talk it is barely audible and mostly boyish. When there are beaming visitors waiting to meet him, he scarcely touches their hands as he leaves his office. Though he is quiet, Bobby is always on the move and is away from his office more than he is in it. In his first six months in the Senate, trips took him to Great Britain, the Canadian Yukon and a dozen states. Of course, there are also the weekly shuttle flights to New York City.

In his first six months as United States Senator, Robert F. Kennedy's impact was largely recognized by the public because his colleagues in the Senate are slow with remarks of recognition for any freshman Senator. Yet, in the summer of 1965, there were grudging admissions heard around the Senate that Bobby would indeed amount to something in the Senate one day. "He has surprised me with his development," said an elder Democrat. "He's done very well. There is reason to think he could become the speaker for the Democratic North." Another Democratic Senator, who says he has mixed feelings about Bobby, said if Bobby has one single, irritating shortcoming as a Senator it is his tendency to get on the telephone with fellow Senators and, instead of discussing the fine points of a question, turn the conversation to which people are for him and which are against him.

A Republican Senator who would like to see the venerable Senate perk up thinks "Bobby could become a useful, stimulating force." This Senator would say no more, but he could well have been suggesting that Bobby's increasing criticism of the Johnson Administration's foreign policy could stir new debate and perhaps realign sentiment on foreign policy to the point of polarizing it as "tough" or "soft," interventionist or neo-isolationist. Bobby, junior as he is, can speak out on foreign policy and command attention for the sole reason that he once sat in the White House's oval office as his brother's adviser during international crises.

Bobby has showed no lack of confidence, and for now, he

seems satisfied with his role of U.S. Senator. Connecticut Senator Abraham Ribicoff, who knows the Kennedy mind as well as anyone, considers the Senate a perfect place "for loners like Bobby." Ribicoff explains, "It has given him a sense of peace. He made it here on his own, and he has become more philosophical." Another Democratic Senator said, after Bobby's first six months: "There is less pressure on him now than any time in the past ten years. The Senate could moderate Bobby's restlessness."

Kennedy, after nine months in the Senate, did seem more relaxed and contented than he had during many of the months when he was Attorney General. In late September, 1965, he was able to express considerable satisfaction with his Senatorial beginnings. He said:

"I enjoyed these first months more than I thought I would. The matters I became involved in were those which I am deeply interested in and which really mean something to me—housing, education and the poverty program. It was all worth while. And all the Senators have been most considerate."

And so it could be that Bobby's personality and creative powers will alter and grow and be expressed in the U.S. Senate. He has showed himself unafraid to speak and act. Some Senators think he is too abrupt, and occasionally haughty. But most would give him good marks for his beginnings as U.S. Senator. He showed minimal ability to charm, but he showed himself to be a man of forceful presence. And almost every Senator would have to conclude that Bobby is his own man—and a man to be reckoned with—beholden to no one and tied in memory only to his dead brother's promise.

XII

BEYOND THE FORTIETH YEAR

A YEAR OR SO AFTER ROBERT KENNEDY became Attorney General in his brother's Cabinet, a reporter prodded him half in jest about persistent stories that the Kennedys planned to put Bobby into the White House someday. Bobby was not amused. "That idea is so obviously untrue," he barked, "that it's foolish even as a rumor."

It isn't any longer.

The assassination of John Kennedy changed Bobby's attitude toward the presidency. As in the past, the death of one Kennedy son profoundly affected the life of another, for it has become a family tradition for the eldest living son to attempt to fulfill the promise of the deceased. The same thing had happened to Jack after Joseph Jr. was killed. While still a Senator from Massachusetts, John Kennedy explained it all quite candidly: "Just as I went into politics because Joe died, if anything happened to me tomorrow, my brother would run for my seat in the Senate. And if Bobby died, Teddy would take over for him."

Bobby Kennedy would very much like to be President. Close friends and members of his family say flatly that this is true.

The public's judgment of Bobby as a possible President will inevitably be influenced by Jack's death. For years there will be a residue of sad memories and unfulfilled hopes associated with Bobby Kennedy. There will always be his resemblance to the unforgettable Jack—in his vocal inflection, his gestures, the cast of his face. There will be endless comparisons between the dead brother and the living. And there will be, for a time at least, Bobby's own reminders in his own speeches of the plans Jack had in mind when he died, of the promise his years in the White House held.

But the charisma of a dead man carries diminishing value for the living. Even when the nation's grief was fresh, there was not enough undisciplined emotion among voters to elect a man to the presidency as a mere act of condolence. And as years pass, the sharp sense of loss felt when John Kennedy was murdered will fade.

If there is to be any continuing impact in the Kennedy name, it will be up to Bobby and the living Kennedys to keep it potent.

Bobby proved when very young that he understood the intricacies of power politics—and on a national level. His organizational work for Jack's presidential campaign was brilliant. Despite his widespread reputation for ruthlessness, he did not alienate people who really mattered. In any presidential quest of his own, Bobby Kennedy would have both the operational know-how and, to a large extent, the personal contacts essential to put together a superb campaign machine.

What was left of the 1960 Kennedy organization was turned over to Lyndon Johnson in 1964. Because Johnson faced such inept competition in Barry Goldwater, the machine never had to operate with the efficiency it produced for John Kennedy. But Bobby could resurrect at least a skeletal structure from it. Such influential Democrats as Chicago Mayor Richard Daley, California State Assembly Speaker Jesse (Big Daddy) Unruh, Connecticut Senator Abraham Ribicoff, Pennsylvania Senator Joseph Clark, Michigan Senator Phil Hart and Bobby's own New York partisans would offer a solid base of support in the nation's most populous states. Also Bobby could probably count on some help from old-time Kennedy loyalists such as Kenneth O'Donnell, Dave Powers, Larry O'Brien, Ted Sorensen and Democratic National Chairman John Bailey.

Beyond that, Bobby can begin to form a new, young Kennedy cadre within the Congress—a network of Democrats on Capitol Hill who would offer additional contact with state organizations around the country. In the early stages of the 1964 elections, Bobby had at least the nucleus for such a pro-Kennedy group in the Senate candidacies of former White House Press Secretary Pierre Salinger from California, Astronaut John Glenn from Ohio, Joseph Tydings from Maryland and, of course, Teddy Kennedy. Unfortunately for Bobby, Salinger lost to one-time Hollywood dancer George Murphy and Glenn bumped his head so badly when he fell in a bathroom that he had to withdraw from the Democratic Senate primary. Only Tydings and Teddy came through.

But there will be other congressional elections before Bobby makes a run for the presidency and there is nothing to prevent his building a loyal Kennedy corps in both House and Senate.

Always, of course, there will be the energetic—and now highly experienced—political campaigners who also happen to be Kennedy family members. Sargent Shriver is a powerful drawing card in himself because of his excellent reputation as Peace Corps director and commander of Lyndon Johnson's war on poverty. Steve Smith has developed into a highly capable political operator. Ethel and the rest of the Kennedy clan have all become pros at political campaigning.

And by the time Bobby is ready to make his move, it is conceivable that Jacqueline Kennedy would be willing and able to lend him a hand, actively and publicly. She abjured politics while Jack was alive, except for occasional campaign trips to stand by his side and offer a few shy handshakes. But since his death, she has clung tightly to his family—to its tradition of public service as well as to its members. She wanted to help Bobby in his campaign for the Senate despite her self-imposed year of mourning for Jack. Bobby kept her out of the public eye lest people think he was coldly using her as a vote getter during her bereavement. In years to come, however, John Kennedy's widow could be an enormous asset to Bobby's campaigns.

And then there is Teddy. Jack Kennedy once said with typical pragmatism, "In politics, you don't have friends. You have allies." Among the Kennedys, Jack found true friends as well as allies—but Bobby was the best of them all, for he committed himself to Jack's campaign and career with a zeal that was all but self-sacrificial. That same relationship does not exist between Bobby and Teddy, for they have pursued distinctly separate careers. Because he was so young, Teddy was never the essential force in John Kennedy's presidency that Bobby was, and after his election to the Massachusetts Senate seat in 1962, Teddy was far too busy with his own life to make any all-encompassing commitment to anyone else.

Thus, Bobby and Teddy never did develop the osmotic relationship, or the mutual dependency that Jack and Bobby had. Yet there is between the surviving Kennedy brothers that unbreakable loyalty that ties together all members of the Kennedy family. And predictably, since Bobby and Teddy get together in the Senate in early 1965, they have constantly consulted each other, advised each other, and helped each other in their Senate functions.

They operate more as equals than Jack and Bobby ever did. Yet there is a rivalry between Teddy and Bobby. It is not one they created by themselves and it is not necessarily one that they welcome, for eventually it could put their family allegiance to a wrenching test that would be unprecedented in brotherhood as well as in American politics. The fact is, both are considered by knowledgeable politicians to be likely presidential timber.

Someday the Kennedys may have to make an incredible choice: which brother—Teddy or Bobby—should run for the presidency first?

Already there are frequent public references to "their" quest for the presidency—as if Bobby and Teddy could mount a double-team attack and get the nomination together. In a *New York Times* story about the Kennedys' impressive effort to push through an amendment to the Johnson Administration's voting-rights bill against Vice President Humphrey's objections, there appeared this sentence: "The consensus was that both Kennedys had picked up considerable support from Negro and civil-rights groups in their potential rivalry with Mr. Humphrey for the Democratic presidential nomination in 1972."

Some influential Democrats in the Senate consider Teddy a brighter presidential prospect than Bobby. And Bobby himself has said, "Teddy is a better natural politician than any of us." Maybe so. But most people who know both brothers say that Bobby is far more intelligent than Teddy. Though Bobby has shown little of the polished caution that Teddy applies to Senate chores, his very abrasiveness, his willingness to scrap like a terrier for what he believes and his almost savage determination to succeed at whatever he does make his younger brother seem bland in comparison.

And what might happen if they arrived neck-and-neck as presidential contenders in some future year? "They would never fight each other for the presidency," said Eunice Shriver. "If it ever came to that, one would give way to the other." Given the Kennedy pragmatism and unrelenting devotion to victory, it is conceivable that the decision might be based on the cold, competitive consideration of which brother had the best chance to win. It is more likely, however, that family tradition would prevail—meaning that the older brother would get the first chance at the best job. Unquestionably, Bobby will do whatever seems best for the Kennedys; his loyalty to the family and his dedication to keeping its name honored—indeed, *hallowed* if that were possible—is an obsession with him. But most people close to the Kennedys are certain that Bobby will run for the presidency before Teddy does.

And when will he try? Bobby is not a patient man, but the facts call for patience. Unless Lyndon Johnson is incapacitated, he would almost certainly retain the Democratic nomination and likely the presidency in 1968. If Johnson is no longer in office due to death or disease, then Hubert Humphrey would be President, with his own nomination all but assured. Except for unforeseeable events, it seems impossible that Bobby Kennedy—or any other Democrat—would stand a chance of snatching the presidential nomination away from Lyndon Johnson or Hubert Humphrey in 1968.

By 1972, the situation could be considerably different. For one thing, a Republican just might win the presidency in 1968— even though that seems a profoundly remote possibility. A G.O.P. victory would mean Johnson or Humphrey had been defeated and Bobby's two major opponents (as of now) would have been removed. But if Johnson served his second full term, he would not be able to run for office again in 1972. The fight for the Democratic nomination would be wide open—although Hubert Humphrey would almost certainly rate as a favorite. Bobby could come out slugging against Humphrey in the presidential primaries, if he chose. By then, Kennedy would have served his first full six-year term in the Senate and run for re-election in 1970, almost certainly without serious danger of losing.

Indeed, by 1972, the muted, but deep-seated antagonism that has existed between Bobby Kennedy and Lyndon Johnson for so long may well have faded for good. It is not unlikely that Johnson, by then a lame-duck President and thus relieved of any anxieties over Bobby as a political rival, might actually become a Kennedy ally. Bobby himself says that he senses at least the beginning of a thaw in their relations. "Johnson isn't as afraid of me as he was," said Kennedy. "He's not so worried that I am going to rise up and run against him. As he has gone along in his job, he has developed more confidence in himself. He is more experienced." And, in a not-so-oblique reference to his own presidential hopes for the future, Bobby added: "I'm not so sure either that he thinks Hubert Humphrey is going to be *the* man to succeed him."

Though 1972 may be the first presidential election year when Bobby Kennedy can realistically expect to be in real contention, it is by no means the last. He is young. He can bide his time. There are the elections of 1967 and 1980. Even in 1984 Bobby will be just 58—not at all too old to run.

Given his name, his political talents, his money, the presidency is by no means beyond his reach. It does lie well beyond his present stature. Even at 40, there is an unsettling aura of immaturity about Robert Kennedy. He is impetuous, impatient, blunt-spoken even when he does not have to be. He has an obsession about winning—whatever the contest. He seems too often to form quick, subjective dislikes for people who offend him quite unknowingly. Sometimes he treats his closest, most able aides as if he were a crown prince and their single purpose on earth were to cater to his every whim.

It is this pervasive impression of callow boyishness that is the most disturbing factor—now—in considering Robert Kennedy for the presidency. For to be a mature man is to display the capacity to forgive, to exercise restraint, to judge other men and their principles from a stance of rational objectivity rather than raw emotion. Tough minded and incisive as he is, Robert Kennedy has yet to show consistently that he has the attributes of full maturity.

In Bobby's new life at 40, there are two places where Americans can watch his presidential potential being developed—or destroyed. One is the Democratic Party of New York State. The other is the U.S. Senate.

In New York, Bobby has entered a searing political caldron where even the strongest men seldom escape without scars. If he were to stay out of the internecine wars there, he could save himself a cruel and possibly devastating test of power and personality. Yet Bobby will almost certainly want control of the New York delegation to the National Convention in 1968, for without it he would have to admit a weakness within his own bailiwick—something he would find extremely painful. To get it, he may have to carry on a rugged battle, and he could do that in two ways: With the offensive emotional tactics of an alley fight, or with the unemotional approach of a field marshal's battle campaign. The tactics he chooses in New York will tell much about Bobby Kennedy—whether he is himself taking on the proportions of a President, or simply retaining those of a man who once helped his brother become one.

In the Senate, Bobby will be visible to the nation as he never has been before as congressional investigator, presidential campaign manager or even as Attorney General. Every speech from the floor, every cloakroom machination, every caucus comment of Bobby's will be magnified and examined. His attendance record will likely be excellent and his voting record will almost certainly show solid Democratic dependability, along with a portion of independence to prove he is willing to dispute the wishes of the Johnson Administration; to prove that Bobby Kennedy is his own man. To some extent, those records in the Senate will reflect political opportunism as much as personal principle, for Bobby's "image" is important to his future—both as a Senator who wants to be re-elected and as a man who wants to be President.

But in Bobby there is a candor, an unrelenting and undeniable compulsion to say what he thinks—right or wrong. That will not be quieted or equivocated. To be successful in the Senate, Bobby must work, one way or another, with 99 other men. The extent to which he offends their sensitivities or captures their loyalties with his capacity for candor will be a measure of Bobby's effectiveness—and his maturity.

Ultimately, Bobby Kennedy's chance to become President rests with what the body politic comes to believe about him. Few men in public life have been the subject of such polemic reactions as Bobby has. He attracts both black hatred and pure love. People who know him and have engaged in struggle with him (such as Jimmy Hoffa, Roy Cohn, Gore Vidal, the old-time politicians of Boston) consider him a ruthless, unscrupulous young man without a hint of charity in his soul. People who know him and have given him their loyalties and their talents (Ed Guthman, Walter Sheridan, Dean Markham) consider him close to a saint, a man of absolute integrity and profound morality.

Obviously, both views are caricatures, drawn from strong and emotional opinions that have more basis in the heart than in fact. As with any man, the truth of Bobby is his own truth and is known—if at all—to him alone. Until his decision in 1964 to place himself in the hands of the electorate, to become a public man committed to the desires of 12 million constituents in New York, Bobby did not need to reveal any more of that truth than he felt personally necessary. That is no longer true—for a man who wants to be President.

As Americans consider Bobby Kennedy for the presidency now, many will have a feeling of ambivalence, of uncertainty. They will see many of the traits they demand of a President and many they could not allow. They do not want a weakling, and Bobby is not one. Neither do they want a man who shoves people around, and Bobby has done that. They want a leader, and Bobby is. But they do not want a man who takes his followers for granted, and Bobby has done that, too. They want a man who understands the anatomy of crisis and can make decisions without personal involvement. Bobby can do that. But they do not want a man who is impetuous and easily angered. And Bobby has been that, too.

Indeed, Americans must wonder whether Robert Kennedy is a man who should be trusted with the presidency.

Trust grows from consistency, from a performance that, if not predictable, is at least dependable. It is up to Bobby Kennedy to prove that he is a man to be relied on. If he wishes to be President, he must make the American people believe that he is at once one of them—and the best of them.

That may be well within the capacities of Bobby Kennedy. Yet, whether or not he is ever destined to be President of the United States, this is a man who has already become one of the powerful people in America. And at 40, Robert Francis Kennedy has really just begun.

INDEX